Roadmap to Job-Winning Military to Civilian Resumes

How to Write Military to Federal, Defense Contractor, and Corporate Resumes Proven to Earn Job Interviews

CareerPro Global's 21st Century Career Series

CareerPro Global Publishing, Georgia

We have been careful to provide accurate and up-to-date information throughout this book; however, it is possible that errors and omissions will still exist. The resume templates and character counts are current at the time of this printing, but federal and private organizations change their application requirements and other details on an ongoing basis. In addition, we presented the resume samples as entry-level (E-1 to E-4), mid-level (E-5 to E-7 and O-1 to O-3), and senior-level (E-8 to E-9 and O-4 and up), but you won't necessarily leave the military and land a job in one of these levels based purely on your highest military rank. You should always double-check with the federal agency or specific company to be sure you are following the most current formatting guidelines. Your own circumstances, accomplishments, resume, and the hiring managers will determine what level position you secure.

Copyright © 2012 by CareerPro Global, Inc.
CAREERPRO GLOBAL PUBLISHING
Published in the United States of America
By CareerPro Global Publishing, a division of CareerPro Global, Inc.
173 Pierce Avenue, Macon, Georgia 31204

Printed in the United States of America
ISBN: 978-0-9823222-2-2

Publication Team:
Proofreader: Carla Lowe
Interior Page Designer: Tracy Reedy
Cover and CD-Rom Designer: Alesha Sevy
Resume Formats: Pat Duckers
Photo Credits: Gerard Steffan and Andrew Brooks

This book is dedicated to all the men and women
who serve in uniform to defend this great nation.
Our special thanks go to the 222nd Field Artillery, Utah Army National Guard, "Triple Deuce,"
and the 1/325th Infantry Regiment, 82nd Airborne Division, "Red Falcons."
Both units returned to Iraq in 2011.

My son, Bryan Adams, preparing for a jump at Fort Bragg
with the 1/325th Infantry prior to its deployment.

My co-author, Lee Kelley, during his deployment to Ramadi, Iraq,
with the 222nd Field Artillery in 2005.

Acknowledgments

This book would not have been possible without the incredible knowledge of the great writing team at CareerPro Global, Inc. (CPG), which has been assisting veterans to transition to the private sector or federal government for more than 25 years. Our team develops thousands of Military Transition Resumes (MTRs) each year and this publication is written from an insider's perspective.

Special thanks go out to my co-author and Iraq War veteran, Lee Kelley, who spent 12 years in the Army and worked his way from Private to Captain. Lee is an expert resume writer, award-winning author, writer training mentor, and editor, and was awarded the TORI for the "Best Military Transition Resume" in 2011. Lee currently serves as CPG's Director of Veterans Transitions and has worked with hundreds of military members and veterans from all services, from E-1 up to O-8. Lee is also a certified Master Military Resume Writer and Master Federal Career Coach.

Much appreciation also goes out to the entire CareerPro Global team, who continue to write the best MTRs in the world and provide world-class customer service to our veterans. Many of them, including Peggi Bass, Gerard Steffan, Fran Sheridan, Patricia Duckers, Lee Kelley, Mark Holmes, Bruce Hillman, Joseph Tatner, Kelly Poltrack, Jeff Nold, Mara Addison, Susie Harris, Karen Silberstein, Ted Telega, Deborah Young, Nancy Segal, Lisa Becker, and Elizabeth Juge, contributed samples for this book.

We would like to especially thank Joseph Tatner for his initiative and expertise in developing builders for the various federal government online resume systems and his astute research and organization during the planning stages of this book. Patricia Duckers did a fantastic job editing and designing sample resumes. We truly appreciate Alesha Sevy for her creative vision in designing the book cover and CD artwork, and Tracy Reedy for designing the book's interior layout. Finally, thanks to Carla Lowe, known for her "eagle eye." Carla's editing and proofreading skills were essential to this project. We also recognize Sarah Vine for her editing and proofreading contributions.

Table of Contents

Samples List

Military to Private-Sector Resume Samples

Veteran's Toolbox CD Contents

Military to Private-Sector Resume Samples
Military to Federal Resume Samples
Cover Letter Samples
Private-Sector Resume Builders
USAJobs Online Resume Template
Vision Statement Worksheet
KSA Worksheet
Accomplishments Worksheet
Action Word List
Resume Builder Worksheet
Tools and Resources
GS-Series Information Sheet
Veterans Employment Program Office Contacts
Federal and State Government Agencies

Explanation of Icons

 **Sample**

 **CPG Exclusive**

 **Decision Time**

Best Practices

Take Note

Introduction

Congratulations on buying this book! In this age, making a successful transition out of the military into the private-sector workforce, the federal government, or the defense contracting industry can be challenging, especially if you don't grab the reader's interest with your resume.

This is the 21st century, and the world (and workplace) is changing. We've been a country at war for the last decade. As a result, plenty of veterans right now are seeking civilian employment. We have veterans at every age, from teens to senior citizens. Many of these are combat veterans with multiple tours in the Middle East. So while our Vietnam and WWII vets are watching the evening news, they are witnessing an entire new generation of vets emerging right before their eyes. This new generation is highly skilled, adaptive, educated, and poised to thrive in the modern workplace.

We are in a new era with almost unlimited new opportunities. The millions of "new" veterans will continue to prosper at virtually every level of society. For example, in the last 10 years, numerous veterans have left the military and used their military skill sets to land jobs with one of the massive defense contractor agencies such as KBR, Inc. (formerly Kellogg Brown & Root). In 2009, President Obama passed legislation to create veterans employment program offices in every federal agency, and to promote hiring more vets. In 2011, President Obama challenged small businesses to hire 100,000 veterans, and those companies that do will receive special tax incentives. More than ever, private organizations are also highlighting the benefits of hiring veterans.

So, if there are so many talented vets ready to lead the way, and so many great opportunities, then why is the unemployment rate among vets (1% of the U.S. population) higher than that of non-vets? Many variables and personal situations cause this, but one clear answer is that many vets don't know how to present their military skills and experience in a way that civilian hiring managers will understand and appreciate. Too often, vets simply slap together a resume that lists their duty stations and job descriptions, and hope that an employer will understand how great they are.

This is not an effective approach. Today's veterans are some of the most highly skilled, dynamic, and experienced the world has ever seen. They can adapt, overcome, and adjust quickly to new and changing environments. Put simply, they are awesome, and have the ability to improve just about any company, project, operation, training program, or planning effort—but none of that matters if they don't land the interview and the job. So how do you do that? With a strong resume. Yes, even in today's technological workplace, the resume is still the most important document you can have to land that job you want. Everything starts with the resume because it is a marketing piece about you and your career.

Many vets have already figured this out, and are landing jobs across corporate America, at all levels of the federal government and overseas with defense contractors. It all started with a resume. These vets have figured out how to create a resume that is "demilitarized" so that civilians can understand it, and that is focused on their specific accomplishments and results (not just general duties and job descriptions).

Since the late 1980s. CareerPro Global, Inc. (CPG) has watched the hiring trends and mastered best practices for writing relevant and effective Military Transition Resumes (MTRs). Through multiple wars and conflicts, and through times of peace, we've worked one-on-one with thousands of military veterans to market their skills, experience, specialized training, and formal education to the civilian sector. Over the years, CPG's team has developed writing strategies, authored more than 300 published military transition career articles, and more.

At CPG, we put our money where our mouth is. We employ veterans from all branches of the service, and these are some of the "best of the best." Our company President has a son in Iraq at the time of this writing. Our Managing Editor was a "military brat." Two of our senior career coaches are Air Force-retired. Many of our writers have military experience, from multiple services and both the enlisted and commissioned officer ranks. Our Director of Veteran Transitions (and the co-author of this book), Lee Kelley, was an Army Captain and Company Commander who spent a year in Ramadi, Iraq.

In service to all veterans, CPG has raised the bar in writing the MTR. In June 2007, our team authored, launched, and currently administers the Master Military Resume Writer (MMRW) credential program in partnership with our credentialing authority, Career Directors International (CDI), one of the leading professional career organizations in the world. In an industry without accountability, CPG chose to be accountable by becoming ISO-9001:2008 Registered and Certified. As of this printing the only career management service in the world to earn this international quality certification. In 2011, we launched our Master Federal Career Coach (MFCC) certification and Train-the-Trainer.

In the past several decades, more than 54,000 military veterans and federal employees have sought our assistance in writing their resumes. You can do that, too. We'd love to hear from you and help you land that sought-after civilian position! But the point of this book is to give you the tools to do it yourself. You don't have to be a professional writer or career expert to create a powerful resume. We believe in you and appreciate your service. And we know that with the right tools, you can make just about anything happen. You have in your hands a current, relevant, comprehensive resource to help you write your resume and cover letter, as well as many insightful tips on how to interview and transition with confidence.

We've organized the book into five check points to make it easy for you to follow and understand. Here's a brief overview:

Check Point 1: Know Your Options and Find Jobs. In this check point, you will learn more about the different options available to you, and where you can find federal or private-sector jobs.

Check Point 2: Identify Your Skills and Write Your Accomplishments. In this check point, you will gain a better understanding of how to match your military skills with government or private-sector positions. You will also learn the absolute importance of writing strong accomplishments.

Check Point 3: Write Your Military to Federal Resume. With a strong understanding of how to capture your accomplishments, here you will learn what goes into a Federal resume, how to use the headline format, and how to write short narratives.

Check Point 4: Write Your Military to Private-Sector Resume. Building on the last one, this check point covers how a private-sector resume is different from a Federal resume, and different ideas for formatting your resumes. Additionally, we share the key steps to writing a private-sector resume and what to include in a cover letter.

Check Point 5: Submit your Application Materials and Prepare for Interview. Finally, in this check point, you will learn more about some of the differences between the federal and private-sector hiring process and application procedures. You will also receive some great guidance about follow-up and interviewing.

Veteran's (Vet's) Toolbox CD: Not only will you find plenty of additional information in Appendix A and B, such as contact information for the new veterans employment offices and federal internship programs, but you will also receive everything in electronic form on your Vet's Toolbox CD. The Vet's Toolbox CD contains more than 25 sample private-sector resumes, including templates for USAJobs online resume builder that you can use to fill in with your own information.

Check Point 1

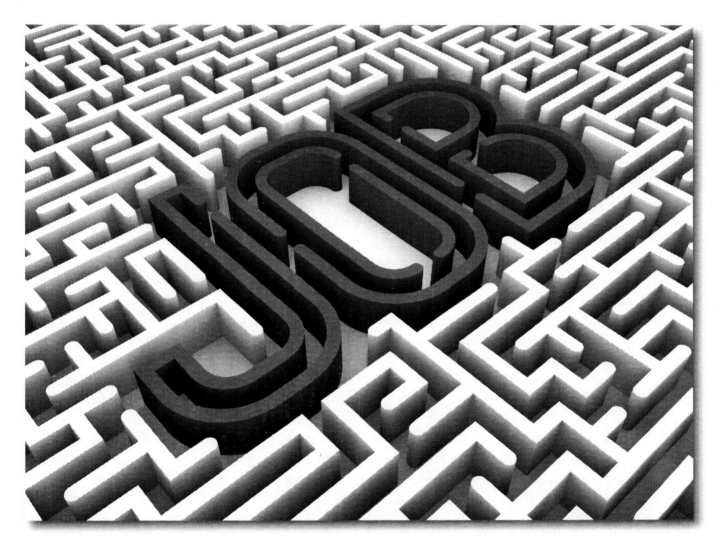

Know Your Options and Find Jobs

KNOW YOUR OPTIONS AND FIND JOBS

If you are a military veteran, you have a lot to offer. If you have served since 2001, it is very likely that you have served in a combat environment—possibly more than once. Whether you spent a couple of years in the military or served in combat and spent several decades in service, you can handle great pressure, learn, adapt, think, and persevere. You represent a new generation of veterans, technically skilled, motivated, and able to overcome challenges of which most people could never imagine. And you have options!

You could start your own business, open a franchise, work for the federal government, work for a defense contracting agency training military personnel, or work in almost countless positions in the private sector. Your potential is limitless, so don't limit your choices. Instead, keep your options open to both the private and federal workforce, and choose what's best for you.

In this check point, we'll discuss the benefits of working in the private sector or the federal government and where to find jobs for both. But before we do that, let's cover some of the reasons why you are such a great asset to the modern-day workforce...

WHY EMPLOYERS WANT (AND NEED) YOU
Depending on your job in the military, you almost certainly have specialized and technical skills to offer to a company or the government. Maybe you were in supply management, in communications, or served as a highly specialized aviation mechanic. On the other hand, maybe you had "additional duties" that provided you with marketable skills.

Even if you didn't work with highly specialized equipment, just serving in the military in today's day and age gives you a high technical aptitude and confidence.

You also have unique traits and values that go beyond specialized skills. These "soft skills" have become part of who you are, and you can apply them to any project, challenge, or position.

Responsibility: You have proven that you can handle responsibility. You may have handled live ammunition in combat. You may have been assigned government equipment and been trusted with classified information during your career. You may have been assigned a task, mission, operation, or challenge in training, and proven that you are responsible enough to carry it out to finish the task. This is a fantastic skill that you should not take for granted. Not every employee out there in the workforce is responsible—but you are.

Integrity/Reliability: Integrity and reliability go hand in hand, and they mean that you can be counted on to do what's right, even when no one's looking. Serving in the military instills a sense of integrity that can last a lifetime, and can certainly assist you in making your career transition. Additionally, you might have a Secret or Top Secret security clearance, which is considered highly valuable to many defense contractor and federal agencies. It also shows that

you can be trusted with sensitive items, equipment, or information.

High Morals/Values: **Regardless of your branch of service, you were taught to maintain a set of morals and values both on a personal level and on a larger scale. This deep-rooted sense of morality and values will help you to represent your organization in a positive way to meet their corporate values.**

Selfless Service: **In the military, you were taught to be a member of a team. Yes, you need to be a strong leader, but you also understand the concept of selfless service, or doing something for the greater good. This awareness will help you make the right decisions in any organization that hires you.**

Cross-Cultural Diversity: **the military is very diverse. You probably worked with people from numerous backgrounds, education levels, cultural backgrounds, personalities, skill levels, ages—you name it. Further, it is very likely that you coordinated with international coalitions and worked with foreign nationals in Iraq and/or Afghanistan. The United States is diverse, too, and your experience and exposure working in such diverse environments will absolutely help you to create a more inclusive and effective workplace in the private sector or the federal government.**

Discipline: **Discipline is a building block of military service. You can't wake up and exercise, make it to formations on time or fulfill your missions without a sense of discipline. If you don't conform, you get counseled and retrained or washed out. Although you want to remain flexible at all times, bringing a sense of discipline to your new career will pay huge dividends.**

Commitment/Dedication: **You have proven that you know how to follow orders, and do so with enthusiasm. You are driven by a commitment to excellence and desire to meet your organization's goals. Not only have you demonstrated a sense of dedication to something larger than yourself, but many employers will hire military personnel out of their own sense of duty, seeking to help a veteran in gratitude for the service you provided to our country.**

Leadership: **In many civilian organizations, an employee can stay in the same position for years. In some cases, people are "stuck" in a certain rank in the military, but for the most part, the entire military structure and culture expects you to continually develop. You are constantly being groomed to become a leader; and you are expected to move up the chain of command. You've probably led numerous projects, operations missions, and training, and have learned from some of the best leaders in the world. Your confidence and leadership will definitely help to propel your career forward.**

Creativity/Versatility: **Military veterans know how to meet short-term and long-term goals by constantly moving toward an objective, even if the mission or conditions change. Most likely, you have been involved in intense training or combat situations and had to deal with far greater stress than you would normally encounter in the civilian workplace. You are versatile and creative, and the corporate and federal workplaces need people who can "think outside the box" to drive momentum toward goals and objectives.**

Team Spirit/Mentoring: **As you know, everyone in the military chain of command is part of a team, and is expected to help develop junior personnel. Military leaders are constantly training and grooming the next generation of leaders. Civilian employers value a "team player" who puts the team first and helps train others to strengthen the overall organization.**

Written and Verbal Communication: **In the military, nearly every action must be properly documented,** and there are mounds of paperwork pertaining to operations, leave requests, personnel evaluations, etc. No doubt you had to maintain and accurately fill out tons of paperwork during your career. You probably also wrote training, briefings, memoranda, or other written materials. Not only did you have to write, but you also gained a lot of experience in reading, analyzing, and interpreting a wide variety of materials, including training manuals, field manuals, regulations, and operations orders. Finally, you had to listen attentively to orders and guidance, then communicate up and down the chain of command.

There are many more skills that you probably possess, but you get the idea. As a military veteran, you have learned to make things happen, overcome obstacles, and think outside the box, all while helping your other team members and moving toward the ultimate goal. And that's the definition of someone who is poised to make a career transition!

WHY WORK IN THE PRIVATE SECTOR?

There are myriad reasons why you might want to work in the private sector, or "Corporate America," which includes retail, blue-collar work, manual labor, temporary work, defense contractor agency work, and white-collar positions. There is a vast amount of career fields, jobs, and projects that you may pursue within the private sector.

Something else to consider is your own personal goals and personality. Let's be honest—the military is so steeped in tradition and organizational structure that it can turn into a love-hate relationship for veterans. On the one hand, vets may miss the structure; on the other hand, some feel like they're free at last! That's why some depart the military, and integrate that sense of order, structure, and discipline into many aspects of their personal and professional lives. Others shift that energy into the creative arts as writers, artists, and graphic designers.

Likely the main benefit of working in the private sector (as opposed to the federal government) is that you have many more options. Just think about all the companies and all the positions available out there in the great big world. Even though the federal government is much larger than most individual companies are, there are still many more opportunities in the private sector.

WHERE DO YOU FIND PRIVATE-SECTOR JOBS?

So, where do you find these private-sector jobs? Again, the answer to this question is very broad, and it depends on where you live and what kind of job you're seeking. There are many, many places to find private-sector jobs, and here are just a few:

- your local newspaper
- online job search engines like Monster.com
- company websites
- professional associations
- networking
- job fairs
- job boards at the unemployment office
- Craigslist
- word-of-mouth
- many others

Wherever you live, it is very likely that you will have access to the Internet. The only limit to finding a job is how hard you want to look for jobs as well as how creative you want to be. This is probably a little bit of urban myth by now, but a few decades ago, it was much more common to simply walk into a business, ask to talk to the manager, stick out your hand, and ask for a job. These days, it seems that the process of applying for a job has been depersonalized a bit—at least for larger companies. There are probably still many small or family-owned companies, such as restaurants or blue-collar companies (construction, landscaping, painting, etc.) whose owners would be more than happy to hear you out and let you know if they're hiring.

But let's say you walk into a large company tomorrow, ask to speak to the manager, and tell him you are seeking employment. Chances are, you would be directed to an online job application system, and the manager would say he'll "let you know" if anything opens up. With such a large amount of people vying for the same job, managers have this luxury. As you'll hear throughout this book, you want to stand out and "brand" yourself. Show your individual value and how you will make an immediate and value-added contribution to the company. And if taking your chances by walking in the door with a fantastic resume in hand is what it takes, then go for it!

Take bold action to show that you are highly confident without being cocky—that you are ready to work and get the job done. So even though the process of finding jobs has been depersonalized over time, by using modern technology and the Internet, you have access to many more jobs than you could ever find just by checking the local ads or walking downtown in your local city. But then again, so do millions of other people.

TOP 10 COMPANIES HIRING VETS IN 2011

Top 100 Military Friendly Employers
Sort by: Rank | Name

Rank	Company	Employees	Revenue
1	Booz Allen Hamilton Inc DEFENSE - www.boozallen.com McLean, Va.	23000	$5.1 billion
2	ManTech International DEFENSE - www.mantech.com Fairfax, Va.	9700	$2.02 billion
3	CSX Corporation TRANSPORTATION - www.csx.com Jacksonville, Fla.	30000	$9 billion +
4	URS DEFENSE - www.urscorp.com Germantown, Md.	13000	$2.5 billion
5	CACI International Inc DEFENSE - www.caci.com Arlington, Va.	12900	$2.7 billion
6	Burlington Northern Santa Fe Corporation TRANSPORTATION - www.bnsf.com/careers Fort Worth, Texas	38000	$14 billion
7	Johnson Controls, Inc. INDUSTRIAL PRODUCTS - www.johnsoncontrols.com Milwaukee	130000	$28.4 billion
8	USAA INSURANCE - www.usaa.com San Antonio, Texas	22200	$17.5 billion
9	Northrop Grumman Corporation DEFENSE - www.northropgrumman.com Century City, Calif.	120000	$33.8 billion
10	Lockheed Martin Corporation DEFENSE - www.lockheedmartin.com Bethesda, Md.	136000	$44.5 billion

To see the complete list of the top 100 companies hiring vets in 2011, and to learn more about how the list is created, visit GIJobs.com http://www.gijobs.com/2011Top100.aspx

SUMMARY: PROS AND CONS OF THE PRIVATE SECTOR

PROS	CONS
Freedom to relocate more often	Potentially less stable jobs
More overall opportunities	Potentially more competition
Fairly simple hiring processes	Less benefits programs
No limit on how much you can make	No guarantee of a paycheck

SPECIAL NEW INITIATIVES FOR VETERANS IN THE PRIVATE SECTOR

In August 2011, President Obama proposed several initiatives aimed at improving employment opportunities for veterans.

First, he proposed a Returning Heroes Tax Credit for businesses that hire unemployed veterans. Under this program, businesses could receive a maximum credit of $2,400 for every short-term unemployed veteran they hire, and $4,800 for every long-term unemployed veteran they hire. Sounds like a good incentive, and good news for veteran job seekers, too.

Additionally, he proposed boosting the Wounded Warriors Tax Credit for businesses that hire veterans with service-connected disabilities and who have been unemployed long term, up to $9,600 per veteran. This can help our wounded warriors to make smooth transitions back into the workplace.

The Department of Defense (DoD) and Department of Veterans Affairs (VA) will also be leading a new taskforce to help exiting service members receive the kind of training, education, and credentials they need to transition into the civilian workforce or pursue higher education. This would include a "Reverse Boot Camp" concept to provide extended career counseling and guidance.

The Department of Labor will develop and launch an "enhanced career development and job search service package" for transitioning vets.

The Office of Personnel Management (OPM) will create a "best practices" guide to help private-sector companies identify and hire more vets.

Finally, President Obama has challenged businesses to commit to hire or provide training to 100,000 unemployed veterans and spouses by the end of 2013. A number of major U.S. firms, including Microsoft, AT&T, and Lockheed Martin, have already committed to the program.

WHY WORK FOR THE FEDERAL GOVERNMENT?

First, the federal government is the country's largest single employer, with approximately 2 million employees and 20,000 jobs posted worldwide on any given day. Even during times of economic hardship, when the news is always talking about federal hiring freezes and pay cuts, the federal government remains a solid place to work.

Just like with anything else, you can find opinions to be a little different for everyone and you might find people who are somewhat disgruntled with the federal government after losing a job. The upside is that you may find other people who were being promoted right up to federal ranks, even during an economic crisis. That all depends on where you work, which government agency you work for, and your own personal circumstances within that organization. There is no single right answer.

Just know that the federal government is vast and highly diverse, and it's not going anywhere. It's a good time for veterans who want to embark on a federal career.

VETERANS' PREFERENCE OVERVIEW

First, you may be eligible for Veterans' Preference. This means you receive a certain amount of points added to your application when you go through the detailed federal hiring process. How many points you'll have for Veterans' Preference depends on whether you separated under honorable conditions, when you served, how long you served, whether you're a combat veteran, and whether you have a disability and how much. For more information on Veterans' Preference, take a look at Appendix A in this book. You can also go to the OPM's website to figure out your exact Veterans' Preference score: http://www.opm.gov/staffingPortal/Vetguide.asp

PRESIDENT OBAMA'S VETERANS INITIATIVE

On November 9, 2009, President Obama issued an Executive Order establishing a Council on Veterans Employment to enhance recruitment of, and promote employment opportunities for, veterans in the government. The goal is to make the federal government a leader in promoting employment for veterans. In addition, 19 federal agencies, including all Presidential Cabinet-level agencies, are required to establish a Veterans Employment Program Office. Essentially, this means that they must designate an agency officer or employee to manage the Veterans Employment Program Office on a full-time basis. The goals of this position are to enhance employment opportunities for veterans within the agency, including developing and implementing the agency's Operational Plan, veterans recruitment programs,

and training programs for veterans with disabilities, as well as coordinating employment counseling to help match veterans' career goals with the needs of the agency. In Appendix A and on your Vet's Toolbox CD, we have included the contact list provided by OPM. Check the website regularly, as the names or agencies may have changed.

Take Note

Review the VetGuide at **http://www.opm.gov/ staffingportal/vet guide.asp,** or contact the Veterans Employment Program Office at the agency of your choice

Not only are there several programs and initiatives designed to bring more vets into the federal government, but there are also a number of great benefits available to all federal employees. The following section lists a few of them:

FEDERAL EMPLOYEES HEALTH BENEFITS PROGRAM (FEHB)

The government's health benefits program offers approximately 180 health plan options throughout the U.S., including consumer-driven healthcare and preferred provider network options. On average, every employee has at least a dozen plan choices, each with varying benefits. None of the federal health plans requires a waiting period or a medical exam for enrollment.

Dental and Vision Insurance

Dental and vision insurance benefits are available to eligible federal and postal employees, retirees, and their eligible family members on an enrollee-pay-all basis. This program allows dental insurance to be purchased on a group basis, which means competitive premiums and no pre-existing condition limitations. Premiums for enrolled federal and postal employees are withheld from salary on a pre-tax basis.

Leave and Holidays

Federal employees are entitled to at least 13 days of vacation leave as well as 13 days of sick leave each year. Depending on years of service, employees can earn up to 26 days of vacation leave each year. In addition, federal employees are entitled to 10 days of paid holiday each year. The rate of a new employee's annual leave accrual rate may be negotiable when an applicant receives a job offer.

Family-Friendly Flexibilities

The federal government provides many programs for workers to support their needs for individual flexibility. For example, Compressed Work Schedules allow employees to adjust their work hours in order to take a day off each pay period. Employees can enjoy 26 three-day weekends each year! Further, the federal government's Alternative Work Schedule (AWS) allows employees to select certain arrival and departure times that best suit their needs within their working day; this is often known as "flextime" (flexible time). Individual agencies also have policies regarding family-friendly work schedules.

Federal Employees Retirement System (FERS)

A federal employee's retirement benefits are based on years of service and salary history.

Thrift Savings Plan (TSP)

With the TSP [similar to a 401(k) plan], an employee can self-direct his/her retirement savings program through multiple investment options.

Social Security

Federal employees hired beginning in 1984 and covered under the FERS earn Social Security credit while working with the government.

Retirement

New employees with previous government service prior to 1984 may be eligible to participate in the Civil Service Retirement System (CSRS). Employees in law enforcement-designated positions are covered under a separate retirement system; certain other positions may offer alternative retirement program options, as well.

Medicare—Part A
Government employees are automatically eligible for Medicare Part A at no cost beginning at age 65.

Federal Employees
Group Life Insurance (FEGLI)
FEGLI is a group term life insurance program. It consists of Basic life insurance coverage and three options. In most cases, new federal employees are automatically covered by Basic life insurance. Three additional forms of optional insurance from which an employee can choose include Standard, Additional, and Family.

Relocation Incentives
In some cases, the government will provide eligible applicants with a one-time incentive to relocate to a geographic area where there has been difficulty in attracting qualified applicants. This varies from a relocation allowance, which some agencies give to qualified candidates to assist them with their relocation expenses.

Incentive Awards
These include: Monetary, Time Off, Honorary, and Non-Monetary, and are given to recognize exceptional accomplishments and/or contributions made on the job.

Employee Development
Federal employees have a myriad of professional enrichment options available to them. These opportunities ensure employees continue to grow and adapt to the changing needs of their jobs.

Support of Community Service
Community leadership is encouraged by the government; as such, the annual Combined Federal Campaign provides federal employees an opportunity to contribute to various charities.

Interagency Transfers
Employees in Competitive Service positions may transfer from one federal agency/position to another without a break in service or seniority.

Student Loan Repayment
Depending on the agency's policies, eligible employees may receive reimbursement for their student loans. This reimbursement is generally granted if the employee went to school for a specific program that is usually hard for the government to fill, but it is also determined on a case-by-case basis.

Some benefits—such as starting salary, annual leave, and recruitment incentives, to name a few—are negotiable. If you are offered a federal position, you should ask about the availability of these options before you make your decision. In general, benefits are available to employees who are appointed to positions for more than one year.

The federal government might change, discontinue, or add new programs at any time. Please check the Office of Personnel Management's (OPM) website often for the most current information.
http://www.opm.gov/index.asp

As you can see, there are many benefits to working in the federal government if that's what you decide is right for you. But once you make that decision, where do you find the jobs?

WHERE DO YOU FIND FEDERAL JOBS?
There are two primary sources where you can find federal jobs. You can either go directly to the agency's website, or use USAJobs.gov.

USAJobs.gov is the official employment website of the federal government, and regularly lists

more than 20,000 vacancies per day in all disciplines and locations, including both the homeland and overseas. In October 2011, OPM launched a streamlined design of the USAJobs website to make it easier to find jobs and apply with just a few keystrokes in most cases.

There is something for practically everyone, no matter what your experience or educational level. And if you are flexible in terms of the location and federal agency in which you want to work, you have even more options.

NAVIGATING AND SEARCHING ON USAJOBS.GOV

If you have even the most basic computer skills, you should have no problem navigating the site and searching for jobs. If you don't, then ask someone to help you. The site even has tutorials and other helpful resources, so within minutes, you should be able to navigate the site and search for jobs in your specialty field or geographical region.

Once you set up an account and build your online resume, you're ready to start applying for federal jobs. You can even sign up to receive email alerts on job openings.

> Check out the USAJobs Info Center for more information on using USAJobs. http://www.usajobs.gov /infocenter/

OTHER FEDERAL SYSTEMS

While most positions are advertised on USAJobs, not all agencies use it for the entire application process. For example, you might start out on USAJobs.gov and be redirected to an agency's specific application system. Some of these other systems include Army Civilian Personnel Online (CPOL), AVUE, and National Aeronautics and Space Administration (NASA) STARS. The Navy CHART system was taken down in October 2011 and now all Navy and Marines jobs are posted on the main USAJobs.gov website. Other agencies, like the Federal Bureau of Investigation (FBI), Social Security Administration (SSA), and Federal Aviation Administration (FAA), also have their own application procedures.

Every system requires a separate account, so it's important to read each individual announcement and to ensure you set up an account on the corresponding system once you have identified the agency in which you're interested. More importantly, each system has different character counts, page limits, and other specific requirements. A good rule of thumb is to read the announcement first to determine what type of application format is required. Learn more about creating a Federal resume in Check Point 3, and about submitting it online in Check Point 5.

SUMMARY: PROS AND CONS OF THE FEDERAL SECTOR

PROS	CONS
Great federal benefits	More difficult and longer hiring process
Dental and vision insurance	Less options for relocation
Leave and holidays	Less creative flexibility
Good pay	Salary freezes

PRIVATE SECTOR VS. FEDERAL RESUME COMPARISON

As you'll learn in Check Points 3 and 4, there are differences between Federal and private-sector resumes. For example, a Federal resume requires more than 40 specific blocks of data, but a civilian resume covers the bare basics, such as employment and education history. Here are some other differences between a civilian and basic Federal resume.

	CIVILIAN RESUME	FEDERAL RESUME
Length	1-3 pages	3-5+ pages, not including supplemental data
Compliance Information	Not applicable	Required, such as employer address, phone number, supervisor, salary, etc.
Social Security Number	Not required	Required
Education and Dates	Dates not required	Required

VISION STATEMENT WORKSHEET

Before you move into capturing your accomplishments and then creating a Federal resume, private-sector resume, or both, you really need to think about some very simple questions first. Use the following worksheet to develop a basic Career Vision Statement. We recommend you do this exercise as many times as you need to until you have a crystal-clear vision. Doing this simple exercise will help you to make decisions as you continue through this book, and in your career transition.

I am really good at:	I am passionate about:	I'd like to live/work in:
1. _____	1. _____	1. _____
2. _____	2. _____	2. _____
3. _____	3. _____	3. _____
4. _____	4. _____	4. _____
5. _____	5. _____	5. _____
6. _____	6. _____	6. _____
7. _____	7. _____	7. _____
8. _____	8. _____	8. _____
9. _____	9. _____	9. _____
10. _____	10. _____	10. _____
(Circle the top 3)	(Circle the top 3)	(Circle the top 3)

My top skills I want to focus on:	The top jobs/companies I want to target are:
1. _____	1. _____
2. _____	2. _____
3. _____	3. _____
4. _____	4. _____
5. _____	5. _____
6. _____	6. _____
7. _____	7. _____
8. _____	8. _____
9. _____	9. _____
10. _____	10. _____
(Circle the top 3)	(Circle the top 3)

Basic Career Vision Statement

I will identify and secure a job in _____ as a _____.
                                    (choose from top 3 locations)   (choose from top 3 job positions)

I know I'd be an ideal candidate because I am good at _____
                                                        (choose from top 3 job skills)

and passionate about _____.
                        (choose from top 3 job passions)

CHECK POINT SUMMARY

After reading this check point, you should be able to see pretty clearly that you have many skills and plenty of options. You have also begun to develop your own vision statement, so you know in which direction you want to go. Of course, every vet is different, but let's face it—you have a lot to offer employers. The first major decision you must make is whether you want to work somewhere in the private sector or in the government. As you can see, each has its own pros and cons. It's your personal decision, and our goal here is to arm you with the tools and resources you need to make a more informed decision.

There is no reason you can't develop a resume for private-sector and government positions, but whichever way you go, the most important thing is to avoid being generic. You need to identify your skills and write strong and compelling accomplishments. That's exactly what we'll cover in the next check point.

Check Point Notes

Check Point 2

Identify Your Skills and Write Your Accomplishments

IDENTIFY YOUR SKILLS AND WRITE YOUR ACCOMPLISHMENTS

Have you noticed that we keep mentioning that all vets are different? Well, obviously, your accomplishments are different, as well. Let's say you are a helicopter mechanic in the Air Force, and we compared your resume to 10 other people stationed around the globe with the same job title. Would there be some similarities in the tools, equipment you used, and the types of engines and aircraft on which you worked? In fact, each military branch has clearly defined "position descriptions" for your Military Occupational Specialty (MOS). But that's two dimensional and generic.

Do you really think that all 10 of you would have the same exact accomplishments to put in your resume? Probably not. It's much more likely that you stand out from the pack. Maybe you thought of a new way to structure the work during a major engine overhaul, or a new method of improving accuracy during highly specialized equipment testing. Maybe you found a way to improve upon the technical manual. Whatever the particular case, you get the point. This check point is about identifying your specialized skills the military taught you, sure, but it's also about digging deep to write accomplishments that really distinguish you from everyone else. And here's a hint about this check point: When you are identifying your skills and writing your accomplishments, you MUST put yourself in the shoes of a civilian reviewer and make sure you present your experience in ways he/she will understand.

IDENTIFY YOUR SKILLS

Before you start capturing and writing your accomplishments, you should have a clear idea of what skills you have to offer and the type of company or position you want to target.

There are approximately 8,500 MOS, more than 40,000 government occupational codes and titles, and almost countless private-sector positions.

The following two tables will give you an overview of some military titles and their civilian counterparts. This is not an exact science. Rather, these tables are designed to help you start thinking in the right way. When "translating" your military job title into terms that civilians can understand, you don't want to go overboard or exaggerate. Not only does your actual specialty come into play, but as you'll see in the chart, your rank can also be a factor.

SAMPLE MILITARY POSITIONS/RANKS AND THEIR RELATED SKILLS

Military Ranks/Job Titles	Possible Civilian-Equivalent Skills/Positions
General Officer/Admiral (O-7 to O-10)	Chief Executive Officer, Chief Financial Officer, Chief Technology Officer, Executive Director, Senior Director, Managing Director/Company President/Vice-President
Field Grade Officer (O-4 to O-6)	Program Director or Manager
Company Grade Officer (O-1 to O-3)	Manager, Project Officer, Instructor
Warrant Officer (WO1 to CWO)	Technical Manager, Specialist
Senior Non-Commissioned Officer (NCO)/Senior Chief (E-8 to E-9)	Operations Manager, Senior Advisor, Project Manager
Platoon Sergeant (E-6 to E-7)	Supervisor, Foreman, Trainer, Personnel Administrator
Squad Leader (E-5 to E-6)	First-Line Supervisor
Intelligence Officer	Security Specialist/Investigator
Assistant Squad Leader (E-3 to E-4)	Section Leader, Task Leader
Crewmember (E-1 to E-2)	Team Member, Production Worker
Recruiter	Sales/Marketing Representative
Mess Cook	Food Service Specialist
Unit Clerk/Financial Specialist	Administrative/Human Resources Specialist
Safety Petty Officer	Safety Coordinator
Bridge Crewmember	Construction Worker
Construction Engineer	Construction Worker
Concrete and Asphalt Equipment Operator	Construction Worker
Signal Officer	Communications Project Manager
Military Police	Law Enforcement Officer/Security Specialist
Cargo/Supply Specialist	Logistics
Human Intelligence Collector	Intelligence Analyst

MOS/Position	Related Skills
Signal Officer	Management, Planning, Communications Planning, Satellite Communications
Non-Commissioned Officer	Training, Counseling, Small Group Instruction, Leadership
Commissioned Officer	Project Management, Advising, Strategic Planning, Team Building, Leadership
Military Police	Law Enforcement, Security Operations, Weapons Training, Self-Defense
Cargo/Supply Specialist	Logistics Planning, Supply Management, Inventory, Inspection, Acquisition, Procurement
Human Intelligence Collector	Intelligence Analysis/Collection, Advising
Infantry Team Leader	Small Group Leadership, Training, Planning, Land Navigation, Weapons Proficiency
Dental Specialist	Dental Operations/Administration
Healthcare Specialist	Hospital Operations/Administration, Patient Assessment, Basic Patient Care
Journalist	Reporting, Writing, Researching, Interviewing, Media Escort
Administrative Specialist	Human Resources, Recordkeeping, Data Entry, Word Processing, Scheduling

TOOLS FOR ASSESSING YOUR MILITARY SKILLS

There are several online tools for identifying your military skills, and you can use these in applying for just about any position:

- Visit the U.S. Office of Personnel Management (OPM) at **http://www.opm.gov/fed-class/html/gsfunctn.asp**, and you can download functional guides (in PDF) of the various MOS. Many of these explain what qualifications, knowledge, skills, and abilities you need in order to be eligible for a specific pay level.

- Another excellent resource is the O*NET Military Crosswalk Search at http://online.onet-center.org/crosswalk/MOC?s=&g=Go. This useful tool, provided by the U.S. Department of Labor, has thousands of listings for the various military branches and their related MOS. Researching on this site can help you think about your military experience in a way that civilian employers can appreciate and understand. You can find even more resources on the Vet's Toolbox CD.

There is a reason we covered matching your skills to a specific field or job before actually writing out your accomplishments. The reason is that you may decide to present your accomplishments in a different way for different jobs. For example, if you were a Platoon Leader in a Military Police organization, then you have experience leading teams and delegating duties, as well as plenty of other leadership skills that you could use in almost any environment. You also have plenty of specialized experience in weapons, tactics, and actual security operations (probably in an intense combat environment).

If you wanted a position as a Small Office Manager, you would focus on your management skills, as well as how successful you were at bringing the team together, mentoring others, and improving morale and productivity.

But what if you were seeking an entry-level position as a Security Specialist with a large corporation? In this case, you might want to place a sharper focus on security procedures, tactics, weapons training, and complex security missions.

WRITING GREAT ACCOMPLISHMENTS

Now that you know how to identify your skills and translate your experience, let's focus on the most important part of any resume: strong accomplishments.

Think about it—hiring managers have to review a plethora of different resumes, and it's probably not the highlight of their day; you can bet that every resume starts to sound the same after a while. Add this to the fact that many people don't give their resume much attention, and you can see how so many resumes don't produce the desired results (an interview and a job!).

So what will make your resume stand out? Lots of fancy graphics and "bells and whistles"? No. Are the resumes that look the best always going to be the best? No. Do you want your resume to be error-free and presentable? Yes, of course! But the way your resume looks isn't the most important factor. What really makes your resume stand out is the inclusion of strong and relevant accomplishments/results that clearly demonstrate what you can do for the potential employer.

Before you start writing your accomplishments, you should gather all your documents in one place.

DOCUMENTS YOU'LL NEED TO GATHER (AND HOW THEY CAN HELP)

VMET (Verification of Military Experience and Training)	Gives you a consolidated view of all your military assignments and training
DD-214 (record of separation)	Gives you dates of service and other basic information
List of Job-Related Skills	Reminds you of what types of positions you want to—and should—target
Letters of Recommendation	Gives you potential quotes and references
Performance Appraisals	Gives you specific accomplishments and possibly some supportive quotes about your performance
College Transcripts	Help you remember specific courses that might be relevant
Training Certificates	Details about what you learned, accomplished/became certified in
Awards Citations and Honors	Shows how you excelled and gives potential quotes about your performance
List of Affiliations	Shows with which organizations you are aligned
List of Publications	Shows that you have been published and possess strong writing skills
List of Speaking Engagements	Shows that you are comfortable and confident speaking in front of people
Official Orders	Can help you remember special assignments/accomplishments

When writing your accomplishments, it's best to focus on the last 10 years or so. When you develop your resume in the following check points, you want to do the same thing. If you have some highly relevant experience that is beyond 10 years, then don't leave it out; just remember that you can't fit everything into a resume—it's designed to grab a hiring manager's attention enough to give you an interview. Once you are sitting down in an interview, that's often a good time to elaborate on the experience you highlighted in the resume.

THE DIFFERENCE BETWEEN DUTIES AND ACCOMPLISHMENTS

By now, you should have gathered all of the information you'll need to write your duties and accomplishments for each position you will include on your resume.

To help you understand the difference between duties and accomplishments, let's use Sergeant Mitchell as an example. He spent five years in the Army as a 25U, Signal Support Systems Specialist, which, in Iraq, basically means that he was the "Commo Dude," asked to fix virtually anything with electricity running through it.

The Army has a specific job description for a 25U. These are Sergeant Mitchell's job duties, but they are also the duties of every other 25U in the Army. Mitchell would definitely want to list some duties in his resume, but would need to be careful that they don't sound too generic or vague.

For example, one of the official duties of a 25U in the Army is to "supervise, install, maintain, and troubleshoot signal support systems and terminal devices, to include radio, wire, and battlefield automated systems." What does that mean? Would a civilian hiring manager understand and appreciate that?

Sergeant Mitchell tweaked this language just a little bit to make it work for his resume, taking out some of the military language and making it easier to understand: "Installed, maintained, and provided training and troubleshooting on a variety of secure and non-secure communications systems." This is a simple example, but you can see how this second version is much easier to understand.

Accomplishments Are Not Generic. Accomplishments are the specific achievements that YOU did, and improvements YOU made. In Sergeant Mitchell's case, he did about a million things in Iraq that were unique to his unit, and they work well in his resume.

Here are a couple of specific accomplishments he might list:

Maintained complex radio communications systems for 30 vehicles (worth more than $400K), troubleshooting and replacing equipment, as

JOB HUNT

needed; developed new system for monitoring communications equipment, resulting in zero radio malfunctions during high-intensity combat assignment.

Overcame a lack of internal communications by coordinating with engineers to cut down old telephone poles on abandoned Iraqi facility and to install telephone poles on base; directed installation of aerial telephone wires and tactical phones at key locations, enhancing productivity and overall resources.

Accomplishments are personalized. And remember, you want to include accomplishments that are also relevant. Sergeant Mitchell's accomplishments might help him land a job in the communications field, but as an accountant? Not so much.

WRITING TIPS AND SAMPLES

The following tips and examples will demonstrate what you should and should not do in your own resume:

- Write your resume in the third-person point of view (POV), not first-person POV.

  Poor: I managed a team of six people in organizing and tracking a major warehouse operation.

  Better: Directed team of 12 personnel in organizing, tracking, and improving a 24/7

warehouse of trucking supplies valued at more than $800K.

- Integrate some action verbs and action-oriented adjectives, but don't overuse them!

Take Note

For your convenience, we have included a list of action verbs and terms in the Appendix and on the Vet's Toolbox CD. Use them, but use them wisely. If a word fits into one of your accomplishments nicely, then great! But when you use too many, it becomes obvious to the reader, and it doesn't work.

Poor: Detail-oriented, versatile, results-focused, and dedicated leader with 20 years of experience. *(uses too many action-oriented adjectives in a row without any specific action verbs that clarify actual tasks)*

Better: Highly skilled electrical engineer with 20 years' experience in designing, evaluating, troubleshooting, and improving complex electrical systems for Fortune 500 companies. *(uses relevant action verbs descriptive of the applicant's tasks)*

- Write strong accomplishments.

  Weak accomplishment: Manage the supply room and help my section chief organize the armory.

  Better: Played a key role in organizing and accounting for more than $200K in government inventory; after only one month of preparation, received "outstanding" rating on official readiness inspection.

- Avoid vague language.

  Example of vague language: Worked with section chief to send tools and equipment to other units in Iraq and the U.S.

  Example of specific language: Planned logistical movement of 50 different tools and pieces of equipment across international boundaries to support the Global War on Terrorism; more

than $1M worth of inventory shipped with 100% accountability.

- In general, choose active voice over passive voice when describing duties and accomplishments.

  Example of passive voice with first-person POV (avoid): In Iraq, as part of my responsibilities, hardware and software were developed and a help desk operated.

  Example of active voice with third-person POV (use): Provided expert technical support and customer service while troubleshooting and solving a broad range of Information Technology (IT) problems.

Use the Accomplishments Worksheet in the Appendix and the Vet's Toolbox CD to write out strong accomplishments for your resume.

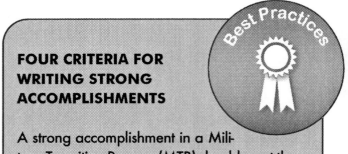

FOUR CRITERIA FOR WRITING STRONG ACCOMPLISHMENTS

A strong accomplishment in a Military Transition Resume (MTR) should meet these four criteria:
1. It is error-free and written in an active voice
2. It is specific to you and what you did, not generic or focused on general duties
3. It has an action and a result
4. It is free of military terminology or excessive acronyms

EXAMPLES OF TRANSLATING YOUR EXPERIENCE

Now you are ready to actually sit down and write your accomplishments for each position. We recommend writing at least 5-10 duties, and 5-10 specific accomplishments. Once you actually format your resume, you might not be able to fit them all, but it will be helpful to have them on hand. As you write them out, remember everything we've said so far about translating your military experience into civilian terminology.

First, most civilian employers won't know what all the acronyms mean. Avoid using them, but if you have to, spell them out the first time they're used. Additionally, you must assume that the person reading your resume does not have military experience, so explain in clear and easy-to-understand terms.

Below, you will find a few examples from several branches of service. There are countless ways to translate your experience, and they really depend on your personal situation. The point here is to show how the military described the positions, and then demonstrate a couple of ways to "demilitarize" those descriptions.

ARMY

Job Title	Infantryman (11B)
Official Description	Protect personnel and property, engaging in direct conflict and combining troubleshooting abilities and situational problem-solving and conflict management skills with training in grounds weapons, counterterrorism, riot control, and sabotage. Operate and maintain weapons, weapons systems, night-vision devices, communications systems, protective equipment, and supplies. Lead or participate in patrols and raids, apprehend insurgents, confiscate weapon caches, locate roadside bombs, and conduct other military operations. Facilitate intelligence operations in hostile environment and for personnel convoying throughout areas of conflict.
Sample Demilitarized Bullets	Provided security and protection for groups of up to 200 people in critical government facilities and vehicles. Applied strong problem solving and situational awareness; responded to dozens of emergencies and resolved each in an efficient manner. Trained and experienced in grounds weapons, counterterrorism, and riot control tactics; led 27 critical assignments in northern Afghanistan in 2010. Operated and maintained weapons, weapons systems, night-vision devices, communications systems, and protective equipment and supplies worth more than $800K. Ensured 100% accountability of all team equipment in every assignment. Performed as viable member of security team and received three awards for outstanding service. Acted as an effective liaison between various agencies to overcome cultural barriers, improve security, and foster productive relationships.
Job Title	Aircraft Electrician (15F)
Official Description	Diagnose and troubleshoot malfunctions in electrical and electronic components, including solid state and transistorized subsystems. Applies principles of electricity/electronics, hydrostatic motion, pneumatics, and hydraulics to repair aircraft instrument systems. Remove, install, repair, adjust, and test electrical and electronic elements of assemblies and components according to technical manuals, directives, and safety procedures. Clean, preserve, and store electrical and electronic components and aircraft instruments. Remove, repair, service, install, and troubleshoot nickel-cadmium batteries. Use and perform operator maintenance on common and special tools for maximum efficiency. Requisition and maintain shop and bench stock for repair of aircraft electrical systems.
Sample Demilitarized Bullets	Diagnosed and resolved malfunctions in electrical and electronic components on critical government aircraft worth billions of dollars. Maintained $3M worth of specialized tools and equipment. Demonstrated deep-rooted knowledge of principles of electricity/electronics, pneumatics, and hydraulics to repair aircraft instrument systems. Received "outstanding" performance evaluations for technical expertise. Read, analyzed, and interpreted a broad range of technical manuals, directives, and safety procedures. Accurately prepared forms and records related to aircraft maintenance.

Air Force

Job Title	Security Forces (3P)
Official Description	Ensure combat capability through the functions of installation security, nuclear and conventional weapon systems and resources security, air base defense, law enforcement, information security, military working dog activities, and combat arms training.
Sample Demilitarized Bullets	Ensured operational capability to military forces in a variety of areas, aligning security considerations with strategic goals and objectives. Applied knowledge of nuclear and conventional weapon systems to improve overall security. Helped to prevent three major attacks on a government facility. Coordinated with Information Technology (IT) personnel to ensure ongoing security of information networks. Trained more than 200 personnel on all aspects of organizational security. Led a team of 16 security specialists and served as key Security Advisor to senior officials.
Job Title	Financial (6F)
Official Description	Receive, disburse, and account for public funds, appropriation and expense, cost, working capital, and real property accounting, including reporting and analyzing costs of programs and operations; formulate, execute, and analyze financial programs.
Sample Demilitarized Bullets	Managed, administered, and justified budgets of up to $10M, cutting overall costs by 16% annually. Received, disbursed, and accounted for public funds for 13K military personnel and families dispersed in 6 locations. Analyzed and reported on program spending to reduce expenditures and advise senior decision makers.

Navy

Job Title	Air Traffic Controller (AC3)
Official Description	Select radar presentation using Fast Time Constant (FTC), Sensitivity Time Control (STC), and Moving Target Indicator (MTI) to enhance radar presentation. Request/obtain/transmit Air Traffic Control (ATC) clearances and releases. Forward departure and arrival times. Notify required personnel of changing weather conditions and duty runway changes.
Sample Demilitarized Bullets	Utilized cutting-edge communications and radar technology to coordinate aircraft movements. Requested, obtained, and transmitted Air Traffic Control (ATC) clearances and releases to ensure smooth flow of numerous aircraft, vehicles, and safety personnel. Coordinated departure and arrival times for 24 months without a single safety violation. Ensured ongoing flight operations by notifying decision makers of changing weather conditions and runway problems.
Job Title	Officer of the Deck
Official Description	Take charge of the safe and proper operation of the ship. Supervise the personnel on watch on the bridge, ensuring all deck log entries are made, and sign the log at the end of the watch.
Sample Demilitarized Bullets	Managed and coordinated a wide range of overlapping logistics tasks and decisions to safely operate government vessels worth more than $50M. Supervised the training, safety, and daily work efforts of up to 30 personnel.

Marines

Job Title	Basic Administrative Marine (0001)
Official Description	Perform administrative and clerical functions: typing; communications; technology; management; personal computer skills; preparation and use of military publications; filing; recordkeeping, etc.
Sample Demilitarized Bullets	Performed a broad range of administrative office assignments in support of records management. Utilized Microsoft (MS) Word, Excel, and Access software to capture and manage sensitive information. Communicated effectively, both verbally and in writing, with personnel at all levels of the organization. Developed a new system for monitoring changes to personnel files. New system was implemented as a model practice across the organization. Skillfully prepared, revised, and utilized publications to comply with organizational policy. Maintained an extensive filing system; recognized for 100% accuracy in organizing personnel records.
Official Title	Maintenance Management Specialist (0411)
Official Description	Provide advice, guidance, and assistance to equipment commodity manager, maintenance manager, and maintenance personnel; supervise and monitor maintenance.
Sample Demilitarized Bullets	Supported managerial staff in assignments to achieve organization's maintenance goals. Assisted in personnel assignments and supervising teams of up to 12 personnel with zero safety violations. Monitored work processes and made recommendations for improvement that led to a 25% increase in overall efficiency.

Coast Guard

Job Title	Information Systems Technician
Official Description	Operate communication equipment; transmit, receive, and process all forms of military records and voice communications. Install and maintain telecommunications equipment ranging from pole lines and underground cables to computer-based data communications.
Sample Demilitarized Bullets	Operated various types of secure and non-secure communications equipment, both in an office and in threatening environments. Received, transmitted, and processed all forms of voice and digital communications to improve Command and Control (C2). Installed, operated, and maintained telecommunications equipment to improve information sharing between key decision makers. Highly proficient in numerous software and computer applications. Troubleshot a major network issue and developed a solution that increased usable bandwidth by 35% and improved information security.
Job Title	Public Affairs Specialist
Official Description	Report and edit news; publish information about service members and activities through newspapers, magazines, radio, and television; shoot and develop film and photographs.
Sample Demilitarized Bullets	Reported and edited news releases, articles, and other correspondence. Published stories and information about personnel and activities in newspapers, magazines, radio, and television. Shot and developed film, and provided photojournalism support during major organizational activities.

Again, these sample bullets would not apply to every person who held these positions—that's because all vets are unique and different. But the point here is that there's a big difference between plain old job descriptions and specific and relevant accomplishments. Do you notice the use of active voice and specific numbers and amounts? Do you notice the focus on actions and results? If you do, then you get the point of these samples and you are ready to start writing your resume.

For an effective tool to help translate your military skills, check out the following website at military.com: http://www.military.com/skills-translator/mos-translator. You can input your Military Occupational Specialty (MOS) number or job title, and military branch, and then conduct a search that will provide a list with equivalent civilian occupations, many of which have federal equivalents.

DUTIES AND ACCOMPLISHMENTS WORKSHEET

Now that you understand where to find and how to write your duties and accomplishments, use the spaces on the next few pages to write out your first drafts. You can refer to the numerous resume samples in Appendix B and on the Vet's Toolbox CD for more examples of good accomplishments. For your convenience, we have also included an electronic version of this worksheet on the Vet's Toolbox CD. This will start you thinking in the right way.

Job Information: (you might want to write in your job title, start and end dates, and any other information to help you be organized for when you actually develop your resume)

_____

_____

Top Duties:

1. _____

2. _____

3. _____

4. _____

5. _____

6. _____

7. _____

8. _____

Top Results/Accomplishments:

1. _____

2. _____

3. _____

4. _____

5. _____

6. _____

7. _____

8. _____

Job Information: (you might want to write in your job title, start and end dates, and any other information to help you be organized for when you actually develop your resume)

_____

_____

Top Duties:

1. _____

2. _____

3. _____

4. _____

5. _____

6. _____

7. _____

8. _____

9. _____

10._____

Top Results/Accomplishments:

1. _____

2. _____

3. _____

4. _____

5. _____

6. _____

7. _____

8. _____

9. _____

10._____

Job Information: (you might want to write in your job title, start and end dates, and any other information to help you be organized for when you actually develop your resume)

_____

_____

Top Duties:

1. _____

2. _____

3. _____

4. _____

5. _____

6. _____

7. _____

8. _____

9. _____

10. _____

Top Results/Accomplishments:

1. _____

2. _____

3. _____

4. _____

5. _____

6. _____

7. _____

8. _____

9. _____

10. _____

Job Information: (you might want to write in your job title, start and end dates, and any other information to help you be organized for when you actually develop your resume)

_____

_____

Top Duties:

1. _____

2. _____

3. _____

4. _____

5. _____

6. _____

7. _____

8. _____

9. _____

10. _____

Top Results/Accomplishments:

1. _____

2. _____

3. _____

4. _____

5. _____

6. _____

7. _____

8. _____

9. _____

10. _____

CHECK POINT SUMMARY

In this check point, you learned that capturing your military accomplishments and then presenting them in the right way is the most important part of writing a great resume. You also learned how to identify your skills and match them with specific companies or career fields in the private sector. Finally, you learned that there is a difference between duties and accomplishments, and saw actual examples of how to demilitarize military experience.

So... you understand your options out there in the civilian world. You know how to gather your documents, and write out your accomplishments for the last 10 years.

Now you're ready to put together your resume!

Check Point Notes

_____

_____

_____

_____

_____

_____

_____

_____

_____

_____

_____

_____

_____

_____

_____

_____

_____

_____

_____

_____

_____

Check Point 3

Write Your Military to Federal Resume

WRITE YOUR MILITARY TO FEDERAL RESUME

There are a number of different Federal resume formats, and each has its own character counts, page limits, and other restrictions. The important thing to remember is that formatting is easy. You should focus on writing great content first, and then format everything to meet the requirements of the specific agency.

Despite the recent attempts to streamline processes (USAJobs went offline for more than a week in October 2011 to make some changes and launch version 3.0), the federal government application process can still be quite tedious. But it's also worth it if you can land one of the great jobs the government has to offer.

 Take Note Probably the single most important thing to remember about formatting your Federal resume is READ THE "HOW TO APPLY" TAB ON THE JOB ANNOUNCEMENT! In fact, read the job announcement in its entirety, but definitely follow the specific instructions in the "How to Apply" tab. If you have questions, email the address on the job well in advance of the job closing date.

COMPONENTS OF A FEDERAL RESUME

Most of the time, you won't have to worry about leaving out a part of the Federal resume, because you will create your resume using an online resume builder. If you are permitted to email, mail, hand-deliver, or fax your resume, then it's a good idea to check the USAJobs system anyway for the required fields. You will also be able to use the USAJobs resume template included on your Vet's Toolbox CD, but make sure it is still accurate, as

the federal government often makes changes to application requirements.

Basically, in a Federal resume, you fill out your personal contact information, and then fill out your work history from most recent job first (going back about 10 years). You don't want to leave employment gaps in your work history, so if there are gaps of more than a couple of months, it's best to give a brief explanation (training, relocation, etc.).

Contact Information. Most federal positions will require you to provide the contact information listed below. Again, check the job announcement to make sure you are including the required information. For example, sometimes you need to include your Social Security Number (SSN), and other times you don't.

- Full name
- Mailing address
- Home, mobile, and work phone numbers (with area code)
- DSN contact phone
- Email address
- Social Security Number
- Country of citizenship
- Veterans' Preference

Employment History. This is the "meat" of your Federal resume, as well as where you will include your duties and accomplishments. You will typically need the following information:

- Job title of your last position at the organization
- Series and grade (if it was a federal position)
- Employer name, full address, and zip code
- Supervisor's name and phone number (make sure it's okay before you list someone as a reference)
- Start and end dates, including month and year (some employers require month, date, and year)
- Hours per week (list "40+" if you worked more than 40)
- Ending salary
- Duties, assignments, and special projects
- Special accomplishments, recognitions, or awards

Education. Include any colleges from which you have earned a degree. USAJobs will typically ask for the college name, city, state, major, and year the degree was earned. You also have the option to list your minor, your GPA, and any relevant coursework. If you have specific classes that are relevant to the position, then list them, too! If you are within 10 credit hours of earning a degree, then it's a good idea to include it in the Education section and input your projected graduation date. However, if you aren't that close to earning a degree, don't list in under Education, because you might be perceived as trying to "fool" the hiring agency. Instead, list the fact that you're working in a degree under the section in Professional Training.

With respect to listing high-school information, we recommend using a case-by-case approach. If you are unsure whether to include this information, then call or email to ask. However, if in doubt, it really shouldn't hurt to list it, especially if you have no college experience yet.

Professional Training. This is where you list any relevant professional training. You should at least list the name of the course, the organization that gave the training, and the year completed. Just as with your work history, training you've taken in

the past 10 years is going to be much more relevant than older training. But if you feel that something is relevant to the position, it can't hurt to include it.

References. Many of these systems will require you to include at least three references, so you should have their names, job titles, organizations, phone numbers, and email addresses. Every once in a while, but not often, you might be asked for the mailing address of your references.

Additional Information. This is an area included in almost all Federal resume systems that people don't use to their advantage. But you should! For example, USAJobs allows only 3,000 characters for each position in your work history, but it allows up to 20,000 more characters in Additional Information! And even though it's at the "bottom" of the resume builder, it should receive just as much attention as the "top" of the resume.

As you have probably seen in resumes in the past, and as you'll learn more in the next check point, the first third of the first page of your resume is a great place to put impactful points and information, such as a Professional Summary and a list of relevant skills. It gives the reader a nice snapshot of your skills and experience, even before he/she dives into the Work History section and sees more of your stellar accomplishments in the Marines (or Coast Guard, Army, Navy, Air Force, course, etc.). In a Federal resume system, you can include that information in the Additional Information section, as long as you follow the rules about character counts and permitted characters. (For instance, some systems won't allow you to use quotation marks.)

> **USE THE "ADDITIONAL INFORMATION" SECTION TO OPTIMIZE YOUR FEDERAL RESUME!**
>
> *Best Practices*

Security Clearance: If you have a Secret or Top Secret clearance, be sure to include that information. It could be yet another element that sets you apart from the competition.

Work History Continued: If you couldn't fit everything in the Employment History section and you think you have relevant information to share in some of the positions, then you can continue them here. Further, if you have positions that go back beyond 10 years, but you think they are important/relevant, you can summarize them here.

Professional Summary: The Professional Summary is a short (maybe one 5- to 10-line paragraph) that gives the reviewer an overview of your profes-

sional background, your relevant skills and experience for the job, and one or two specific examples to back up those claims. Think of it as a short marketing piece that's all about you. See the Federal resume samples in the Appendix and on the Vet's Toolbox CD.

Career Highlights: Listing 5-10 of your top career achievements (that are relevant to the job) is another good way to entice reviewers to call you in for an interview.

Performance Quotes: Try including a couple of short quotes about you from your official performance evaluations. As always, you should only include information in your resume that is honest and relevant. If you couldn't provide evidence if asked to do so, then don't include it.

Awards and Recognition: Civilian employers may not appreciate exactly what it takes to obtain a Bronze Star or another military award, but it still serves to show that you were recognized for outstanding performance. Don't go overboard here, but it certainly can't hurt to list 10 or more awards that you've earned. To make it a little easier for employers to understand, you can give a very brief explanation, such as "Army Commendation Medal for outstanding support during major training exercise, 2008."

Computer and Technology Skills: This is a good place to list any software, machinery, tools, testing equipment, or other specialized equipment in which you are proficient.

Publications: If you have been published in trade or professional publications, or even if you've written press releases for your unit, this is a good place to highlight these publications. As with everything else, you shouldn't list anything that is completely irrelevant to the job you're seeking.

Professional Licenses and Certifications: If you have computer certifications or other professional licenses, list their titles and year completed here.

USING KEYWORDS TO YOUR ADVANTAGE

First, what are keywords? They are simply the important terms and phrases in the job announcement. Another way to say it is this: Keywords are words and phrases that correspond to what the job announcement is calling for, and that will stimulate a hiring agent's interest in you. So if the job is for a contracting specialist and it mentions "cost analysis" many times, then you can bet that's an important keyword to the hiring manager.

Here's the deal: Not only are keywords logical ways to match your skills to the information in the job announcement, but they are a way to make life a little bit easier for Human Resources (HR) professionals who probably read the most resumes. HR professionals are generally the first people to screen incoming resumes, and they have learned to use technology to speed up the process. In the past, they would have to read every application to weed the best job candidates from the rest.

With the advent of computers and searchable software programs, some agencies use an optical scanning program to search for predetermined qualifications and keywords in resumes. By using this system, they "weed out" many applicants who might not be qualified. However, the Navy CHART system is now using USAJobs and Army CPOL is projected to completely transition to the USAJobs system in 2012.

So how and where do you find keywords? They are actually right in the job announcement! Now, they aren't going to be listed for you, but with a little common sense, you should be able to spot them fairly easily. First, you should either print it

out and highlight/circle the keywords, or use a separate sheet of paper and write a list. Starting at the top of the job announcement, review each section, especially the Major Duties, Qualifications Required, and any narrative statements you have to answer. This isn't rocket science; you should simply be looking for the words and phrases that are repeated, or seem the most important to the position. Once you have your list, you can see which ones apply to you, and try to use them in describing your duties and accomplishments.

> *Take Note*
>
> Below is a sample from an actual announcement, with suggested keywords italicized.
>
> QUALIFICATIONS REQUIRED: Have one year of specialized experience, equivalent to the GS-12 level in the Federal Service, *managing, directing,* or *supervising* work to include duties such as *development of strategic plans, budget formation and administration and fiscal management, human resources administration, project planning and execution,* and *program evaluation*, etc.
>
> Based on the above sample, your keywords might include *staff supervision, strategic planning, fiscal management, human resources, project planning,* and *program evaluation*. With these keywords identified, you now have a general blueprint on what areas you need to explore in your background.

If your goal is to become an aircraft mechanic, important keywords might be hydraulics, airframe and power plant, structural repair, operational testing, inspections, or the names of specific tools and equipment used in that profession.

You don't want to become *too* caught up in worrying about keywords, because matching your skills with the right job in the first place is much more important. No amount of keywords is going to land you a job or take you through an interview unless you really have the skills they're seeking. However, there is one effective a way to use and integrate keywords into your Federal resume—it's called the headline format.

THE HEADLINE FORMAT-STYLE RESUME

CareerPro Global, Inc. (CPG) developed the Headline Format-Style Resume in the early 1990s to assist veterans returning from Operations Desert Shield and Desert Storm. When the SF-171 was eliminated and regular paper Federal resumes and RESUMIX systems were launched in 1995, we adapted the headline format on all Federal resume applications, as well. The headline format-style resume is an easy and effective tool to help organize your duties and accomplishments, and integrate keywords and phrases into your resume. The headline format also helps those overworked HR representatives to easily find the relevant skills and accomplishments they are seeking; you definitely want to do whatever you can to make it easy for them!

What does the headline format look like? It's simple, really. Under each job, instead of just listing bullets or having random blocks of text, you organize your duties and accomplishments into headlines and put those headlines into capital or bold text, or both. For example, if you were an Instructor and First Sergeant, the headline for that section might be "translated" to TRAINING AND LEADERSHIP.

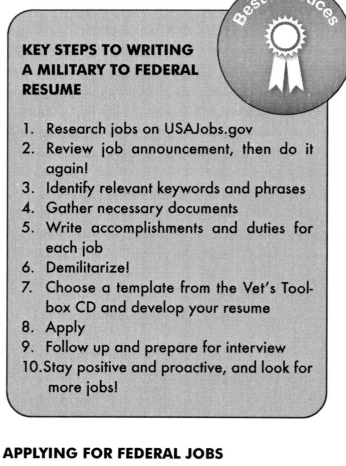

Take Note

Note that Federal resumes typically don't require cover letters, but if they do, then follow the cover letter-writing instructions found in Check Point 4. For your convenience, you will also find sample cover letters on the Vet's Toolbox CD.

SAMPLE FEDERAL RESUME WITH HEADLINES/KEYWORDS

On the next page is an example of how you can use keywords to create headlines within the Employment section of a resume. Note how the "headline"" is followed by a brief description that captures the key points or accomplishments within the headline and does not just restate basic job description (see Check Point 2 for a refresher).

Notice also how the text is left-justified with no formatting (highlights and bold for illustration purposes); this is the recommended format for federal electronic applications. The information at the beginning of the section—including position title, employer, hours per week, salary, supervisor name, and contact information—is required for Federal resumes.

Best Practices

KEY STEPS TO WRITING A MILITARY TO FEDERAL RESUME

1. Research jobs on USAJobs.gov
2. Review job announcement, then do it again!
3. Identify relevant keywords and phrases
4. Gather necessary documents
5. Write accomplishments and duties for each job
6. Demilitarize!
7. Choose a template from the Vet's Toolbox CD and develop your resume
8. Apply
9. Follow up and prepare for interview
10. Stay positive and proactive, and look for more jobs!

APPLYING FOR FEDERAL JOBS

As you learned in Check Point 1, you will typically apply for a federal job through the USAJobs.gov website or another agency website.

HQ U.S. Special Operations Command (USSOCOM), 06/22/2007 to Present, Future Operations officer MacDill Air Force Base (AFB), Tampa, FL, United States, 40+ hours/week, $60,000 per year, Supervisor: John Joes, 222-222-2222, may contact.

DUTIES: Serve as Strategist planning future operations and coordinating with overall Department of Defense (DoD) initiatives of the Global War on Terrorism (GWOT).

PROGRAM PLANNING/EXECUTION: Conduct security-sensitive planning. Coordinate and execute biweekly Join Synchronization Bard comprised of up to 20 executive-level leaders ranging from colonels to three-star generals, Orchestrate the coordination and synchronization of Combatant Command, Joint Staff, and Office of the Secretary of Defense (OSD) actions, provide consultation and analysis-based options, recommendations, and solutions.

FINANCE OVERSIGHT/CONTRACT ADMINISTRATION: Develop and manage large-scale contracts, such as Global Analysis Cell production initiative and Battle Staff Support Cell totaling $1M+.

REPRESENTATION: Lead concept development for a GWOT prioritization tool, a strategic innovation designed to provide links between GWOT assessments and program prioritization.

IMPROVEMENT MANAGEMENT: Standardize National Implementation Plan (NIP) language across 56 sub-objectives; enable reliable, uniform, results-based assessment for the GWOT. Provide development and implementation contributions to create Special Operations Staff Officer Courses to prepare inbound officers for duty.

ACCOMPLISHMENTS:
*Developed model for evaluating input provided for the national Defense Authorization Act 2006, Section 1206 report; influenced resourcing for emerging counterterrorism projects.
*Provided authorial and editorial contributions during revisions of policy, such as for US Directive 71-4; refined its overall instructiveness and applicability.

You are often given a choice to use a resume (which we recommend always doing), or the Optional Application for Federal Employment form (OF-612), or any other written format of choice. Other times, a resume (and resume only) is required, and it must be submitted through a specific website and meet all formatting requirements. Cover letters are usually not required or requested.

There are also rare cases in which a federal agency will require you to mail in your resume. If this is the case, you can either print out your USAJobs resume or develop a better-looking one. The important thing to remember is to keep it simple. Don't bother with fancy graphics or anything like that. The federal government typically frowns on flashy or distracting resume formats (which is probably why almost all resume are submitted electronically).

If you do have to mail or fax your resume, these simple formatting steps can help to ensure a clean and comprehensive resume:

• Read the job announcement for any specific information they require.
• Read the "How to Apply" tab again!
• Submit your resume on plain white paper. No crazy colors!

- Use half-inch margins and Times New Roman, Courier, or Arial font, size 11 or 12.
- Keep the resume looking professional and clean.
- Call or email the contact in the job announcement if you have questions.

When you are developing your resume for a federal job, go to the job announcement and click on the "Apply Now" button to see exactly what will be required. You may have to use their online resume builder, or you may be able to upload your own resume. This can also show you which online system is being used, so you will be able to research the formatting requirements.

Take Note

Shameless Disclaimer: The authors of this book are in the resume-writing and career-coaching industry, and we are always adjusting our products to keep up with current trends and changes. The information about the different online systems below is very accurate, but not guaranteed to be accurate forever and not intended to describe every online system. Instead, it is designed to show you how some of them work, and to encourage you to think about an agency's requirements as you develop your application materials. It is up to you to check the agency's website, read the job announcement (especially the "How to Apply" tab), and research their application instructions to ensure you meet all the formatting requirements, such as character counts. Having said that, the information below, as well as the USAJobs resume template on the Vet's Toolbox CD, will assist you in preparing a professional and properly formatted resume.

SELECTED ONLINE FEDERAL SYSTEMS REQUIREMENTS AND RESTRICTIONS

While most federal agencies use the system established on USAJobs.gov for their application process, a few use their own systems. These other systems include CPOL and AVUE. Specific agencies, such as the Federal Bureau of Investigation (FBI), Social Security Administration (SSA), and Federal Aviation Administration (FAA), also have their own application procedures. A good rule of thumb is to read the announcement to determine what type of application format is required.

USAJobs (http://www.USAJobs.gov)
Overall Length: No overall limit, except for certain rare individual agencies and job announcements
Work Experience: 5,000 characters per work experience
Education (includes relevant coursework, licenses, and certifications): 2,000 characters to describe coursework
Job-Related Training: 5,000 characters
Professional Publications: 5,000 characters
Additional Information: 20,000 characters; enter job-related honors, awards, leadership activities, skills, and professional profile here; KSAs (statements of Knowledge, Skills, and Abilities) may be copied and pasted into this field, depending on the announcement's instructions
Other Information: Up to five separate resumes may be maintained on the USAJobs.gov website
Organizations: 4 maximum
References: 5 maximum

U.S. Army Civilian Jobs - Civilian Personnel Online (CPOL, https://acpol.army.mil/employment/)
Overall Length: 20,000 characters or 6 pages, excluding the Supplemental Data information
Work Experience: 12,000 characters
Education: 2,000 characters
Additional Information (training, licenses, certifications, awards, etc.): 6,000 characters
Cover Letter: 1,500 characters

AVUE Digital Services
(http://www.avuedigitalservices.com)
Overall Length: N/A

Work History: 4,000 characters; as many jobs as necessary

Additional Information: Unlimited characters; enter performance appraisals, leadership activities, and special skills not covered elsewhere

Some agencies that use AVUE Digital Services include:
- Library of Congress - http://www.loc.gov/hr/employment
- U.S. Forest Service - http://www.fs.fed.us/fsjobs
- U.S. Agency for International Development - http://www.usaid.gov/careers/
- Department of Justice, Justice Management Division - http://www.usdoj.gov/jmd
- AVUE Technologies Corporation - http://www.avuetech.com/current-opportunities
- Drug Enforcement Administration - http://www.usdoj.gov/dea/resources/job_applicants.html
- Architect of the Capitol - http://www.aoc.gov/employment/index.cfm
- Defense Intelligence Agency - http://www.dia.mil/careers/
- Securities and Exchange Commission - http://www.sec.gov/jobs.shtml
- Office of Federal Housing Enterprise Oversight - http://www.fhfa.gov
- Peace Corps - http://www.peacecorps.gov/index.cfm?shell=pchq.jobs

QUICKHIRE

QuickHire does not have a website; instead, individual agencies have a built-in online application system that resembles the QuickHire resume format that is accessible via their respective websites.

Overall Length: N/A

Character Limit: 16,000 characters

Resume Headings and Section: Flexible (all one field)

Some agencies that use QuickHire include:
- Federal Deposit Insurance Corporation (FDIC)
- U.S. Department of Transportation - http://www.careers.dot.gov (uses "Careers in Motion")
- U.S. Coast Guard - http://www.uscg.mil/hq/cgpc/cpm/jobs/vacancy.htm

Central Intelligence Agency (CIA, https://www.cia.gov/careers/index.html)
Overall Length: N/A

Skills/Professional Licenses and Certifications: 1,000-character limit

Work Description: 1,000-character limit per position - three positions

Overseas Experience: 1,000-character limit per position - two regions

Military Experience: 1,000-character limit; include any special qualifications or certifications

Defensive Information Systems Agency (DISA, www.disa.mil/careers/index.html)
Work Experience: List five to eight years of relevant experience

Total Length: Five pages plus one supplemental data page

FEDERAL BUREAU OF INVESTIGATION (FBIJOBS.GOV)
Overall length: 16,000 characters and spaces total, or approximately 8 single-spaced pages of text. You should provide the following information in order:

- Contact Data
- Education (chronically arranged, starting with high school)
- Employment History: job title and grade level, if it was a federal job; duties and accomplishments; employer's name and address; supervisor's name and telephone number; starting and ending dates (month and year); hours worked per week; and salary

- Other Qualifications: Include such items as job-related training courses, job-related skills (e.g., typing speed), computer software/hardware skills, foreign language proficiency, job-related honors, awards, special accomplishments, publications, memberships in professional or honor societies, leadership activities, and performance awards

FEDERAL AVIATION ADMINISTRATION (HTTP://JOBS.FAA.GOV/ONLINE APPLICATIONS.HTM)

The Federal Aviation Administration (FAA) introduced the Automated Vacancy Information Access Tool for Online Referral (AVIATOR) in late December 2010. This system replaces the old ASAP and is used for the majority of the FAA vacancy announcements. AVIATOR allows applicants to access announcements on the Internet and link directly to the questionnaire to complete and submit their application.

The FAA also uses the Centralized Applicant Pools (CAPS) system for select jobs, including Electronic Technician (GS-0856) and non-executive-level Airway Transportation Safety Specialists (GS-2101). CAPS is primarily used to rate and rank applicants for "Open Continuous" vacancies, and is similar in concept and information requirements to the old ASAP system.

For your convenience, we have included a US-AJobs resume template on the Vet's Toolbox CD, since this is by far the most popular one you'll see out there. By developing your Federal resume using this template, you will find it much easier to copy/paste your information into the online system once you're ready. Again, don't assume that the template will always be current. Online systems are often changed, updated, or discontinued, so please check with the agency to make sure you meet all of the requirements and that your resume is properly formatted.

Federal Resume Do's and Don'ts Table

Do:	Don't:
Read the vacancy announcement	Assume the requirements are all the same
Reread the "How to Apply" tab	Assume all vacancy announcements use the USAJobs online system
Use keywords	Make up keywords or use them randomly
Use the headline format	Use a big block (paragraph) format
Verify formatting requirements	Assume your resume will fit in all builders
Verify vacancy closing date	Assume the system will take late applications
Customize your resume for each job announcement	Use a general resume for all federal positions

OCCUPATIONAL QUESTIONNAIRES AND KSAS

In the past, written essays known as Knowledge, Skills, and Abilities (KSAs) statements were often required. However, recent developments in federal hiring mandate that KSAs no longer are required for initial applications as of November 2010. At least 89% of federal agencies no longer request KSAs. However, some vacancy announcements "suggest" that you address certain KSA qualifications, and you must incorporate the answers within your Federal resume.

One of the biggest differences between a vacancy announcement for the federal government and the private sector is that federal jobs often require additional documentation of your qualifications.

This additional documentation can take many forms, and the current trend is to use questionnaires to elicit additional information. Despite the recent move from requiring KSA essays to using multiple-choice questionnaires, most agencies are still identifying KSAs in their announcements under "How You Will Be Evaluated." In such cases, agencies are looking not for written essays but instead for the specific knowledge, skills, and abilities to be addressed through the resume.

Keep a close eye on the recent shift to "no KSAs." There have been a number of federal job vacancies that removed the KSAs from the main announcement only to replace them within the occupational questionnaire, which are questions that still require essays. Whether it's a KSA or an occupational questionnaire response, you need to know how to write an effective essay response that uses specific and relevant examples to demonstrate your knowledge, skills, and abilities.

DEFINING "KNOWLEDGE, SKILLS, AND ABILITIES"

Knowledge: An organized body of information, usually of a factual or procedural nature, which, if applied, makes adequate performance on the job possible. Examples include knowledge of:

- Administrative practices
- Budget and accounting principles
- Federal regulations and directives
- Operational systems and procedures
- Environmental compliance law

Skills: The manipulation of data, things, or people through manual, verbal, or mental means. Skills are measurable through testing, can be observed, and are quantifiable. A skill is often referred to as expertness that comes from training, practice, etc. Examples include skill in:

- Electronic or computer repair
- Carpentry, plumbing, and/or HVAC repair
- Managing multiple priorities
- Weapon usage
- Motor vehicle operation

Abilities: The capacity to perform a physical or mental activity at the present time. Typically, abilities are apparent through functions completed on the job. Abilities and skills are often interchanged. Examples include the ability to:
- Organize and plan work (observed at work)
- Analyze situations, programs, and problems
- Coach and mentor others

- Communicate orally and in writing

Simply mentioning that you have a specific knowledge, skill, ability, or characteristic is not enough. You'll want to focus on demonstrating how you applied your specific knowledge, skill, ability, or other characteristic to solve a particular challenge.

WHAT ARE NARRATIVES?
Short narratives are typically included as part of the online assessment questionnaire that agencies are now including as part of the application process.

As a result of the federal hiring reform initiative, agencies are switching to a format in which they ask an applicant to complete multiple sections of an online assessment consisting of multiple-choice questions and then ending with a short narrative to demonstrate the multiple-choice response.

PREPARING NARRATIVE RESPONSES
Maybe you hated essay questions in high school or college, and you are intimidated by having to write one for a federal position. Don't worry; you don't have to be a professional writer (although it's a good idea to find some professional help to give you that extra edge). Just keep it simple and use a current example of something

Take Note

Always maintain your honesty and integrity when writing narratives, and include only factual information and experience. If you are selected for an interview, you will need to be able to defend your statements and possibly even provide more details.

SAMPLE NARRATIVE RESPONSE
The following is an example of a multiple-choice question that requires you to provide an essay response:

Select the statement that best describes your knowledge of the agency mission, operations, policies, and procedures.

A. *I have extensive knowledge of agency programs/policies/procedures on an operational level gained through executing special assignments related to agency programs (e.g., determining the requirements or procedures for implementing major new programs at the local and national level; providing technical advice and assistance to other agency personnel, industry representatives, or special-interest groups; or providing information to media regarding initiatives and special programs w/ various offices).*

B. *I have knowledge of agency programs, policies, and procedures on an operational level gained through assisting in executing special assignments or activities related to agency programs.*

C. *I have limited knowledge of agency mission, operations, policies, and procedures.*

D. *I have no knowledge of agency mission, operations, policies, and procedures.*

If you chose responses A, B, or C in the previous question, provide several brief examples of your accomplishments that demonstrate this experience. If you chose response D, indicate "not applicable."

As you can see by the above example, a short narrative statement will be necessary only if you answered A, B, or C. If you have to write an essay response, pay close attention to any character/space limitations. This information will generally be included below the textbox field on the online assessment or may be included in the vacancy announcement itself.

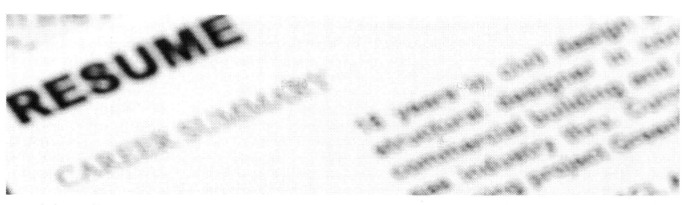

you did to tell a story. Not only can you include specific examples that demonstrate your possession of the knowledge, skill, or ability, but you can also use your paid and unpaid experience, education (degrees, courses, and research projects), awards and recognitions, and quotes from endorsement letters or letters of recommendations.

The easiest—and most preferred—method of writing a strong narrative statement is using the Challenge-Context-Action-Result (CCAR) format. In some military branches, they use a similar technique to capture tasks and accomplishments, called Situation-Task-Action-Result (STAR). The CCAR format is similar, and provides a logical outline to present your information.

THE CCAR FORMAT
CHALLENGE: Describe a specific problem or goal faced in the assignment and why it was difficult/unique/challenging. What was your job title? When did this happen?

CONTEXT: Why was this a problem? What did the organization need you to accomplish?

ACTION: Describe the specific actions you took to resolve the challenge.

RESULT: Provide examples of results with numbers to quantify the result, if possible.

Here's an example of a "before-and-after" written narrative statement:

BEFORE (poor):

"I have written numerous policies, letters, and memoranda. These written documents cover a variety of complex topics and I have never had a complaint from a reader. I am a good writer, pride myself on my creativity and writing skills, and never suffer from writer's block. My work is always grammatically correct and there are no spelling errors."

This is a poor example because it doesn't really tell the hiring official anything. It's not specific, and won't set you apart from the rest of the applicants.

AFTER (better!):

As a Human Resources Specialist (E-6) in the Department of Defense (DoD) in 2007, my leadership challenged me to update all of our organizational policies after an audit identified major deficiencies in our current policies. I was required to prepare policies and procedures on performance management, staffing, and employee relations [*challenge/context*].

I researched the old policies and the finding of the audit, and then wrote new policies that corrected misunderstandings that many employees had concerning performance management [*actions*].

I received the agency's Plain English Award for the performance management policy I wrote, and the other policies I prepared were also well received. The employee relations policy I prepared is seen as a model program, and I was asked to discuss it at a recent DoD-wide Human

Resources (HR) meeting. It is now under consideration for department-wide adoption [results].

In this second example, the story follows the CCAR format and is much more effective. If you don't provide a specific example, you might as well be saying, "Oh yes, I do that; trust me, I do it well..." Rather than taking this ineffective approach, simply state what you can do, then PROVE it with a relevant example.

KSA Do's and Don'ts Table

Do:	Don't
Use specific examples	Be too general or vague
Be factual	Stretch the truth
Use keywords from the job announcement	Use totally unrelated or irrelevant information in your examples
Use CCAR	Just list a few random bullets or sentences
Spell out all terms before using acronyms	Use too many acronyms or technical terms

KSA WORKSHEET

For each KSA or other essay question you might need to write, the following worksheet will help you to write your response. You will also find an electronic version of this worksheet on the Vet's Toolbox CD.

Question: _____

Your Topic or Example: _____

CHALLENGE: Describe a specific problem or goal and the obstacles, problems, and challenges you faced in achieving your goal.

_____

_____

_____

CONTEXT: Title of your job or role you are playing in this example. Talk about the individuals and groups with whom you worked and/or the environment in which you worked to tackle a particular challenge.

_____

_____

_____

ACTIONS: Discuss the specific actions you took to address a challenge. Describe your role and actions in resolving the problem or meeting the outcome goals.

_____

_____

_____

RESULTS: Describe results, outcomes, or long-term impacts of your efforts.

_____

_____

_____

Question: _____

_____

Your Topic or Example: _____

_____

CHALLENGE: Describe a specific problem or goal and the obstacles, problems, and challenges you faced in achieving your goal.

_____

_____

_____

CONTEXT: Title of your job or role you are playing in this example. Talk about the individuals and groups with whom you worked and/or the environment in which you worked to tackle a particular challenge.

_____

_____

_____

ACTIONS: Discuss the specific actions you took to address a challenge. Describe your role and actions in resolving the problem or meeting the outcome goals.

_____

_____

_____

RESULTS: Describe results, outcomes, or long-term impacts of your efforts.

_____

_____

_____

Question: _____

_____

Your Topic or Example: _____

_____

CHALLENGE: Describe a specific problem or goal and the obstacles, problems, and challenges you faced in achieving your goal.

_____

_____

_____

CONTEXT: Title of your job or role you are playing in this example. Talk about the individuals and groups with whom you worked and/or the environment in which you worked to tackle a particular challenge.

_____

_____

_____

ACTIONS: Discuss the specific actions you took to address a challenge. Describe your role and actions in resolving the problem or meeting the outcome goals.

_____

_____

_____

RESULTS: Describe results, outcomes, or long-term impacts of your efforts.

_____

_____

_____

Question: _____

_____

Your Topic or Example: _____

_____

CHALLENGE: Describe a specific problem or goal and the obstacles, problems, and challenges you faced in achieving your goal.

_____

_____

_____

CONTEXT: Title of your job or role you are playing in this example. Talk about the individuals and groups with whom you worked and/or the environment in which you worked to tackle a particular challenge.

_____

_____

_____

ACTIONS: Discuss the specific actions you took to address a challenge. Describe your role and actions in resolving the problem or meeting the outcome goals.

_____

_____

_____

RESULTS: Describe results, outcomes, or long-term impacts of your efforts.

_____

_____

_____

Florence Dominguez

1749 West 800 South St., George, UT 84770, United States
Email: email@usa.com
Day Phone: 123-456-7890
Mobile Phone: 123-456-7890
Highest Federal Civilian Position Held: GS-7

WORK EXPERIENCE:

Veterans Affairs (VA) Police Department	03/2002 to Present
Tacoma, WA, United States	
Federal Police Officer (GS 6/7)	Average hours per week: 40
Scott Blanchard	Phone: 123-456-7890

Duties, Accomplishments, and Related Skills:

The organization provides uniformed police service for the U.S. Department of Veterans Affairs (VA). As a Federal Police Officer, enforce federal laws, determine when a crime has been committed, and apprehend suspects.

KNOWLEDGE OF SECURITY AND LAW ENFORCEMENT: Apply 30 years of comprehensive security and law enforcement knowledge pertaining to following arrest procedures, collecting evidence, conducting investigations, writing reports, and determining jurisdiction. Perform criminal investigations, enforce federal laws, and apprehend suspects. Conduct interviews, examine documents, take statements, and file complaints.

PHYSICAL SECURITY: Utilize Closed Circuit Television (CCTV), Intrusion Detection System (IDS), and alarm systems to ensure access control and physical security of healthcare facility. Conduct security surveys of all areas of the medical center to detect opportunities for pilferage, theft, and other crimes. Carry out threat procedure plans for large, complex organization.

COMMUNICATIONS: Demonstrate outstanding oral and written communication skills. Interview suspects and witnesses in the investigation of federal crimes. Draft extensive written reports detailing the specifics of the alleged criminal activity and facility security. Provide depositions and testify in court to aid in the prosecution of criminal cases.

TRAINING: Develop and conduct numerous training courses for police and security personnel. Teach courses in First Aid, Automated External Defibrillators (AED), Cardiopulmonary Resuscitation (CPR), Handcuffing, Pepper Spray, and Night Stick. Maintain proper records of training courses and documentation in accordance with state regulations.

ACCOMPLISHMENTS:
*   Demonstrated exceptional ability to handle high-threat situation when successfully talking down suspect threatening to harm hospital employee; resolved conflict peacefully.
*   Conducted numerous criminal investigations leading to arrests and convictions in child molestation, narcotics, theft, and driving under the influence.

- Received Outstanding Service Award, 2006.
- Chosen to train other law enforcement personnel for the State of Washington in investigations and firearms.

American Security Company   09/1997 to 03/2002
Ithica, NY United States
Operations Manager   Average hours per week: 40
Johnny Walker   Phone: 123-456-7890

Duties, Accomplishments, and Related Skills:
Organization provides uniform security for private, corporate, and commercial clients.

OPERATIONS MANAGEMENT: Managed day-to-day security operations for 215 law enforcement officers. Developed goals and plans for the organization. Assigned workloads and ensured personnel had proper training to cover all aspects, both planned and emergency, of security and patrol work. Provided background checks, internal investigations, surveillance, countersurveillance, loss prevention, security analysis, civil and criminal investigations, and weapons instruction.

HUMAN RESOURCE (HR) AND BUSINESS MANAGEMENT: Managed HR duties for organization, including hiring and firing personnel. Conducted cold calls with potential clients and sold security services to private, corporate, and commercial customers. Led patrol programs to prevent and control unauthorized entry, balancing operational and budgetary needs and abilities of the customer.

TRAINING: Demonstrated a combination of practical knowledge of instruction and of subject matter in training security personnel. Developed training program to ensure personnel could meet the needs of customers.

COMMUNICATIONS: Consulted with clients to evaluate security procedures and to determine weaknesses. Provided guidance to management officials in all aspects of security activity. Liaised with customers to ensure positive relationships and high satisfaction rates.

ACCOMPLISHMENTS:
- Adapted immediately to several high-intensity situations, resolving each without any harm to personnel, facilities, or equipment.
- Ensured customer satisfaction by analyzing security needs and establishing a program to meet those needs; streamlined overall security operations and saved $10K per year.
- Drafted Standard Operating Procedures (SOPs), regulations, and policies for personnel pertaining to new client facility security.

EDUCATION:
University of New Orleans   Major: Business
New Orleans, LA, United States
Master's Degree   GPA: 3.0
Completion Date: 05/2009

University of Montana   Major: English
Missoula, MT, United States
Bachelor's Degree   GPA: 3.5
Completion Date: 08/2003

JOB-RELATED TRAINING:

Interview and Investigation Techniques; Basic Law Enforcement; Hostage Situation; Drug Enforcement; Loss Prevention and Control; Doppler Radar Operation; Child Abuse Investigation; Customer Service; Time Management; Lie Deception Detection; Psychological Stress Evaluator Technique; Loss Prevention and Control; Civil Treatment for Managers; Bomb School; Burglary Investigation; Report Writing Advanced Course; Security Camera and Equipment School; Advanced Patrol Course

---

AFFILIATIONS:

Fraternal Order of Police	Member
American Legion	Member
Veterans of Foreign Wars	Member

ADDITIONAL INFORMATION:

Secret clearance

PROFESSIONAL SUMMARY:

Proven Law Enforcement Professional with more than 30 years' experience enforcing laws and providing security. Outstanding investigative skills; able to conduct civil and criminal investigations as well as lead other investigators. Adept at gathering evidence, performing interviews, and writing reports. Excellent communicator, equally capable testifying in court or handling a threatening situation. Expert trainer, utilizing law enforcement and security knowledge to instruct other officers in investigations and weapons training.

PROFESSIONAL HIGHLIGHTS:

- Demonstrated exceptional ability to handle high-threat situations
- Conducted numerous criminal investigations leading to arrests and convictions in child molestation, narcotics, theft, and driving under the influence.
- Chosen to train other law enforcement personnel in investigations and firearms.
- Ensured customer satisfaction by analyzing security needs and establishing a program to meet those needs.
- Drafted Standard Operating Procedures (SOPs), regulations, and policies for personnel pertaining to new client facility security.
- Reduced crime levels by analyzing high-risk areas and adjusting assignments accordingly.
- Implemented child fingerprinting community crime-prevention program.
- Improved reporting process, utilizing secretaries to transpose oral reports into written reports, increasing amount of time officers could be on patrol.

SUPERVISOR QUOTES AND RATING TEAM COMMENTARY:

"Florence has done outstanding work in organizing the Police Department and supervising the officers.

[She] was not only the head of the Police Department, but also conducted all investigations involving both felony and misdemeanor cases. She is a true professional and conducts herself in a straightforward and determined manner."

- Lars Ulrich, Town Board President, Ivins, UT

"Florence has demonstrated a high degree of initiative and competency in the performance of her duties... She has always rendered superior performance."

- Gerard Stefanovich, Chief of Police, Springdale, UT

AWARDS:
- Outstanding Service Award, 2006
- National Rifle Association (NRA) Legion of Honor Award
- Purple Heart
- National Defense Service Medal
- Vietnam Campaign Medal
- Vietnam Cross of Gallantry with 3 Bronze Stars
- Combat Action Ribbon
- Vietnam Service Ribbon
- Civil Action Ribbon

PROFESSIONAL LICENSES/CERTIFICATION:
- "C" Private Investigator License, Current
- Weapons Instructor, Current
- Firearms Instructor (Home Firearm Safety, Pistol, Rifle, Personal Protection in the Home); NRA Certified
- Basic Life Support Instructor, Current
- Cardiopulmonary Resuscitation (CPR) Instructor, Current
- Automated External Defibrillator (AED) Instructor, Current
- First Aid and First Responder Certified Instructor, Current
- Certified Handcuffing Instructor
- Certified Pepper Spray Instructor
- Certified Night Stick Instructor
- Certified in Hypnotherapies
- Federal Law Enforcement Certified
- Florida Notary
- Deputy Coroner
- Class "M"-Management Private Investigator License (Class "A" and "B" Agency)
- Doppler Radar Instructor

MILITARY EXPERIENCE:
U.S. Army Reserve, 1982 to 1995
U.S. Army Active Duty, 1968 to 1982

CHECK POINT SUMMARY

In this check point, you learned about the different components of a Federal resume, and the different requirements for some of the online systems. You also learned how to identify and use keywords and the headline format to optimize your resume. Next, we reviewed how to use the CCAR (remember, Challenge-Context-Action-Result) format to write narrative responses. When it comes to writing your Federal resume, the focus is the same as any resume—presenting your skills and accomplishments in a way that hiring managers will appreciate and understand. But you also have to think about formatting or other agency-specific requirements.

Along with following the guidance in this check point, here are two of the most important things to remember:

1. Read the "How to Apply" tab!
2. Call/email the contact on the job announcement if you have any questions.

Finally, don't forget to use the Federal resume samples and templates on the Vet's Toolbox CD.

Check Point Notes

_____

_____

_____

_____

_____

_____

_____

_____

_____

_____

_____

_____

_____

_____

_____

_____

_____

Check Point 4

Write Your Military to Private-Sector Resume

WRITE YOUR MILITARY TO PRIVATE-SECTOR RESUME

Many people transitioning out of the military look forward to working in the private sector as a change in atmosphere from the government. As you learned in Check Point 1, you have plenty of options and lots to offer private-sector organizations. You might want to move back to or near your hometown and start a career in the retail industry. You might want to launch an executive career. Or, you might want to leverage your military skills and work for a defense contractor, supporting or training military units. Either way, as you've heard repeatedly in this book, the content of your resume is much more important than the way it looks (as long as it looks clean and professional).

Everything you learned in Check Point 2 about matching your experience with the right jobs, and writing and demilitarizing your accomplishments, all applies to private-sector resumes. In this check point, we'll review the most important components of a private-sector resume, discuss the steps to developing your resume, and then provide you with a wide range of samples to use as a guide, or to fill in with your own duties and accomplishments. As we'll discuss later, cover letters are also much more popular in the private sector.

Tip: If you are going to develop a Federal resume as well as a shorter, more targeted resume, it can help to develop the more detailed and lengthy Federal resume first. Then, you can use it almost like a personal database, copying and pasting specific parts of it to build your private-sector resume.

FORMATTING YOUR PRIVATE-SECTOR RESUME

First, how long should your resume be? There is a lot of debate about this, but here's the easy answer: Less is more. With the large amount of resumes the reviewer has to read, you should avoid presenting him/her with a "novel." After serving more than 30,000 veterans in the past several decades, CareerPro has come up with a good "rule of thumb" on this subject. If you have fewer than five years of military experience, then you can probably fit everything into a concise, one-page resume. If you have five or more years of experience, then you should probably go with a two-page resume. Note: It looks much better if you pick one or two pages and format everything to fill up those pages. A resume with only half of the second page filled in doesn't look nearly as nice, and creates the perception that it's an unfinished document. Play around with fonts and margins to try to make it fit better.

When you print out your private-sector resume or view it on your computer screen, it should have a balanced look. For example, you don't want too much white space, or it will look like you are trying to "stretch" your experience to make it look like more than it is. Then again, you don't want to overwhelm readers with so much text that there's hardly any white space peeking through. Readers won't be impressed by all that text; they will just be annoyed that they have to read it all. You should try to find just the right balance of text and white space so that your resume looks presentable and professional. Hint: If you are going with a two-page resume and there is too much white space, you might want to try a one-pager.

Compared to a Federal resume, you have much more flexibility in how you present your information in a private-sector resume. Further, you typically don't need to provide quite as much detail in the contact information. Your name, address, and email address are usually enough. You also can be a little more creative or "flashy" with the look of your resume, but your focus should still be on high-quality and relevant content. In other words, no matter how "cool" your resume looks, it won't help you find a job unless the hiring manager can clearly see what you can bring to his/her company. If you want to use a resume format that integrates colors or charts, or other graphics, then go for it! Just make sure you feel comfortable with it. If you think it's a bit too flashy or just obnoxious, then the person reading it will probably feel the same way.

Be proactive: Contact the company you want to work for and ask the HR department what information they would like to see in your resume. Do they want a cover letter? Do they want references?

MAJOR COMPONENTS OF A PRIVATE-SECTOR RESUME

You have almost unlimited options when it comes to formatting, fonts, margins, and overall look and feel. In general, there are four main parts to a private-sector resume, as described below: Contact Information, Professional Summary, Employment History, and Additional Information.

1. Contact Information

Be straightforward in the header section of your resume. Simply include your name, any security clearance you have, mailing address, phone number, and email address. Don't use funny, "cute," or "clever" email addresses like sniper4life@ yahoo.com. If your personal email address is humorous, it could come off as unprofessional or even inappropriate to a hiring manager. It's a good idea to create a new email address solely for the purpose of your job search.

2. Professional Summary

There are a number of ways to handle this section, and you can see many examples in the Appendix and on the Vet's Toolbox CD. In general, the Professional Summary section should take up no more than the top third of the first page. Here are some great ideas of what to include in your Professional Summary:

A "Presidential" or "Branding" Statement. This is a short, concise summary of your work ethic and experience, usually no more than one or two sentences. If an employer asked you to tell him/her about your experience in fewer than 20 words, what would you say?

Again, there are countless ways to write such a statement, but here are some examples:

- Skilled Project Management Professional, leading more than 15 technology projects in the last 3 years with budgets exceeding $2.5M and teams of up to 30 personnel.

- Dynamic Security Professional; led a peak-performing team in Iraq, securing critical government property and facilities worth in excess of $5M.

In the past, everyone liked to write their "objective" statement across the top of the resume, and some still do. Here's an example: "I am seeking an organization in which I can use my skills and grow professionally."

As a vet, you might assume writing an objective makes perfect sense, right? Your mission is to find a new job and you have a clear objective. But this is the civilian workforce, and trends are always changing. These days, we believe it's best to keep the focus on what you can do for potential employers, rather than on what you want from them. For that reason, we recommend using an energetic and confident Presidential Statement that tells the reader what you bring to the table, rather than an Objective Statement that tells the reader what you want.

Bulleted List of Your Skills and Qualifications. This is a good way to highlight some of your relevant private-sector and specialized skills. For example, if you're pursuing a security position, you might want to list the weapon systems and tactics in which you are proficient.

Career Highlights. Simply choose three to five bullets from your work history that you think are most relevant to this position, and list them right up front! Or, you can do higher-level career overview statements that don't necessarily apply to one job, such as, "In past positions, received outstanding performance awards and trained a total of 4,532 personnel in information security and awareness."

- *Performance Quote.* Why not include a brief quote that really says it all? Of course, you need to make sure that the quote is accurate and from a real (and relevant) source, and that you can show a hiring manager where it

came from, if asked. But imagine if you were applying for a job as a dental assistant, and you had something like this right above the work history:

"Jane Doe is the best Dental Medicine Specialist I have worked with in my 26-year career. Her combination of customer service, communication, and technical skills had a positive impact on the entire clinic!"
– Colonel John Davis, U.S. Air Force

Again, there are many ways to develop your Professional Summary, but we do recommend including one. At the very least, it will make it easy for a reviewer who is sick of reviewing to see a snapshot of your skills and qualifications. That might be just enough to grab his/her attention and keep reading!

3. Employment History
After the Professional Summary, use a reverse-chronological timeline (most recent job first) and go back about 10 years. This is the most important part of your resume, because it shows in detail what you've been doing. Employers will look at your jobs and your accomplishments, and decide whether they would like to call you in for an interview.
For each job, start by clearly listing your job title, organization, location, and dates of employment (month and year is usually sufficient). Next, include a one- to three-sentence synopsis of your duties, including the numbers/amounts of personnel and/or resources you managed. Next, use bullets to list your most significant accomplishments. Refer back to Check Point 2 for a refresher on writing strong accomplishments.

4. Additional Information
This is generally the last part of a private-sector resume, and again, there is more than one way to put it together. Here are some of the items you might want to include, depending on your own experience and what kind of job you are trying to land:

Education: List any degrees you have earned (or are close to completing). Usually it's enough to list

---

the name of the school, the city and state, the degree, and the year completed. If you have only a high-school diploma, you can list that here, as well.

Training: You can also list relevant training here. Just remember, not all of your training will necessarily be relevant. For example, it may not be necessary to list your marksmanship training or Ranger tab if you are trying to land a job as an office manager. Just as with your accomplishments, you should try to only include training that is relevant to the position.

Awards: Although many civilian employers don't understand or appreciate military awards, you can still use them to demonstrate that you were recognized for your performance. Further, some awards are self-explanatory, such as "Humanitarian Award" or "Overseas Campaign Ribbon." Still other awards are widely known, such as the "Bronze Star." If an employer really wants to know, then he/she can ask about the award in an interview situation. If you have room, provide a brief description of why you received the award, such as, "Awarded Bronze Star for exemplary service managing four infrastructure rebuilding initiatives in Iraq."

Take Note

As you've learned, there is a variety of Federal resume styles and formats. No matter which one you use, at some point, you will still need to gather your information. You may choose to do that directly into the resume template you are using. On the other hand, you might like to have a larger "general" resume document on which all of your information is organized, and then use that document to develop your specific resumes for specific jobs. To make this easier for you, we have included a basic resume builder worksheet on the Vet's Toolbox CD.

References: If the employer wants you to include references in the resume, this is where you would list them.

Computer and Technology Skills: If relevant, this is a good place to list your specialized computer and technology experience.

Professional Licenses and Certifications: If you have achieved certifications that apply to the civilian world, then go ahead and list them (if you think it's relevant to the job, of course), but don't list items that are military-specific. For example, stating that you are "Nuclear, Biological, and Chemical Inspector certified" might not help you to land that job managing the local Barnes & Noble. However, if you hold Information Technology (IT) certifications, most of those are also valid and well respected in the private sector.

KEY STEPS TO WRITING A PRIVATE-SECTOR RESUME

Best Practices

1. Research and choose jobs to apply for

2. Review the job announcement or company's website (or call) to identify any specific application requirements

3. Identify relevant skills and keywords they are looking for

4. Gather documents

5. Write accomplishments and duties for each job

6. Demilitarize!

7. Choose a format from the Vet's Toolbox CD and develop your resume

8. Apply

9. Follow up and prepare for interview

10. Stay positive and proactive, and look for more jobs!

PRIVATE-SECTOR RESUMES DO'S AND DON'TS TABLE

Do	Don't
Research and tailor your resume to the company or job you want	Send out a generic resume to all companies and hope you get a "bite"
Be proactive and positive	Be passive
Use relevant and specific accomplishments	Use vague or generic language that could apply to anyone
Demilitarize your experience	Use lots of acronyms and military jargon

SAMPLE PRIVATE-SECTOR RESUME

CHARLES VICKNAIR
777 Brown Cow Drive | Tacoma, WA 77629 | 123-456-7890 | chuckv@gmail.com

WELL-ROUNDED WAREHOUSE MANAGER WITH 16 YEARS OF HONORABLE EXPERIENCE
IN U.S. ARMED FORCES. LEAD INNOVATIVE LOGISTICAL AND OPERATIONAL STRATEGIES IN
SUPPORT OF TRAINING AND DEVELOPMENT OF A HIGHLY SKILLED MILITARY FORCE.

LOGISTICS/ADMINISTRATIONS MANAGER	*Active "Secret" clearance*

- *Logistics Management*
- *Communication and Coordination*
- *Recruiting and Retention*
- *Training and Development*
- *Project Management*
- *Management and Leadership*
- *Administrative Management*
- *Partnership and Collaboration*
- *Inventory Management*

- **Logistics Management**: Hands-on Team Leader and Manager, coordinating and improving logistics processes for up to 900 personnel

- **Training and Development**: Distinguished record of intense dedication to value-added training and development programs for up to 250 personnel

- **Recruiting and Retention**: Proven ability to provide effective leadership in recruiting and retaining a quality workforce. Oversaw high-volume regional Recruit Sustainment Program process for more than 150 personnel

- **Inventory Management**: Adept at organizing and streamlining inventory management processes. Coordinated daily logistical operations for more than $2.8M in supply and equipment assets

PROFESSIONAL EXPERIENCE & ACHIEVEMENTS

WAREHOUSE MANAGER   10/2006 to Present
United States (U.S.) Army, Ramadi, Iraq
Warehouse Manager charged with leading 14 personnel in daily logistical operations, supporting military operations by ensuring on-hand inventory/supply for more than 800 detainees and 900 personnel.
- Led 90-day contingency supply program to ensure availability of supplies for personnel
- Developed and facilitated inventory management training programs for up to 15 personnel
- Coordinate daily logistical operations for more than $2.8M in supply and equipment assets
- Provide expertise and leadership adhering to established Standard Operating Procedures (SOPs)

Accomplishments:
→ Recognized by supervisor for successfully leading purchase agreement valued at $180K (largest fund in Iraq) and the requisition of $400K in inventory/supplies
→ Praised for leading inventory operations setup for 6,000-sq.-ft. warehouse
→ Commended for assuming the role of logistics operations leader prior to being formally trained, and initiating and developing warehouse safety SOP

RECRUITING/HUMAN RESOURCES MANAGER   04/2004 to 10/2006
U.S. Army, North Augusta, SC
Recruiting Sustainment/Human Resources (HR) Manager serving to consistently retain personnel. Provided leadership in maintaining effective training programs, administrative support, and personnel activities.
- Oversaw high-volume regional Recruit Sustainment Program process for more than 150 personnel
- Maintained accountability for administrative, payroll, and procedural compliance
- Partnered with guidance counselors in the coordination of training activities for personnel
- Provided HR management, administration, and leadership to more than 300 personnel

Accomplishments:
→ Commended for developing and implementing a new tracking process to reduce pay inconsistencies
→ Recognized for value-added facilitation of sales and recruiting operations training
→ Repeatedly recognized for approachable demeanor and positive attitude among peers and personnel vital to role as Recruiter and HR Manager

HUMAN RESOURCES MANAGER   01/2003 to 04/2004
U.S. Army, Colorado City, AZ

Personnel Service Sergeant leading personnel assignments and administrative functions for regional headquarters and subordinate facilities.
• Provided leadership in training program execution and administrative functions for up to 250 personnel
• Key contributor to the development and facilitation of official Evaluation Report training manuals
• Established and maintained tracking system utilized in performance review follow-up and execution

Accomplishments:
→ Repeatedly recognized by supervisors for superior presentation skills and technical training abilities
→ Accomplished below a 2% rejection rate upon producing and delivering more than 200 evaluation reports
→ Achieved a 56% reduction in past-due evaluation reports

RETENTION MANAGER/RECRUITING MANAGER   02/2001 to 01/2003
U.S. Army, Paddington, Kansas

Personnel Retention Manager overseeing retention initiatives to maintain appropriate staffing. As Recruiting Manager, led recruiting activities to obtain quality applicants for enlistment to the Army National Guard (ANG).
• Coordinated training and development activities for all newly enlisted personnel
• Provided leadership in the training and development of recruiters in technical disciplines
• Key contributor to managing sponsorship programs
• Led recruiting events, distributed recruiting materials, conducted interviews, and prepared and processed documentation for newly enlisted personnel

Accomplishments:
→ Recognized by supervisor for significant contributions to training quality and efficiency of organization, increasing student pass rates and reducing labor costs
→ Demonstrated commitment to continual learning by completing more than 130 hours of correspondence courses within a 12-month period
→ Recognized for graduating with honors in Human Resources Training
→ Achieved 100% accountability for more than $25K in recruiting equipment/supply

PROFESSIONAL DEVELOPMENT

2004: Caplan University, Bachelor of Arts degree in Homeland Security
2000: Salt Lake Community College, Associate's degree in Applied Science

Antiterrorism Awareness Training, Defense Security Service Academy; Information Assurance Security Officer Certification Course; Total Army Instructor Trainer Course; Personnel Service Specialist; Unit Attrition Management Course; Recruiting & Retention Course; Primary Leadership Development Course (PLDC); Hazardous Materials (HAZMAT) Waste Management Course; Combat Engineer; U.S. Marine Corps Infantry School

WRITING A COVER LETTER

In many cases, private-sector companies welcome you to include a cover letter with your resume. If you are required to submit a resume to their custom online resume builder, you may not be able to include a cover letter. Professional protocol is to include a customized cover letter detailing your interest in working for the company and why they should hire you by including a few quantitative or qualitative bullets. Cover letters can serve as the hiring manager's first impression of you, so you want to make it memorable. Don't worry about any fancy formatting; simply make sure the content, font, and overall look complement the resume.

A cover letter should not be more than one page (unless specifically required or requested), and it should have a good balance of white space and text. Just a few short and engaging paragraphs will usually work. Although it is probably fine to use similar cover letters for multiple positions, you still want to target each different organization by doing a little research and then tweaking each cover letter accordingly. That way, you can show in your cover letter how your unique skills and experience make you a perfect candidate for the position. Always remember that templates and samples can definitely help you to format your cover letter (or resume) and give you ideas, but everything must be completely personalized and unique to your situation. There are countless ways to write a strong cover letter. Be professional, but let your own personality, experiences, and work ethic shine through.

COMPONENTS OF A COVER LETTER

Header/Contact Information: Include the same contact information you have on the resume, but also include the date and a "To" section before your first paragraph. Openings like "To Whom it May Concern" have been widely overused, so it's best to examine the job announcement or the agency, find the Point of Contact (POC) for the position to which you are applying, and address the letter specifically to that person.

Introductory Paragraph: Introduce yourself in a professional manner with a brief summary of your main accomplishments and level of experience, and express a strong interest in candidacy for the position. It's best to reference the actual position title here.

Second (and Maybe Third) Paragraph: Just as you learned about using a Presidential Statement instead of an Objective Statement, this area of your cover letter is all about convincing the reader to read your resume because you are such a strong candidate. A good way to do this is by including a short summary of what you have been doing professionally for the past 5-10 years and how that experience can help the organization meet its objectives (which you already know because you did your homework, right?).

Closing Paragraph: This section of the cover letter should quickly review why you would be such a great asset to the organization and include a call to action. Don't just say "thanks for your consideration"—that's too passive. Instead, say something like, "I look forward to hearing from you soon so that we can discuss how I can help your organization meet and exceed its goals."

[DATE]

[NAME, TITLE]
[ORGANIZATION]
[ADDRESS]
[CITY, STATE ZIP]

Dear [NAME]:

I am writing to explore employment opportunities within your organization, and would like to be considered for the Security Manager position. My background includes hands-on experience in law enforcement, security, and force protection. Enclosed please find a copy of my resume for your review and consideration.

Recognized as a dedicated, results-oriented professional, I have made numerous positive contributions throughout my career. Currently, as Ground Operations Specialist in the United States Marine Corps (USMC) at Camp Pendleton, CA, I provide support for the operation section and participate in activities to protect base personnel, equipment, and resources.

I have successfully completed challenging assignments in the U.S. and abroad, providing me with the opportunity to participate in critical support operations in time-sensitive situations. I served in Iraq from 2006 to 2007, providing security and force protection support for Operation Iraqi Freedom (OIF). My experience includes force protection, facility security, and personal security, and I have consistently received ratings as a top performer. My current security status is Secret.

My broad-based experience and training in the aforementioned fields have positioned me for various career avenues. I feel certain I would be a viable asset to a progressive organization such as yours and am prepared to apply my skills and experience to help you meet and exceed your goals. I look forward to hearing from you soon so that we can set up an interview and discuss the position in more detail.

Respectfully submitted,

Marc Geolo

Enclosure

CHECK POINT SUMMARY

In this check point, we reviewed how a private-sector resume is different from a Federal resume. We also reviewed similarities between all resumes (it's all about the content). Next, you learned about the different ways to format your resume and the major components you should include.

Additionally, you now know the top steps to writing a private-sector resume and what to include in a cover letter. You can find more sample resumes, cover letters, and templates in Appendix B and on the Vet's Toolbox CD. Now you are all ready to submit your resume and prepare for the interview.

Check Point Notes

Check Point 5

Submit Your Application Materials and Prepare for Interview

SUBMIT YOUR APPLICATION MATERIALS AND PREPARE FOR INTERVIEW

There are literally thousands of different federal agencies and private companies out there. As you learned in Check Point 3, many federal agencies use USAJobs for their application process, but not necessarily. That's why it's so important to apply for specific positions and research the application requirements, not just throw a resume on the Internet and passively wait for something to happen.

THE FEDERAL APPLICATION PROCESS

Your application materials will be sent to the federal agency, generally through the online application process. This will include the Federal-style resume, any occupational questionnaires and narrative statements, and other documentation (such as transcripts, DD-214, SF-50, etc.) called for in the announcement.

The HR Review Process for determining your qualifications and for rating and ranking your KSAs is as follows:

Step 1: Application Review. A personnel staffing specialist will review the application package to make sure it has been correctly completed and includes all of the appropriate documentation requested (many people don't progress beyond this point). If the application is complete and correct, the specialist will review the resume to decide if you possess the basic qualifications for the position, in accordance with the Qualifications Handbook.

Step 2: Resume Review. The staffing specialist will then review the application to determine if you meet the specialized experience qualifications for the job. This qualification information can be found on every vacancy announcement. Occupational questionnaires and any narrative statements will also be reviewed for both the quality of response and to ensure answers to questions are supported by the resume (so don't mark "expert" in all cases with nothing supporting that answer in the resume).

Step 3: *Rating* (if applicable). Resumes, questionnaires, and short narrative statements will be reviewed by Human Resources (HR) staff or a panel of Subject Matter Experts (SMEs) and assigned to a rating category using a crediting plan or "scorecard." Candidates will be placed in one of three categories, generally called "Best Qualified," "Well Qualified," and "Qualified"—or Gold, Silver, and Bronze.

Step 4: Veterans' Preference (if applicable). Applicants with preference eligibility are provided with that "credit." Candidates with 10-point preference generally are placed in the top category; candidates with 5-point eligibility are placed in their assigned category. Only candidates in the highest category may be referred to the hiring manager. Non-veterans in a category may not be selected over veteran candidates in that same category.

APPLYING FOR PRIVATE-SECTOR JOBS

In the private sector, the hiring process is not so transparent or standardized. There is also no centralized hiring site such as USAJobs. You might be able to find thousands of job boards online, but each company is likely to have its own application process. There is also no standardized hiring process. Some companies might have formal and efficient process in place, while others may simply be the owner reading resumes him/herself on the weekend. You just never know, so the best thing you can do is read the job announcement, research the specific company, and then apply, following its instructions.

HOW LONG WILL IT TAKE TO LAND AN INTERVIEW?

We wish there were a simple answer to this question, but there are just too many variables such as the number of applicants, budget or staffing issues at the agency, changes in position requirements, and new government initiatives.

Currently, there is no standard timeframe for how long it can take a federal agency to fill a vacancy. The good news is that President Obama has signed a new Executive Order ordering agencies to shorten the hiring process, with a goal of hiring within 80 days of the initial job posting. On average, the federal hiring process can last anywhere from two weeks to a year, depending on the type of job being sought and the number of other applicants.

For example, positions with an agency that require a clearance will probably require you to be able to secure a Secret security clearance at a minimum. If your military job did not require one, this process can take from several months up to a year to complete. By contrast, the more stringent Top Secret clearance can take up to 18 months to obtain, with certain situations requiring a length of up to three years.

There is also no standard time for interviewing or hiring in the private sector. Depending on the agency, the process can be very fast or extremely slow. But one thing is certain with federal and private-sector positions: There will always be some type of interview before a hiring decision is made (this could be in person, by phone, or a combination of both).

SHOULD YOU FOLLOW UP?

Yes, you should definitely be proactive and professional and send a follow-up email after four to six weeks. Alternatively, you can send a handwritten thank-you note to stand out from other applications. If you have the contact information of a particular individual, call him/her directly and politely ask for the status of your application.

Just remember, hiring decisions are often made behind closed doors, and there are numerous factors involved such as stiff competition, internal politics, and personal preferences of the hiring manager. If you are not called in for an interview or not hired, the most detail you will probably receive is, "You were not selected based on....." In the private sector, companies don't always give applicants any feedback.

In some cases, you may receive a response of, "We thank you for applying, but we have hired someone whose qualifications better matched our needs at this time." If something like this happens to you, don't take it personally. Stay positive and keep moving forward toward that next great opportunity.

Whether you are applying for federal jobs, private-sector jobs, or both, you should maintain a list of all the positions you've applied for, and when, along with the agency contact information. You can then check your list every couple of weeks and determine when you should follow up. The more organized you are about it, the better.

HOW TO BE EFFECTIVE DURING AN INTERVIEW?

Federal agencies realize that resumes are only snapshots of the applicants and that interviews are needed to better understand a person's capabilities and to learn if he/she would fit well into the work environment. For this reason, most (but not all) government agencies conduct interviews. Typically, government agencies conduct panel interviews, with anywhere from two to five people interviewing you at the same time. Interviewers ask all candidates the same questions, which are typically about the position, rather than an individual applicant's specific qualifications.

Government agencies are encouraged to use what is called Behavioral-Based Interviewing to ensure fairness. Second interviews, while allowable, are not common for most federal positions. Some agencies conduct telephone interviews or ask a candidate to travel to a local facility where videoconferencing may be available.

In the private sector, companies have complete flexibility on how to interview. You could have a one-on-one interview, a panel interview, or a combination of both.

Whether you are going into a structured federal interview or meeting with a manager in his/her office, all interviews are essentially the same. They are a chance for potential employers to ask you questions, observe the way you speak and act, and decide whether you are a good fit for their agency.

Let's face it—some of us are natural interviewers. Our confidence and friendly manner shine through and we perform well. But some of us don't like being in the spotlight, and interviewing does not come as naturally. Whichever group you fall into, and whether you are applying for federal or private-sector jobs, you can use the following methods to be more prepared and ace that interview!

BEHAVIORAL-BASED INTERVIEWING

Once upon a time, interviewers used to rely on bland, generic questions to determine whether someone is qualified. And this still happens all the time. (For example, "Why should I hire you?") These days, more and more government and private agencies have gravitated toward more of a Behavioral-Based Interviewing approach.

Here's how it works: You are presented with a scenario or asked to identify a situation in which you demonstrated a particular knowledge, skill, ability, or experience, training, etc. to prove that you can handle that kind of situation or challenge.

For example, you might be asked to give a response to an imaginary situation. "We've had some issues with network security breaches and viruses in our office. How have you handled this kind of challenge in your past jobs?"

While you could speak in general terms about how to resolve the infiltration of security breaches and viruses on a network, a stronger and better response would be to talk about a specific example from your own professional experience that demonstrates not only the behavior exhibited to solve the problem, but also the quantifiable (and verifiable) results.

You will be expected to provide answers to specific past scenarios. Employers are looking for four pieces of information: the situation or task assigned, the challenges faced in completing it, the actions taken to address the challenge(s), and the result. Sound similar? That's because it's the same format you learned for writing narrative responses— CCAR (Challenge-Context-Action-Result). And it works for verbal responses, as well. Interviewers don't want to hear "fluff"; they want to hear specific examples, and using CCAR is the best way to provide them.

Here are some more examples of the CCAR technique in action:

Provide an example when you were challenged with meeting a critical deadline and what actions you took to meet the deadline.

Challenge/Context: While working for Macy's as an Information Technology (IT) Specialist, I was challenged with programming coding to calculate accumulated monthly totals for a specific product.

Action: Phoned software vendor for assistance in coding programming roadblock.

Result: Resolved coding roadblock; launched new program that reported monthly and accumulated product totals.

Ability to solve employee communication problems.

Challenge/Context: When I was a manager with ABC Company, I supervised six subordinates. Whenever I encountered a conflict, I sat down individually with specific team members and discussed conflicts or situations.

Action: After reviewing all sides of the conflict, I brought the team members together to professionally discuss the conflict and without taking sides, I led the meeting by defining and clarifying project scope.

Result: The team members talked through their situation and bought into a new plan together to complete the project. There were no further conflicts on this project.

When you are asked these types of behavioral-based questions, you should be as thorough as possible. In many cases, there are no wrong answers—just a lack of answers. You should state what you would do in any situation using a step-by-step process, if possible. The more specific and job-related the answer, the better. Behavioral-based questioning may also require you to remember instances in the past and relate how you and others reacted. Chances are, you have a lot of experience working on teams to solve problems, but employers want to know specifically what you—not the team—did.

EXAMPLE: PROJECT MANAGEMENT

Below is an example of the type of question a job candidate may be asked when applying for a project management position. It includes the key behaviors the interviewer is looking for and the behavioral-based questions that may be asked:

PROJECT MANAGER

Creates and maintains an environment that guides a project to its successful completion.

Key Behaviors:

- Explains the processes involved in the initiation phase of a project and the development of an overall project plan
- Identifies key stakeholders in the project
- Identifies and analyzes environmental influences impacting on the project
- Develops and manages the scope of a project
- Describes in detail the process of resource allocation, including human resources, and how

cost, work, and time estimates are developed

- Understands the risks involved in starting a project
- Understands the importance of quality assurance and control
- Develops effective communication skills to interact with members of the project team

Interview Questions:

1. Describe a time when you were responsible for managing a project with varying priorities that included staggered milestones. What was your approach? What steps did you take to ensure the appropriate stakeholders were involved? How did you ensure that you effectively communicated with your team?

2. Provide an example of a time when you were responsible for managing a project during which conflicts within the team developed. How did you handle this situation? What was the result/outcome?

Take Note

Popular Interview Questions You Can Expect and Prepare For:

1. Tell me about yourself.
2. What are your career goals?
3. Name three transferable skills that you bring to the civilian sector.
4. How efficient and knowledgeable are you regarding computer software?
5. How would your subordinates describe you?
6. What would you like to change about yourself?
7. What drove you to achieve E-9?
8. Are you attracted to working for the federal government?
9. What type of pleasure are you seeking to experience in your next work environment?
10. Do you accept "no" for an answer? If not, provide a situation in which you did not, and describe the issue and result.
11. Provide an example of how you motivated under-motivated personnel, how you approached the subject with them, and what you did to turn them around.
12. With your recent degree in Information Systems Management w/ concentration in Information Security, what prompted you to select this major, and is this where you hope your future career will allow you to go?
13. Where do you see yourself, career-wise, in the next three to five years?
14. How would you handle working with "slackers" if you weren't their supervisor or manager? How would you handle the day-to-day interaction and frustration that they weren't carrying their weight to achieve a team goal?
15. List your top three attributes and your top three weaknesses.

---

3. What has been your approach for monitoring and controlling risks throughout a project?

CREATING AN INTERVIEW SCRIPT

While there is no way to correctly forecast what questions will be asked during an interview, another great way to be prepared is to put together a loose script that addresses the following areas:

Key Areas of Interest. **Most agencies' interview questions are based on the keywords and specialized experience requirements found in the announcement and questionnaire. You should be prepared with specific examples that address the keywords.**

Your Presidential Statement. **What do you bring to the organization? This is your chance to introduce a summary of your qualifications to the employer.**

Topics covered should include experience, quantifiable strengths, signature achievements, and—if applicable to the job being sought—personal interests and hobbies.

Your Top Success Stories. **You should list your top achievements that relate to the announcement and be prepared to talk about them. If you created your resume in the right way, and tailored it to the specific job and agency, then this part should be easy to think through. Achievements can include specific accomplishments on the job (e.g. saving time or money); earning a rapid promotion; introducing a new system or process; earning responsibilities normally held for persons at a higher level, etc.**

Your Career Goals. **You should think about what you would say if asked about your goals, and align your answer with the organization's goals (which you should already know from your extensive research). For example, if you are trying to become a supervisor at your next employer, you might say, "Over time, I hope to inspire enough confidence in my skills, abilities, and contributions to where I might be given additional responsibilities to help the organization continue to meet its service needs."**

Your Weaknesses. **This particular question is bound to come up in one form or another. The trick is to turn a weakness into a strength. For example, if you tend to micromanage employees, you might say something like this:**

"While I tend to micromanage employees initially, I find that this happens when we take on a new challenge because I want to ensure everything goes according to expectation. Over time, however, I gradually build the trust and confidence in my staff to let them take on the various project segments to which they've been assigned; this trust has resulted in the foundation for many productive project teams, who went on to produce some amazing results, such as..."

Interview Preparation Tips

Dress in a professional manner. This should be obvious. Using your best judgment, make sure you look clean, well groomed, and presentable. Sometimes, an agency will give you guidance, such as "business casual." But a good rule of thumb is that it's better to be a little overdressed than a little underdressed. If other applicants are wearing jeans and sandals, and you're wearing nice pants and a shirt and tie, who do you think looks more professional and more serious about the job?

Show up early. Do you really want to start the interview by being late? Make a good first impression but showing up before the interview starts (but no more than 10 minutes).

Rehearse with family or friends. This can be fun and helpful, and it's a vital part of almost any military operation. Why not use it to land a job? Sit around with family or friends and have them ask you questions you think you might be asked in the interview, and then rehearse your answers a few times.

Create an interview script (see previous section).

Demilitarize your experience and speak in terms that any government or private hiring manager can understand and appreciate.

Be likeable. If you had a bad drive over to the interview, or you are just generally down because this is your third interview in a week, then put on a happy face and fake it! Don't be too obvious about it, but you certainly don't want to come across as negative or pessimistic. The savvy interviewer knows exactly how to trick people into showing their true colors; one such tactic is initiating small talk about such trivial matters as the weather, traffic, or construction. The goal here is to see if you are negative or a complainer.

Be human. Oftentimes, people are so nervous or afraid of saying or doing the wrong thing that they come off as robotic. It's okay to laugh during an interview (employers are human, after all). It's also okay to open or hold doors when moving to the interview room (it shows courtesy) and to accept a cup of water, if offered, especially if the interviewer has a mug filled with a beverage on his/her desk.

Be attentive. You should devote your full attention to the interviewer. That means cell phones should be turned off and BlackBerry devices and other Personal Digital Assistants (PDAs) put away. If you would like to take notes and the interviewer agrees to that, don't overdo it with endless, distracting doodling. Make eye contact, smile, and be positive in your answers to ensure the best possible experience and to eliminate nervousness.

Be polite. Finally, don't forget to thank the interviewer(s) at the end of the interview. You should take the time to shake hands with everyone present and thank them for their time with a smile.

The day after the interview, why not compose a brief note to follow up? This extra step can set you above the other candidates and, if nothing else, shows appreciation. The note should be brief, since most employers will have little time to read them, but should include three paragraphs.

The first paragraph should thank the interviewer for the interview. The second paragraph should briefly review key points of your resume, cover letter, and interview. This paragraph should remind the hiring agency that you are the best candidate for the job. In the last paragraph, thank the interviewer again and provide your phone number or email address and the best time to be reached.

CHECK POINT SUMMARY

In this final check point, you learned about some of the differences between the federal private-sector hiring process and application procedures. You also learned some great tips on following up and interviewing. Using the guidance in this check point, you should be able to prepare for and rock that interview!

Check Point Notes

Final Thoughts

Here we are at last. By now, you should now have a much better understanding of your options for transitioning from the military to the federal or civilian workforce, and you definitely have plenty of practical information, samples, and templates to guide you through the process. By following the information laid out in the five check points, and then using the resume samples and templates on the Vet's Toolbox CD, the process of developing your federal or private-sector resume will be much easier, and your resume will be much more effective.

As we mentioned in the beginning of the book, we have used the information and techniques in this book to help thousands upon thousands of vets just like you. There are currently about 23 million Iraq and Afghanistan vets, and you're part of that new generation. You weren't trained to be passive; you were trained to be highly skilled and proactive, ready to handle your mission or adapt to any mission given to you in a moment's notice. So don't wait for the right time to achieve your career goals—CREATE it!

Decision Time

Whenever you complete a training course or a book like this one, the ball is in your court. It's decision time. So, what are you going to do next? Are you going to develop a high-energy set of well-written duties and accomplishments for each job? Are you going to research companies or federal agencies and then match your resume with those positions? Are you going to target the federal government, the private sector, or both? Whatever you decide, you will succeed, because you are part of our new generation of vets and we believe you can do anything!

First, you should follow the final checklist below, then make a decision. Once you've selected a job and developed a resume you can be proud of, apply for civilian positions with confidence. You are capable of great things, and you deserve great opportunities. Go out and grab them. One of the most important transitions of your life has officially begun!

Final Checklist

Check Point 1: Know Your Options and Find Jobs

Do you understand all of the different options you have as a vet, and where you can look for federal or private-sector jobs? Do you have a clear vision statement?

Check Point 2: Identify Your Skills and Write Your Accomplishments

Do you understand how to identify your military skills and match them with the right kinds of jobs, agencies, or companies? Do you know how to write strong accomplishments that a civilian employer will appreciate and understand?

Check Point 3: Write Your Military to Federal Resume

Do you have a better understanding of the Federal resume, how to use keywords and the headline format, and how to use the CCAR (Challenge-Context-Action-Result) approach to writing essay responses? Have you used the samples to write your resume yet?

Check Point 4: Write Your Military to Private-Sector Resume

Do you understand what goes into a private-sector resume and cover letter? Have you used the samples and templates in the book and on the Vet's Toolbox CD to write your resume yet?

Check Point 5: Submit Your Application Materials and Prepare for Interview

Do you understand the differences between applying for a federal job and a private-sector job? Do you feel more confident about preparing for and then conducting the interview? Have you written an interview script and followed the other steps in this check point for becoming prepared?

Appendix A: Tools and Resources

VETERANS EMPLOYMENT PROGRAM OFFICE CONTACTS

Below is a list of Veterans Employment Program Offices created following the President's Executive Order on the hiring of veterans. These individuals are responsible for promoting veterans' recruitment, employment, training and development, and retention within their respective agencies. If you are a veteran, you are encouraged to contact these individuals for specific information on employment opportunities in these agencies. The following contact information was current as of the printing of this book; check the Office of Personnel Website (OPM) website (**www.fedshirevets.gov/AgencyDirectory/index.aspx**) for the most current information.

Agency	Name	Email	Phone
Agency for International Development (USAID)	Tom Davis	vets@usaid.gov	202-712-5663
Department of Agriculture (USDA)	David Dissinger	VeteransEmploymentProgram@dm.usda.gov	202-690-3420
Department of Commerce (DOC)	Sabra Street	sstreet@doc.gov	202-482-4270
Department of Defense (DoD)	Karen Hannah	hiringheroes@cpms.osd.mil	888-363-4872
Department of Education	Len Clark	len.clark@ed.gov	202-401-3855
Department of Energy	Donna Friend	donna.friend@hq.doe.gov	202-586-5880
Department of Health and Human Services (HHS)	Kelly Williams	Mailbox.Vetsa@hhs.gov	202-260-6117
Department of Homeland Security (DHS)	Kimberly Burney	vets@dhs.gov	202-357-8620
Department of Housing and Urban Development (HUD)	Anthony L. Johnson	anthony.l.johnson@hud.gov	202-402-2018
Department of Interior (DOI)	Martin Pursley	vep_hr@ios.doi.gov	877-227-1969
Department of Justice (DOJ)	Cortez Puryear	cortez.puryear@usdoj.gov	202-514-0349
Department of Labor	Anthony Camilli	Camilli.Anthony@dol.gov	202-693-0260
Department of State (DOS)	Denise Wright	vets@state.gov	202-663-2182
Department of the Treasury	Ernie Beltz, Jr.	vets@do.treas.gov	202-927-VETS
Department of Transportation (DOT)	Brenda Adams	vetemployment@dot.gov	202-366-1779
Department of Transportation, Federal Aviation Administration (FAA)	Austin Lewis	austin.lewis@faa.gov	501-918-4415
Department of Veterans Affairs (VA)	Dennis May	vecs@va.gov	866-606-6206
Environmental Protection Agency (EPA)	Terry Jones	EPAVeterans@epa.gov	202-564-5233
General Services Administration (GSA)	Edner Escarne	hiringvets@gsa.gov	202-694-8137
National Aeronautics and Space Administration (NASA)	Krystal Hall	nssc-contactcenter@nasa.gov	202-358-1297
National Science Foundation	Annette Taylor	vepo@nsf.gov	703-292-7893
Nuclear Regulatory Commission	Leonard Carsley	leonard.carsley@nrc.gov	301-415-7400
Office of Personnel Management (OPM)	Kelly Woodall	kelly.woodall@opm.gov	202-606-2825
Small Business Administration (SBA)	Dianna Burrell	vets@sba.gov	303-844-7787
Social Security Administration (SSA)	Sandra Seymour	sandy.seymour@ssa.gov	410-965-0479

GS-SERIES INFORMATION SHEET

The General Series (GS) comprises 23 occupational families that are further divided into more than 400 white-collar occupations under the General Schedule—GS-000 through GS-2200. The following are the core GS descriptions:

GS-000: Miscellaneous
This group includes all classes of positions, the duties of which are to administer, supervise, or perform work that cannot be included in other occupational groups.

GS-100: Social Science, Psychology, and Welfare Group
This group includes all classes of positions, the duties of which are to advise on, administer, supervise, or perform research or other professional and scientific work, subordinate technical work, or related clerical work in one or more of the social sciences: psychology, social work, recreational activities, or the administration of public welfare and insurance programs.

GS-200: Personnel Management and Industrial Relations Group
This group includes all classes of positions, the duties of which are to advise on, administer, supervise, or perform work involved in the various phases of personnel management and industrial relations.

GS-300: General Administrative, Clerical, and Office Services Group
This group includes all classes of positions, the duties of which are to administer, supervise, or perform work involved in management analysis; stenography, typing, correspondence, and secretarial work; mail and file work; the operation of office appliances; the operation of communications equipment, use of codes and ciphers, and procurement of most efficient communications services; the operation of microfilm equipment, peripheral equipment, duplicating equipment, mail-processing equipment, and copier/duplicating equipment; and other work of a general clerical and administrative nature.

GS-400: Biological Sciences Group
This group includes all classes of positions, the duties of which are to advise on, administer, supervise, or perform research or other professional and scientific work or subordinate technical work in any of the fields of science concerned with living organisms, their distribution, characteristics, life processes, and adaptations and relations to the environment; the soil, its properties and distribution, and the living organisms growing in or on the soil; and the management, conservation, or utilization thereof for particular purposes or uses.

GS-500: Accounting and Budget Group
This group includes all classes of positions, the duties of which are to advise on, administer, supervise, or perform professional, technical, or related clerical work of an accounting, budget administration, related financial management, or similar nature.

GS-600: Medical, Hospital, Dental, and Public Health Group
This group includes all classes of positions, the duties of which are to advise on, administer, supervise, or perform research or other professional and scientific work, subordinate technical work, or related clerical work in the several branches of medicine, surgery, and dentistry or in related patient care services such as dietetics, nursing, occupational therapy, physical therapy, pharmacy, and others.

GS-700: Veterinary Medical Sciences Group

This group includes all classes of positions, the duties of which are to advise and consult on, administer, manage, supervise, or perform research or other professional and scientific work in the various branches of veterinary medical science.

GS-800: Engineering and Architecture

This group includes all classes of positions, the duties of which are to advise on, administer, supervise, or perform professional, scientific, or technical work related to engineering or architectural projects, facilities, structures, systems, processes, equipment, devices, materials, or methods. Positions in this group require knowledge of science or art—or both—by which materials, natural resources, and power are made useful.

GS-900: Legal and Kindred Group

This group includes all classes of positions, the duties of which are to advise on, administer, supervise, or perform professional legal work in the preparation for trial and the trial and argument of cases; the presiding at formal hearings afforded by a commission, board, or other body having quasi-judicial powers, as part of its administrative procedure; the administration of law entrusted to an agency; the preparation or rendering of authoritative or advisory legal opinions or decisions to other federal agencies or to administrative officials of own agency; the preparation of various legal documents; the performance of other work requiring training equivalent to that represented by graduation from a recognized law school and, in some instances, requiring admission to the bar; or quasi-legal work that requires knowledge of particular laws, regulations, precedents, or departmental practices based thereon, but that does not require such legal training or admission to the bar.

GS-1000: Information and Arts Group

This group includes positions that involve professional, artistic, technical, or clerical work in (1) the communication of information and ideas through verbal, visual, or pictorial means; (2) the collection, custody, presentation, display, and interpretation of art works, cultural objects, and other artifacts; or (3) a branch of fine or applied arts such as industrial design, interior design, or musical composition. Positions in this group require writing, editing, and language ability; artistic skill and ability; knowledge of foreign languages; the ability to evaluate and interpret informational and cultural materials; the practical application of technical or aesthetic principles combined with manual skill; and dexterity and related clerical skills.

GS-1100: Business and Industry Group

This group includes all classes of positions, the duties of which are to advise on, administer, supervise, or perform work pertaining to and requiring a knowledge of business and trade practices, characteristics and use of equipment, products, or property, or industrial production methods and processes, including the conduct of investigations and studies; the collection, analysis, and dissemination of information; the establishment and maintenance of contracts with industry and commerce; the provision of advisory services; the examination and appraisement of merchandise or property; and the administration of regulatory provisions and controls.

GS-1200: Copyright, Patent, and Trademark Group

This group includes all classes of positions, the duties of which are to advise on, administer, supervise, or perform professional scientific, technical, and legal work involved in the cataloging and registration of copyright, in the classification and issuance of patents, in the registration of trademarks, in the prosecution of applications for patents before the Patent Office, and in the giving of advice to government officials on patent matters.

GS-1300: Physical Sciences Group

This group includes all classes of positions, the duties of which are to advise on, administer, supervise, or perform research or other professional and scientific work or subordinate technical work in any of the fields of science concerned with matter, energy, physical space, time, nature of physical measurement, and fundamental structural particles as well as the nature of the physical environment.

GS-1400: Library and Archives Group

This group includes all classes of positions, the duties of which are to advise on, administer, supervise, or perform professional and scientific work or subordinate technical work in the various phases of library archival science.

GS-1500: Mathematics and Statistics Group

This group includes all classes of positions, the duties of which are to advise on, administer, supervise, or perform research or other professional and scientific work or related clerical work in basic mathematical principles, methods, procedures, or relationships, including the development and application of mathematical methods for the investigation and solution of problems; the development and application of statistical theory in the selection, collection, classification, adjustment, analysis, and interpretation of data; the development and application of mathematical, statistical, and financial principles to programs or problems involving life and property risks; and any other professional and scientific or related clerical work requiring primarily the understanding and use of mathematical theories, methods, and operations.

GS-1600: Equipment, Facilities, and Services Group

This group includes positions, the duties of which are to advise on, manage, or provide instructions and information concerning the operation, maintenance, and use of equipment, shops, buildings, laundries, printing plants, power plants, cemeteries, or other government facilities, or other work involving services provided predominantly by people in trades, crafts, or manual labor operations. Positions in this group require technical or managerial knowledge and ability in addition to a practical knowledge of trades, crafts, or manual labor operations.

GS-1700: Education Group

This group includes positions that involve administering, managing, supervising, performing, or supporting education or training work when the paramount requirement of the position is knowledge of—or skill in—education, training, or instruction processes.

GS-1800: Investigation Group

This group includes all classes of positions, the duties of which are to advise on, administer, supervise, or perform investigation, inspection, or enforcement work primarily dealing with alleged or suspected offenses against the laws of the U.S., or such work primarily relating to determining compliance with laws and regulations.

GS-1900: Quality Assurance (QA), Inspection, and Grading Group
This group includes all classes of positions, the duties of which are to advise on, supervise, or perform administrative or technical work primarily concerned with the QA or inspection of material, facilities, and processes, or with the grading of commodities under official standards.

GS-2000: Supply Group
This group includes positions that involve work regarding finishing all types of supplies, equipment, material, property (except real estate), and certain services to components of the federal government, industrial, or other concerns under contract to the government, or receiving supplies from the federal government. Included are positions concerned with one or more aspects of supply activities from initial planning—including requirements analysis and determination—through acquisition, cataloging, storage, distribution, and utilization to ultimate issue for consumption or disposal. The work requires knowledge of one or more elements or parts of a supply system and/or supply methods, policies, or procedures.

GS-2100: Transportation Group
This group includes all classes of positions, the duties of which are to advise on, administer, supervise, or perform work that involves two or more specialized transportation functions or other transportation work not specifically included in other series of this group.

GS-2200: Information Technology (IT) Group
This group includes all positions for the administrative work in Information Technology (IT). The primary subcategory is 2210, which covers IT management. Within IT management are 11 possible areas of responsibility (or combination of responsibilities), including:

Policy and Planning (PLCYPLN)
Enterprise Architecture (EA)
Security (INFOSEC)
Systems Analysis (SYSANALYSIS)
Applications Software (APPSW)
Operating Systems (OS)
Network Services (NETWORK)
Data Management (DATAMGT)
Internet (INET)
Systems Administration (SYSADMIN)
Customer Support (CUSTSPT)

WAGE GRADE TRADES AND LABOR JOB FAMILIES AND OCCUPATIONS
The Wage Grade (WG) group offers an additional 36 occupational families: WG-2500 through WG-9000. These are typically considered the blue-collar positions. The following is a list of the WG groups:

WG-2500 Wire Communications Equipment Installation/Maintenance Family
WG-2600 Equipment Installation and Maintenance Family
WG-2800 Electrical Installation and Maintenance Family
WG-3100 Fabric and Leather Work Family
WG-3300 Instrument Work Family

WG-3400 Machine Tool Work Family
WG-3500 General Services and Support Work Family
WG-3600 Structural and Finishing Work Family
WG-3700 Metal-Processing Family
WG-3800 Metalworking Family
WG-3900 Motion Picture, Radio, TV, and Sound Equipment Operation Family
WG-4000 Lens and Crystal Work Family
WG-4100 Painting and Paperhanging Family
WG-4200 Plumbing and Pipefitting Family
WG-4300 Pliable Materials Work Family
WG-4400 Printing Family
WG-4600 Woodwork Family
WG-4700 General Maintenance and Operations Work Family
WG-4800 General Equipment Maintenance Family
WG-5000 Plant and Animal Work Family
WG-5200 Miscellaneous Occupations Family
WG-5300 Industrial Equipment Maintenance Family
WG-5400 Industrial Equipment Operation Family
WG-5700 Transportation/Mobile Equipment Operation Family
WG-5800 Heavy Mobile Equipment Mechanic
WG-6500 Ammunition, Explosives, and Toxic Materials Work Family
WG-6600 Armament Work Family
WG-6900 Warehousing and Stock-Handling Family
WG-7000 Packing and Processing Family
WG-7300 Laundry, Dry Cleaning, and Pressing Family
WG-7400 Food Preparation and Servicing Family
WG-7600 Personal Services Family
WG-8200 Fluid Systems Maintenance Family
WG-8600 Engine Overhaul Family
WG-8800 Aircraft Overhaul Family
WG-9000 Film-Processing Family

VETERANS' PREFERENCE INFORMATION

Veterans' Preference gives eligible veterans preference in appointment over many other applicants. Veterans' Preference applies to virtually all new appointments in the Competitive Service and many in the Excepted Service. Veterans' Preference does not guarantee veterans a job, and it does not apply to internal agency actions such as promotions, transfers, reassignments, and reinstatements.

Not all veterans receive preference for federal civilian employment, and not all active-duty service qualifies for Veterans' Preference. Only veterans discharged or released from active duty in the Armed Forces under honorable conditions are eligible for Veterans' Preference. This means preference eligibles must have been discharged under an honorable or general discharge. If you are a "retired member of the Armed Forces," you are not included in the definition of preference eligible unless you are a disabled veteran, or you retired below the rank of major or its equivalent.

There are two types of preference eligible: those with a service-connected disability and those without.

If your active-duty service meets any of the following, and you do not have a disability rating from the Department of Veterans Affairs (VA) of 10% or more, you have preference. This preference entitles you to be hired before a non-veteran whose application is rated in your same category. To meet these criteria, your service must meet one of the following conditions:

1. 180 or more consecutive days, any part of which occurred during the period beginning September 11, 2001 and ending on a future date prescribed by Presidential proclamation or law as the last date of Operation Iraqi Freedom (OIF), or

2. Between August 2, 1990 and January 2, 1992, or

3. 180 or more consecutive days, any part of which occurred after January 31, 1955 and before October 15, 1976.

4. In a war, campaign, or expedition for which a campaign badge has been authorized or between April 28, 1952 and July 1, 1955.

If you served at any time, you have a service-connected disability of at least 10%, and you meet basic qualifications for the position and any Selective Placement Factors (SPFs), you are placed at the top of the highest category on the referral list (except for scientific or professional positions at the GS-9 level or higher).

If you:

1. received a Purple Heart, or

2. are the spouse, widow, widower, or mother of a deceased or disabled veteran (derived preference),

... then you are placed above non-preference eligibles within your assigned category.

If you are not sure of your preference eligibility, visit the Office of Personnel Management (OPM) website, Feds Hire Vets at www.fedshirevets.gov/Index.aspx and/or the Veterans Guide at www.fedshirevets.gov/hire/hrp/vetguide/index.aspx. You can also contact the designated veterans' hiring program coordinator for your agency of interest; agency coordinator contact information can be found in Appendix A.

In addition, there are special hiring programs for veterans. These include:

Veterans Recruitment Appointment (VRA). VRA is an excepted authority that allows agencies to appoint eligible veterans without competition. If you:

• are in receipt of a campaign badge for service during a war or in a campaign or expedition; or

- are a disabled veteran, or

- are in receipt of an Armed Forces Service Medal for participation in a military operation, or

- are a recently separated veteran (within the last three years), and

- separated under honorable conditions (this means an honorable or general discharge), you are VRA eligible.

You can be appointed under this authority at any grade level up to and including a GS-11 or equivalent. This is an Excepted Service appointment. After successfully completing two years, you will be converted to the Competitive Service. Veterans' Preference applies when using the VRA authority.

There is no limit to the number of times you can apply under VRA.

VETERANS EMPLOYMENT OPPORTUNITIES ACT (VEOA) OF 1998, AS AMENDED

VEOA is a Competitive Service-appointing authority that can be used only when filling permanent, Competitive Service positions. It cannot be used to fill Excepted Service positions. It allows veterans to apply to announcements that are open only to so-called "status" candidates, which means "current Competitive Service employees."

To be eligible for a VEOA appointment, you must have your latest discharge issued under honorable conditions (this means an honorable or general discharge), and you must be either:

- a preference eligible as discussed above, or
- a veteran who substantially completed three or more years of active service.

When agencies recruit from outside their own workforce under merit promotion (internal) procedures, announcements must state VEOA is applicable. As a VEOA eligible, you are not subject to geographic area of consideration limitations. When applying under VEOA, you must rate and rank among the "Best Qualified" when compared to current employee applicants in order to be considered for appointment. Your Veterans' Preference does not apply to internal agency actions such as promotions, transfers, reassignments, and reinstatements.

Current or former federal employees meeting VEOA eligibility can apply. However, current employees applying under VEOA are subject to time-in-grade restrictions like any other employee.

"Active Service" under VEOA means active duty in a uniformed service and includes full-time training duty, annual training duty, full-time National Guard duty, and attendance while in active service at a school designated as a service school by law or by the secretary concerned.

"Preference eligible" under VEOA includes those family members entitled to derived preference.

"30% or More Disabled Veteran" allows any veteran with a 30% or more service-connected disability to be non-competitively appointed.

You are eligible if you:

- retired from active military service with a service-connected disability rating of 30% or more; or
- you have a rating by the Department of VA showing a compensable service-connected disability of 30% or more.

This authority can be used to make permanent, temporary (not to exceed one year), or term (more than one year, but not more than four) appointments in the Competitive Service. There is no grade-level restriction.

When using this authority to appoint on a permanent basis, you are first placed on a time-limited appointment of at least 60 days and then converted to a permanent appointment at management's discretion. When the authority is used for temporary or term appointments, you will not be converted to a permanent appointment.

DISABLED VETERANS ENROLLED IN A VETERANS AFFAIRS (VA) TRAINING PROGRAM

Disabled veterans eligible for training under the VA vocational rehabilitation program may enroll for training or work experience at an agency under the terms of an agreement between the agency and VA. While enrolled in the VA program, the veteran is not a federal employee for most purposes, but is a beneficiary of the VA.

Training is tailored to the individual's needs and goals, so there is no set length. If the training is intended to prepare the individual for eventual appointment in the agency, rather than just to provide work experience, the agency must ensure the training will enable the veteran to meet the qualification requirements for the position.

Upon successful completion of the training, the veteran receives from the host agency and VA a Certificate of Training, displaying the occupational series and grade level of the position for which the veteran trained. The Certificate of Training allows any agency to appoint the veteran non-competitively under a status-quo appointment, which may be converted to career or career-conditional at any time. In all cases, you must provide acceptable documentation of your preference or appointment eligibility. The Member 4 copy of your DD-214, "Certificate of Release or Discharge from Active Duty," is necessary to document the character of service. If claiming 10-point preference, you will need to submit a Standard Form 15, "Application for 10-point Veterans' Preference."

OTHER USEFUL INFORMATION:

The Veterans Employment Opportunities Act (VEOA) makes a willful violation of Veterans' Preference a prohibited personnel practice. If you are preference eligible and you believe an agency violated any of your rights under the Veterans' Preference laws or regulations, you may file a formal complaint with the Department of Labor's Veterans Employment and Training Service (VETS). If VETS is unable to resolve the complaint within 60 days, you may appeal to the Merit Systems Protection Board (MSPB).

The Uniformed Services Employment and Reemployment Rights Act of 1994 (USERRA) prohibits discrimination in employment, retention, promotion, or any benefit of employment based on your uniformed service. The Department of Labor, through the VETS, assists all persons with USERRA claims.

If you are a disabled veteran and you believe an agency discriminated against you in employment because of your disability, you may file a disability discrimination complaint with the offending agency under regulations administered by the Equal Employment Opportunity Commission (EEOC).

Examinations for custodians, guards, elevator operators, and messengers must be filled by preference-eligible veterans (5 USC 3310).

As a 10-point preference eligible, you may file an application at any time for any position that was filled on a non-temporary basis in the preceding three years, provided that a register (list) of eligibles is maintained that is closed to new applications or if a register is about to be established. If you want to file after the closing date of the register, you should contact the agency that announced the position for further information.

Finally...
The President's Executive Order regarding hiring of veterans in the federal government did not create any new hiring authorities, but it did reinforce our country's commitment to hiring veterans. Key agencies are now required to establish a plan for recruiting and training veterans as well as implementing annual training at the agency level to ensure Human Resources (HR) personnel and managers fully understand Veterans' Preference as well as associated hiring programs. In order to ensure you receive the preference to which you are entitled, you should read the announcement carefully, ensure you meet the qualifications for the position, follow the instructions in the announcement specifically, and include all required documentation to document your preference eligibility.

FEDERAL STUDENT AND OTHER INTERNSHIP PROGRAMS
The federal government offers several internship programs designed to help aspiring students gain a taste of the federal culture as they prepare for a prospective full-time career in the government. Applicants interested in various internship programs should visit http://www.usajobs.gov/studentjobs/, as well as individual agency websites. If you had college credit before you joined the military, before you earned a degree, or if you are currently working on a degree, one of the following programs might be a good fit:

Student Temporary Employment Program (STEP)

STEP provides for students part-time, paid federal jobs that can last as little as one summer or as long as the duration of their college career. The work is not necessarily related to a student's field of study, which is a benefit because it provides the student with the opportunity to gain experience in other fields.

Who Is Eligible: Full-time high-school, college, vocational school, or graduate-school students who are U.S. citizens are eligible for STEP. However, there are some instances in which an agency's appropriation act will permit non-citizen employees to apply; if this is the case, you must provide proof he/she is eligible to work under U.S. immigration laws in order to be considered for the program.

STEP positions are not always listed on http://www.USAJobs.gov; for example, if you're interested in gaining experience in the Department of Justice (DOJ), you should check with the agency directly to see if it participates in STEP.

For more information on STEP, visit http://www.opm.gov/employ/students/intro.asp.

Student Career Experience Program (SCEP)
SCEP allows a student to gain experience working for the government in a job that is related to his/her field of study. Many of the positions are paid and some may provide academic credit toward the degree requirements.

Who is Eligible: In order for a student to be eligible for SCEP, his/her educational institution must have a formal agreement with the hiring agency. SCEP positions are available to both undergraduate and graduate students. In most cases, U.S. citizenship is required; however, if the hiring agency's appropriation act permits non-citizen employees, and the student is eligible to work under U.S. immigration laws, he/she can participate in the program.

Once a SCEP candidate successfully completes 640 hours of work within the program's guidelines, he/she becomes eligible to be hired to a permanent position without going through the traditional hiring process. Recent modifications of SCEP allow agencies to waive up to half of the required 640 hours for students with certain job-related experience acquired in a structured work-study program, or inactive military service, or if they have delivered exceptional job performance and academic excellence (3.5 GPA out of a 4.0 scale, are in the top 10% of their graduating class, and/or are inducted into a nationally recognized scholastic honors society during their enrollment in the program). For more information on SCEP, visit http://www.opm.gov/employ/students/intro.asp.

Presidential Management Fellows (PMF) Program
The PMF Program is a prestigious two-year program that prepares students for upper-level management positions in the federal government.

Who is Eligible: To be eligible, a student must be in the final year of a graduate program and must receive a nomination from his/her school. Eligible students must submit their application packages in the fall. For more information, visit https://www.pmf.opm.gov.

The PMF Program is structured by individual agencies; however, all PMFs receive training opportunities and developmental assignments, either within the agency or to another agency or branch of the government. PMFs are usually appointed at the GS-9, 11, or 12 levels. In some cases, a PMF candidate may be eligible for rapid annual or accelerated promotions up to GS-13 during the program.

After two years, PMFs are eligible for conversion to permanent positions. While the number of PMF positions varies every year according to agency—and not all agencies participate in the program—some of the agencies that have been the most active in terms of the program include the DOJ, Department of State (DOS), Department of Health and Human Services (HHS), U.S. Agency for International Development (USAID), Department of Defense (DoD), Department of Commerce (DOC), and Department of Homeland Security (DHS).

Searching for Federal Jobs by College Major
To help students choose the right career field, the Office of Personnel Management (OPM) has prepared an extensive table that groups federal jobs that are often filled by college graduates

with appropriate academic majors. The jobs provided on this table, found at http://www.USAJobs.gov/EI/jobsbycollegemajor.asp#icc, are not all-inclusive, as a student can qualify for a large number of administrative jobs with a degree in any academic major. Most of the jobs listed do not require a college degree.

Summer Employment

The federal government, much like private sector, offers a limited number of summer employment opportunities to eligible applicants. These temporary/seasonal assignments are typically found on http://www.USAJobs.gov as well as the individual agencies' websites. As a rule of thumb, applicants desiring summer employment are advised to begin their search and application process early, as many agencies look to conclude their hiring for the summer well before the end of the school year.

Pathways

Introduced by President Barack Obama via an Executive Order on December 27, 2010, the Pathways Program, which replaces the former Federal Career Intern Program (FCIP), encourages federal agencies to diversify their respective workforces with both students and new graduates. Whereas in the past, a new graduate or a student might struggle to meet minimum qualifications for a position, this Executive Order eliminates these barriers by offering positions that "provide meaningful training, mentoring, and career-development opportunities" via internships.

If a student employee is deemed to "have what it takes" as far as the potential to be successful in the federal government employment structure, the student is given additional training and advancement opportunities accordingly.

You can read more about this new program at http://www.whitehouse.gov/the-pressoffice/2010/12/27/executive-order-recruiting-and-hiring-students-and-recent-graduates.

HELPFUL WEBSITES FOR VETERANS

Find a list of all federal and state government agencies here: http://www.usa.gov/Agencies/Federal/All_Agencies/index.shtml

- Veterans Transition Headquarters blog: www.veteranstransitionhq.wordpress.com
- O*NET: http://online.onetcenter.org/
- FASCLASS: https://acpol2.army.mil/fasclass/inbox/default.asp
- OPM: http://www.opm.gov/
- USAJobs (federal government's official jobsite): http://www.usajobs.opm.gov/
- Army Civilian Personnel Online (CPOL): http://www.cpol.army.mil/
- Military Skills Translator: http://www.military.com/skills-translator/mos-translator
- National Resources Directory: www.nrd.gov
- Military Resume Writers: http://www.militaryresumewriters.com
- Federal Job Resumes: http://www.federaljobresume.com
- USAJobs Info Center: http://www.usajobs.gov/infocenter/
- VetGuide: http://www.opm.gov/staffingportal/vetguide.asp
- Veterans' Preference score: http://www.opm.gov/staffingPortal/Vetguide.asp
- G.I. Jobs: http://www.gijobs.com/2011Top100.aspx

VISION STATEMENT WORKSHEET

I am really good at:

1. _____
2. _____
3. _____
4. _____
5. _____
6. _____
7. _____
8. _____
9. _____
10. _____

(Circle the top 3)

I am passionate about:

1. _____
2. _____
3. _____
4. _____
5. _____
6. _____
7. _____
8. _____
9. _____
10. _____

(Circle the top 3)

I'd like to live/work in:

1. _____
2. _____
3. _____
4. _____
5. _____
6. _____
7. _____
8. _____
9. _____
10. _____

(Circle the top 3)

My top skills I want to focus on:

1. _____
2. _____
3. _____
4. _____
5. _____
6. _____
7. _____
8. _____
9. _____
10. _____

(Circle the top 3)

The top jobs/companies I want to target are:

1. _____
2. _____
3. _____
4. _____
5. _____
6. _____
7. _____
8. _____
9. _____
10. _____

(Circle the top 3)

Basic Career Vision Statement

I will identify and secure a job in _____ as a _____.

                                          (choose from top 3 locations)   *(choose from top 3 job positions)*

I know I'd be an ideal candidate because I am good at _____

                                                                     (choose from top 3 job skills)

and passionate about _____.

                            (choose from top 3 job passions)

ACTION WORD LIST –

accomplished	calculated	delegated	engineered	honest
achieved	capable	delivered	enlisted	hypothesized
acted	catalogued	demonstrated	enterprising	identified
activated	chaired	dependable	enthusiastic	illustrated
active	charted	described	established	Imaginative
adaptable	checked	descriptive	estimated	imagined
adapted	clarified	designed	evaluated	implemented
addressed	classified	detailed	examined	improved
adjusted	coached	detected	executed	improvised
administered	collected	determined	expanded	incorporated
advised	communicated	developed	expedited	increased
aggressive	compared	devised	experimented	independent
aided	competent	diagnosed	explained	industrious
alert	competitive	diplomatic	explored	influenced
allocated	compiled	directed	expressed	informed
altered	completed	disciplined	extracted	initiated
ambitious	composed	discovered	extroverted	innovated
analytical	computed	discreet	fabricated	inspected
analyzed	conceived	dispatched	facilitated	inspired
anticipated	conceptualized	dispensed	fair	installed
applied	conducted	displayed	familiarized	instituted
appraised	confident	disproved	fashioned	instructed
approved	conscientious	dissected	filed	integrated
arbitrated	conserved	distributed	financed	integrated
arranged	consistent	diverted	fixed	interpreted
ascertained	consolidated	documented	followed	interviewed
assembled	constructed	drafted	forceful	introduced
assertive	constructive	dramatized	forecast	invented
assessed	contracted	drew	forecasted	inventive
assigned	controlled	drove	formed	inventoried
assisted	coordinated	earned	formulated	investigated
attained	coordinated	economical	founded	judged
attentive	corresponded	edited	friendly	kept
audited	counseled	educated	gathered	launched
authored	created	efficient	gave	learned
balanced	creative	eliminated	generated	lectured
bought	critiqued	empathized	guided	led
broad-minded	dealt	enabled	handled	leveled
brought	debugged	encouraged	headed	lifted
budgeted	decided	energetic	helped	listed
built	defined	enforced	helpful	listened

 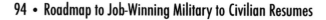

loaded	performed	reconciled	sensed	taught
logged	personable	recorded	sensible	teachable
logical	persuaded	recruited	separated	tended
loyal	photographed	reduced	served	tested
made	piloted	reevaluated	set goals	tolerant
maintained	planned	referred	sewed	traced
managed	planted	refined	shaped	trained
manipulated	played	reflective	shared	transcribed
marketed	pleasant	rehabilitated	showed	translated
mature	positive	rejected	simplified	transmitted
measured	practical	related	sincere	traveled
mediated	precise	reliable	sketched	treated
memorized	predicted	remodeled	sold	troubleshot
methodical	prepared	rendered	solved	trustworthy
modeled	prescribed	renegotiated	sophisticated	tutored
moderated	presented	reorganized	sorted	typed
modified	printed	repair	specified	unified
molded	prioritized	repaired	spoke	united
monitored	processed	reported	sponsored	updated
motivated	produced	represented	stable	upgraded
navigated	productive	researched	started	upheld
negotiated	programmed	resolved	stimulated	used
objective	projected	resourceful	streamlined	utilized
observed	promoted	responded	strengthened	validated
obtained	proofread	responsible	studied	verbalized
offered	protected	restored	successful	verified
operated	provided	retrieved	summarized	versatile
opportunistic	prudent	reunited	supervised	volunteered
optimistic	publicized	reviewed	supplied	warned
ordered	published	revised	supported	washed
ordered	purchased	revitalized	supportive	weighed
organized	questioned	rewrote	surveyed	will relocate
original	quick	risked	symbolized	wired
originated	raised	saved	synergized	worked
outlined	rational	scheduled	synthesized	wrote
overhauled	read	screened	systematic	
oversaw	realistic	searched	systematized	
painted	realized	selected	tabulated	
patient	reasoned	self-confident	tactful	
perceived	received	self-reliant	talented	
perceptive	recommended	sense of Humor	talked	

GRAMMAR AND PUNCTUATION TIPS/RESOURCES

As you probably already know, the English language has seemingly countless rules on grammar and punctuation. On top of that, there are a number of different accepted styles based on industry. For example, journalists might use one style, technical writers might use another, and professional resume writers might use a combination of several different styles to meet their clients' needs.

When it comes to writing your resume and other application materials, there may be lots of bullets (which can be incomplete sentences) and acronyms. We recommend that you minimize the use of acronyms, but when you need to use them, spell them out the first time. And most importantly, be consistent! If you use one space after each period, then do that for the entire document. Make sense?

If you don't feel confident about checking your own grammar or punctuation, here are a few tips:

1. Have a friend, family member, or colleague who has some writing or editing experience check your work

2. Use the grammar and spell checker in Microsoft Word or another program (but be careful; it doesn't catch everything)

3. Hire a professional resume writer and/or proofreader

4. Go to the library or research grammar and punctuation rules online

5. Use helpful websites like the ones below. Remember, even professionals sometimes refer to sites like these, so there is no shame in doing so.

Resources:

Grammar Girl: http://grammar.quickanddirtytips.com/

Grammarly.com (an automated proofreader and your personal grammar coach): http://www.grammarly.com/?q=grammar&gclid=CInt59mpm6wCFZJS7AodV29-IQ

Strunk and White's The Elements of Style: http://www.bartleby.com/141/

Appendix B: Samples

Disclaimer: We have been careful to provide accurate and up-to-date information throughout this book; however, it is possible that errors and omissions will still exist. The resume templates and character counts are current at the time of this printing, but federal and private organizations change their application requirements and other details on an ongoing basis. In addition, we presented the resume samples as entry-level (E-1 to E-4), mid-level (E-5 to E-7 and O-1 to O-3), and senior-level (E-8 to E-9 and O-4 and up), but you won't necessarily leave the military and land a job in one of these levels based purely on your highest military rank. You should always double-check with the federal agency or specific company to be sure you are following the most current formatting guidelines. Your own circumstances, accomplishments, resume, and the hiring managers will determine what level position you secure.

Whether you are writing a resume or other application materials, or preparing for an interview, there is not just one correct way to do anything. There are only good ideas, tactics, and best practices, many of which you have learned in this book. Obviously, we encourage you to use the guidance and resume samples in this book. But we also advise you to avoid using them "as is," without integrating all of your own skills and experience. They are designed to give you ideas and help your own resume development go much smoother.

Samples List

Military to Private-Sector Resume Samples

Military to Federal Resume Samples

Cover Letter Samples

Narrative Samples

Military to Private-Sector
Resume Samples

LISA KINGSTON

173 PIERCE AVENUE, MACON, GA 31204
Home: 478-742-2442 ■ Cell: 555-123-4567 ■ Email: info@careerprocenter.net

~ EXECUTIVE ASSISTANT ~
(Secret Security Clearance)

■ Project Coordination/Management	■ Leadership/Team Building
■ Budgeting and Cost Control	■ Operations/Executive Advisor
■ Best Practice Standards/Process Improvements	■ Human Resources/Training

- **Executive/Administrative:** Eight years' experience, including recent work with major Fortune 500 corporation, excelling in communicating vision, instilling team culture, and igniting competitive drive. Drove major projects, programs, and initiatives from planning through tactical execution.
- **Quality Improvements:** Driving force behind strategy, planning, and launch of operational enhancements. Proven track record in six-year career developing/implementing effective process improvements through Total Quality Management/Lean Six Sigma.
- **Operations Management:** Director of Leadership programs in managing Human Resources (HR) and postal operations in a military setting, servicing both military and civilian clientele. Controlled $50K budget.
- **HR Administration:** Experience monitoring and processing personnel actions for as many as 65 staff members. Facilitator of strategic alliance and channel development through morale building and training.
- Computer Skills: Proficient in Microsoft (MS) Office (MS Word, Access, Excel, and PowerPoint).

PROFESSIONAL EXPERIENCE

CIVILIAN CONTRACT POSITIONS   12/2008 to 09/2011

Executive Assistant, Logistics Specialists, Macon, GA   *02/2010 to 09/2011*

Managed a wide range of critical and time-sensitive executive and administrative details in support of the Commander.
- Sought-after by executive management to facilitate multiple priority activities concurrently.
- Served as first Point of Contact (POC) with internal/external staff, managers, and agents, requiring extreme tact/diplomacy.
- Recognized for highest levels of integrity, ethics, judgment, work ethic, discretion, professionalism, and maturity.
- Managed Commanding Officer's daily calendar/schedule and facilitated military business arrangements.
- Remained accountable for funds allocated for travel, supplies, awards, and overtime, ensuring no fraud, waste, or abuse.
- Coordinated complex meetings, overseeing the setup of all VIP conference room briefings.
- Designed/implemented a Standard Operating Procedure (SOP) to improve continuity of reporting with regulations/guidelines.
- Streamlined travel, lodging, itineraries, and security for VIPs, dignitaries, and Heads of State.

Executive Assistant, Military Department, Afghanistan   *12/2008 to 01/2010*

Provided Deputy Project Manager high-level administrative assistance for up to seven different departments.
- Compiled confidential daily personnel reports to Army Materiel Command (AMC) Headquarters (HQ), ensuring data accuracy.
- Appointed as company historian based on superior work performance, attention to detail, and research capability.
- Sharp focus in compiling and generating weekly corporate project status corporate reports.

LISA KINGSTON   PAGE TWO

U.S. ARMY   **01/2004 to 10/2008**

Human Resources Specialist/Office Manager, U.S. Army, Macon, GA   *10/2007 to 10/2008*

Supervised the administrative office for a Major Command jointly staffed with military and civilian personnel.
- Served as advisor to Chief of Staff and senior management on administrative and personnel operations.
- Controlled $1.2M budget for operations/office equipment and maintained accountability of all government property.
- Streamlined personnel action authorizations, reducing the lag time for authorization from six weeks to two weeks.
- Coordinated removal of old computers with the Recycling Program, ensuring crediting of budget for returned equipment.

Supervised U.S. Army Forces Command (FORSCOM) Leaderships Awards Programs.

Director, Army Command, Leadership Programs and Operations, Macon, GA   *08/2005 to 10/2007*

- Advised Directorate Chief, subordinate organizations, and external agencies on policies/procedures, ensuring continuity.
- Enhanced morale throughout the command by revising leadership regulations for award processes.
- Planned and developed policies, procedures, and programs for 52 postal units, raising overall standards of operation/delivery.

Organized and managed all administrative actions, programs, and support services for the executive director.

Executive Services Officer, Fort Macon, GA   *02/2004 to 07/2005*

- Served as Program Manager for all government credit card purchases with the responsibility for consolidating, balancing, paying, and maintaining account transactions records with accuracy and accountability.
- Supervised the overall support for U.S. and International Military Students and distinguished civilian guests/visitors.
- Coordinated, planned, and executed all installation-level ceremonies and social functions.

Served as the HQ Training Leader/Supervisor, ensuring Department of the Army standards were met for 200+ soldiers.

Operations Manager, Fort Macon, GA   *04/2003 to 02/2004*

- Managed Common Task Testing, Dental, Hearing, Conservations, HIV, Immunizations, Weapons Qualifications, and Army Physical Fitness Testing.
- Maintained a 100% incident-free drug urinalysis testing program while serving as the Drug and Alcohol Coordinator.
- Avoided the escalation of 10% of cases as the appointed HQ Equal Opportunity Advisor.

EDUCATION AND SPECIALIZED TRAINING/CERTIFICATIONS

Associate in General Studies, Georgia University College, Macon, GA

Safety/Occupational Safety & Health Administration (OSHA) Training, 2006 ~ Sexual Harassment ~ Consideration of Other Facilitator Course ~ Advanced Non-Commissioned Officer (NCO) Course ~ Basic NCO Course ~ Primary Leadership Development Course

HONORS/AWARDS

Bronze Star Medal ~ Meritorious Service Medal (3) ~ Army Commendation Medal ~ Joint Commendation Medal ~ Joint Achievement Medal ~ Army Achievement Medal (2) ~ NCO of the Year

TERRELL P. KNOX

173 Pierce Avenue | Macon, GA 31204 | 478-742-2442 | info@careerprocenter.net

"Motivated and challenged; coordinates through leadership by example. Willing to sacrifice time and effort to attain unit goals. Always placed subordinates' needs above his own; extraordinary motivator; and constantly leads by example."

■ JOHN SMITH, MSGT, United States Army

- *Security Clearance: Secret*
- *Training and Development*
- *Management and Leadership*
- *Administrative Management*
- *Operations and Supply*
- *Inventory Management*

- **Training and Development:** Distinguished record of intense dedication to value added training and development programs for up to 46 personnel monthly.
- **Inventory Management:** Adept at organizing and streamlining inventory management processes. Maintained 100% inventory accountability for company assets worth $350K.
- **Operations and Supply:** Managed daily meal distributions to 1,200 personnel during deployment, providing critical sustenance and allowing for team goal accomplishment.

■■■ EMPLOYMENT HISTORY ■■■

UNITED STATES ARMY 2005 to 2011
OPERATIONS AND TRAINING MANAGER, FORT SILL, OK 1/2009 to 2011
Coordinate, implement, and track necessary performance training and schedules for personnel, including professional qualification, physical fitness, and other task benchmarking, to guarantee readiness at a moment's notice. Ensure quality control while delivering on time and according to procedures. Resolve problems and guide others in improving performance and meeting goals for optimum career progression.
- Recognized for 100% accountability and serviceability of all team equipment, valued at $50K.
- Selected over four training supervisors to create and administer physical fitness program.
- Recognized by senior leadership for the development and results of organization's Energy Conservation Program.
- Commended by Directorate of Operations and Training for dedicated, specific assignment training program.

FOOD SERVICE MANAGER, FORT SILL, OK 4/2007 to 1/2009
Managed daily food preparation for 700+ personnel, training and supervising assistant food service workers and facility attendants. Maintained pristine sanitation standards, quality food preparation, and equipment maintenance. Oversaw food service supply in excess of $300K, forecasting demand and creating supply plans to ensure availability. Supervised Information Security System, cash control, fire prevention, and energy conservation teams, and supply and administrative performance.
- Oversaw $300K+ of food service supplies, employing advanced cooking techniques, resulting in <5% waste.
- Maintained 100% accountability of section equipment worth $800K during change of division inventories.
- Received Silver Medal in Presentation category of Advanced Culinary Skills Training Course.

FOOD SERVICE MANAGER, CAMP EAGLE, KOREA 4/2006 to 11/2006
Oversaw daily meal preparation for more than 1,200 personnel, supervising preparation of meals in both base camp and in the field. Conducted daily inspections of personnel, food preparation, storage areas, and facilities. Managed six food service workers, guiding morale, welfare, counseling, and training on standard policies and procedures and creation of recipes; encouraging engagement in correspondence courses for continued self-development; and developing and implementing continual on-the-job training.
- Maintained $350K in field food service equipment and monthly inventory of $90K, with no loss of resources.
- Led shift during dining facility inspections, winning unit director's "Best Restaurant in Town" 3rd and 4th quarter, 2006.
- Upheld section's 100% operational readiness, ensuring no delay in deployment of critical personnel.

■■■ EDUCATION, TRAINING, & AWARDS ■■■

Quartermaster School, Advanced Culinary Skills Course and Quartermaster School, Food Service Specialist Course

Commendation Medal ■ *Achievement Medal*

Ronald Dell

✉ info@careerprocenter.net

173 Pierce Avenue ◆ Macon, GA 31204 ◆ Phone: 478-742-2442

Investigator ◆ Law Enforcement Officer
Security Clearance: Secret

AREAS OF EXPERTISE AND TECHNICAL SKILLS

- Leadership/Management
- Program/Project Management
- Written/Verbal Communications
- Mentoring/Guidance

- Law Enforcement
- Accountability/Quality Assurance
- Team Building/Personnel
- Training/Instruction

- Tactical Planning
- Intelligence/Surveillance
- Physical Fitness
- Safety Awareness/Training

PROFESSIONAL BACKGROUND

Team Supervisor, Fort Bragg, NC   *12/2009-Present*

- Lead and supervise 23 paratroopers in a combat zone located in an airborne Military Police Company, currently serving in Iraq in support of Operation Iraqi Freedom (OIF).
- Ensure personnel and equipment are prepared, maintained, and ready for combat patrols in a hostile setting.
- Maintain accountability for equipment, vehicles, and weapons systems valued at more than $500K.
- Guide and mentor personnel to pursue educational opportunities and achieve to the best of their ability.
- Inspire team efforts to ensure safety while meeting the highest standards and achieving 100% of mission goals.
- Supervised Iraqi Police Station and administered contracts valued at more than $750K for station.
- Conducted numerous investigations in criminal matters to include homicide and assault; mentored Iraqi Police in investigation techniques and aided them in conducting their own procedures.

NOTABLE EVALUATION COMMENTS: "Unsurpassed leadership ability . . . steadfast leader throughout combat operations."

Lead Trainer, Fort Jackson, SC   *08/2008-11/2009*

- Taught, led, and mentored 15 training candidates under rigorous conditions in a nine-week revolving cycle.
- Provided instruction in tactical training, methods of training, integrated training management, stress management, leadership, counseling, fitness, weapons systems, and a variety of other subjects.
- Trained more than 20 training candidates to proficiency in teaching basic combat training skills.
- Consistently inspired cooperation and confidence; ensured safety was paramount in all training situations.

NOTABLE EVALUATION COMMENTS: "Displays strengths of an exceptional leader; tireless in the pursuit of mission accomplishment."

Human Resources (HR) Advisor, Fort Polk, LA   *10/2005-07/2008*

- Maintained and controlled movement on main supply routes; planned operation of operations area checkpoints.
- Performed duties of a Headquarters (HQ) Team Supervisor, directing 7 sections and activities of 35 personnel during deployment to Iraq.
- Directed day-shift Tactical Operations Center (TOC) functions during combat operations.
- Planned and coordinated resources for law enforcement certification for more than 75 personnel.

EDUCATION AND TRAINING

BACHELOR OF ARTS, CRIMINAL JUSTICE, American Public University, WV

Professional Army Training:
Staff and Faculty Development Course: Instructor/Developer, U.S. Army Staff Sergeant School
Military Police Advanced Non-Commissioned Officer Course, Non-Commissioned Officer Academy
Drill Sergeant Course, U.S. Army Drill Sergeant School
Graduated, U.S. Army Military Police School

AWARDS

Manager Development Course, Army Institute for Professional Development
Bronze Star Medal, Purple Heart, Meritorious Service Medal

MARK AMES

Active Secret Security Clearance Holder
173 Pierce Avenue
Macon, GA 31204

478-742-2442   info@careerproplus.net

LAW ENFORCEMENT AND SECURITY

Extensive hands-on experience in security and force protection, applying knowledge of laws, processes, and procedures to provide security for personnel, property, and institutions.

Demonstrated self-defense expertise and high-level proficiency with weapons; trained in hand-to-hand combat and self-defense; qualified with a variety of weapons/firearms. Experience with Microsoft (MS) Office (Word, Excel, Outlook). Expertise in…

Security Operations	Law Enforcement	Force Protection
Entry Control	Personnel Protection	Weapons and Self-Defense
Convoy Support	Equipment Accountability	Administrative Support

PROFESSIONAL EXPERIENCE

Ground Operations Specialist, United States Marine Corps (USMC), Camp LeJeune, NC   7/2009 to Present
Participate in the establishment and maintenance of the operation section's installation in the field, and prepare and maintain operation and situation maps.

- Maintain pertinent information obtained from intelligence and reconnaissance reports, complete operations journal containing briefs of important messages, and generate associated reports.
- Perform force protection and entry control and participate in activities to secure the base and provide security for personnel, equipment, and resources.
- Participate in training exercises and security operations, providing assistance in the execution of tactical operations and security support.
- Account for the security, maintenance, and operational readiness of personal equipment and weapons and follow security directives and safety regulations to ensure the highest levels of security.

Security Specialist, USMC, Camp LeJeune, NC   2/2008 to 7/2009
Performed law enforcement, force protection, and entry control and participated in individual and team patrols to secure the base and provide security for personnel, equipment, and resources.

- Participated in training exercises and security operations, assisted in the execution of tactical operations, and provided support to ensure the highest level of security and readiness.
- Deployed to Afghanistan to provide force protection and security support for the Global War on Terrorism (GWOT) (06/2008 to 06/2009), providing support for offensive and defensive operations.
- Served as a key member of a company-level personal security detachment, providing security for high-ranking individuals and dignitaries; participated in base and convoy security.
- Received training in ground operations and obtained a secondary occupational specialty.
- Maintained training records for the battalion, enforced military standards, and accounted for equipment.

EDUCATION/TRAINING

Chaulker High School (member, JROTC)

Specialized Training and Certifications: Ground Operations Specialist Course; Mine Resistant Ambush Protected (MRAP) Vehicles Course; Biometric Automated Tool Set Basic User Course; Anti-Tank Assaultman Course; Ground-Based Operational Surveillance System Course

AWARDS & RECOGNITION

Junior Reserve Officer Leadership Medal; USMC Certificate of Commendation; GWOT Service Medal; Afghanistan Campaign Medal; Sea Service Deployment Ribbon (2); National Defense Service Medal

AMBER JOHNSON

173 Pierce Avenue | Macon, GA 31204 | 478-742-2442 | info@careerprocenter.net

PARALEGAL
Legal Claims Management / Evaluation and Review / Partnership and Collaboration / Administrative Management

Confident in leading broad-scope paralegal/military justice division operations in support of high-priority military assignments. Provided supervision for the full spectrum of military justice administration to sustain 17 organizations. Distinguished history of facilitating value-added legal and regulatory training and development programs for up to 150 individuals. Motivating team leader, advisor, and mentor with a strong ability to build and sustain working relationships with leaders, colleagues, and personnel. Led team to earn top honors as the AMC Gold winner for the 1st quarter of 2011.

CAREER HIGHLIGHTS

- Lauded as the top AMC Military Justice Section; honored with the AMC Gold for the 1st quarter of 2011.
- Recognized by senior leader for managing the execution of more than 800 general/special courts-martial.
- Notarized 35 powers of attorney and legal documents, and witnessed 40+ wills, resulting in $10K in legal fee cost savings.
- Processed more than 2,625 tort claims related to the Tuckerton fires; $3M+ paid to victims.
- Performance rated as "Excellent" by the Command Judge Advocate for Combined Joint Task Force 101.
- Enhanced international relations by managing 1,670+ foreign nation legal reviews.
- Praised for motivating the team to achieve a 2.8-day average processing time for 450 claims.
- Drafted 75 powers of attorney, notarized 160 documents, and processed 114 Article 15s at a 97%, 20-day completion rate.

PROFESSIONAL EXPERIENCE

LAW OFFICE MANAGER/MILITARY JUSTICE OFFICER   6/2009 to Present
U.S. Air Force (USAF), New York

- Provided supervision for the full spectrum of military justice administration to sustain 17 organizations.
- Led the execution of adverse, judicial/non-judicial actions performed by a justice team of four individuals.
- Supervised non-judicial punishment processes and courts-martial cases for military personnel.
- Conducted reviews of evidence for factual sufficiency and jurisdiction, recommending case disposition.
- Evaluated and analyzed complex military justice data to deter adverse trends and promote fairness.
- Managed accountability for Status of Discipline and Article 137 briefing programs for four teams/wings.
- Instructed up to 150 personnel in Article 137 rights, rules, and consequences.
- Authored newspaper articles focused on crime and punishment as well as deterrence factors for discipline issues.
- Controlled a $24K witness funding budget, maintaining 100% voucher reconciliation.

PARALEGAL/CLAIMS OFFICE MANAGER   9/2004 to 6/2009
USAF, North Carolina

- Oversaw the investigation and administration of claims for and against the U.S. government.
- Evaluated and reviewed laws and regulations for legal precedents and rulings associated with claims issues.
- Notarized documents for 250 personnel to increase legal readiness and to provide superior customer service.
- Coordinated and presented Law of Armed Conflict (LOAC) briefings for up to 450 personnel.

CLAIMS RECOVERY MANAGER   9/2004 to 8/2006
USAF, Andersen Air Force Base (AFB), Guam

- Presided over claims recovery processes for the largest team in the USAF, serving a population of 21.5K personnel.
- Performed claims recovery, witness interviews, and inspections; ensured compliance with applicable laws and regulations.

PROFESSIONAL DEVELOPMENT

Paralegal Craftsman Course; Advanced Contingency Skills Training; Operations Law Course; USAF Non-Commissioned Officer (NCO) Academy; Military Justice Administration Course; Technical Publications; Paralegal Apprentice Course; Paralegal Craftsman Course; Human Relations; Department of Defense (DoD) Information Assurance Awareness Course

JANET SPEARS

173 Pierce Avenue | Macon, GA 31204 | 478-742-2442 | info@careerprocenter.net

"Janet excels in leadership. She saved our office over 15% in production costs by streamlining procedures. I recommend her highly."
- John Dean, Lt. Col., U.S. Army

NETWORK SYSTEMS ENGINEER

- *Project Management*
- *Supervision and Leadership*
- *Biometrics Automation*
- *Information Technology*
- *Hardware/Software*
- *Networking Systems*
- *Language/Scripts*
- *Operating Systems*
- *Project Coordination*
- *Database Platform/Architect*
- *Database Administration*
- *Team Leadership*
- *Budget/Finance Analysis*
- *Configuration Management*
- *Website Construction*
- *Troubleshoot and Repair*
- *Medical Evacuation*

- **Hands-on Database Systems Administrator**: Hardware and software servers, workstations, laptops, PDAs, printers, digital copiers, storage cards, card readers, DSL, cable modems, controllers, switches, direct attached storage, network appliance, peripheral devices, BIOS, Firmware, Microsoft (MS) Office Suite, Open Office, Data mining, VERITAS backup, VMware, NetApp, Active Directory, DATA On-Tap, Symantec, Norton, Web Root Antivirus, Internet Explorer, Firefox, Lotus, Document Management, Battlefield Simulator Software

- **Demonstrated capacity to plan, support, and oversee operating systems and supporting software, to include**: Microsoft (MS) Windows 2000, 2003, 2007, XP, Vista; UNIX, Linux, RedHat, Solaris, capable of performing administration from Command Line Interface (CLI) in MS Windows, MS Office Suite to include Excel, Access, Word, PowerPoint, Outlook, Visio, Visual, and Project; Norton Utilities, Antivirus, Ghost, Remedy Dameware, Symantec Corp Security, HP JetAdmin, WinZip, CorelDRAW Suite, Remote Anywhere, Fireworks, Combat Track II,TMIP, DCAMS, AHLTA-T, AHLTA-M, JMeWS, TMDS, CHCS/TC2, Alta Point 6.0

- **Networking and language proficiency, to include**: NIPRNet/SIPRnet, Centrix, Dentrix, Wireless Networking, LAN/WAN/MAN, TCP/IP, Subnets, Intrusion Detection, IEEE 802.1, Active Directory, User Account Management, Data Links, Remote Access, Virtual Services Hosting, Network Database Management, WINS, and Network Security, DSL/Cable, routers, Ethernet 802.11, Bluetooth, C++, CSS, Java Script, SQL, NET, ECC, BAT files, scripting in Notepad

PROFESSIONAL EXPERIENCE AND ACHIEVEMENTS

Combat Medic/Biometrics Collector
United States (U.S.) Army, Macon, GA

10/2008 to Present

Manage Biometric Automated Toolset (BAT) and perform Database/System Administration. Maintain and support base services relating to planning, scheduling, operations, Information Technology (IT) security provisions and protocols, maintenance, and repair. Highlighted duties include:

- Database operations, administration, maintenance, procurement, watch list documentation, and reporting. Perform troubleshooting and connectivity issues relating to security and management. Provide management configuration for all systems and peripherals and ensure storage and optimization for storage.
- Evaluate, test, and upgrade database programs and network support programs and equipment to include Handheld Interagency Identity Detection Equipment (HILDES) and Discovery Synchronization Service (DSS). Performed Communication Intelligence (COMINT) collection of local national and hostile personnel.

Accomplishments:

⇒ Awarded Army Commendation medal for leadership and development of training relating to medical evacuation operations; enhanced 95% efficient standardization for airlift support.
⇒ Selected to participate in Tactical Operation Center (TOC) during convoy missions, enhancing processes and performance-based operations score.

JANET SPEARS, PAGE 2

478-742-2442 | info@careerprocenter.net

Information Systems (IS) Assistant Manager	7/2006 to 10/2008
Georgia Community Bank, Macon, GA	

Managed IS and IT over bank portfolios and financial functions, reports, evaluations, and support. Provided privacy and security in compliance with all federal regulatory requirements relating to Bank Security Act (BSA), ChexSystems, and National Homeland Security Knowledgebase (NHSK). Developed audit reports for evaluation and assessment of transactions to identify suspicious activities. Supervised Lead Teller, opening accounts and overseeing redemption of bonds and tax origination, life insurance sales, mortgage and auto loans, annuities, college loans, and investment options. Utilized Oracle web and database programs.

Accomplishments:
⇨ Selected as Employee of the Month for Top Performance, 07/2007.
⇨ Established audit/evaluation reports to identify suspicious transaction; increased identification by 45%.

PROFESSIONAL TRAINING AND DEVELOPMENT

Graduate of the Army Basic Instructor Course (ABIC), 2010
Combat Medic/Emergency Medical Technician, 2008
Fire Marshall/Fire Warden, Certified for 62nd Medical Brigade in support of 575th ASMC Company, 2008
Certified Trainer of MC4 software ALTHA & TC2, 2008
Certified Trainer, BAT and HIIDE, 2008

EDUCATION

M.B.A. and Master's of Computer Science/ITM, City College, Cypress, California, 2008-Present

Computerized Medical Billing and Coding, Technical Institute, Macon, Georgia, Graduated 2007

B.A. Economics/Business Administration, Georgia State, Atlanta, Georgia, Graduated 2007

COMPUTER SKILLS AND CERTIFICATIONS

Software: Certifications - CompTIA Security+, A+, Network+, Microsoft Certified Systems Engineer (MCSE) in progress, Microsoft Certified Systems Administration (MCSA). Certificated Oracle9i Database Administrator Associate. Graduate Certificate in Information Security/Assurance and Digital Forensics. Certified Emergency Medical Technician under National Registry No. B1887473. OPSEC; HIPAA; IA Certified; Microsoft (MS) Word, Excel, PowerPoint, and Outlook; SQL security server; BAT systems and networks; website construction; S/HTTP, HTTPS, HTML, XML, Java, JavaScript, APPLET Web

AWARDS AND HONORS

Army Commendation Medal (2)
Army Achievement Medal, Outstanding Performance
Army Achievement Certificate, leadership support for NATO forces in support of Operation Enduring Freedom (OEF)
Honor Graduate, Army Basic Instructor Course

GABRIELLA C. JIMINEZ

173 Pierce Avenue | Macon, GA 31024 | 478-742-2442 | info@careerprocenter.net

RECRUITING
*Multidimensional professional with demonstrated experience and education
in recruiting and retention and team leadership*

Fluent in Oral and Written Spanish Language

- *Psychology*
- *Recruiting and Retention*
- *Training and Mentoring*
- *Partnership and Collaboration*
- *Communication and Coordination*
- *Team Leadership*

- **Team Leadership:** Motivating team leader, advisor, and liaison with a strong ability to establish working relationships with leaders, colleagues, and personnel.

- **Recruiting and Retention:** Results-oriented recruiter, building high-performance teams to accomplish organizational goals and objectives.

- **Training and Development:** Distinguished history of leading value-added training, development, and mentoring programs.

EXPERIENCE & ACHIEVEMENTS

RECRUITER TEAM LEADER   2/2008 to Present

U.S. Army, Fort Hamilton, Brooklyn, NY

Market military career opportunities within a 481-square-mile area.
- Lead and perform recruit prospecting, candidate interviewing, and processing of qualified applicants.
- Conduct presentations with enlistees, educators, and the community; convey the benefits of a U.S. Army career.
- Design and integrate strategic prospecting plans using key community and environmental data.
- Canvass and post recruiting materials throughout the region, averaging 15K miles annually.
- Oversee government equipment and supplies valued in excess of $40K.

Accomplishments:
- Recipient, Recruiter Gold Badge with 3 Sapphire Stars and the Recruiter Gold Ring for performance excellence.
- Selected over 224 individuals as the Recruiting Top Non-Commissioned Officer (NCO) of the Year.
- Praised for motivating the team to exceed recruiting goals by 108%.
- Maintained a 94% retention rate for newly enlisted personnel transitioning to Basic Training.
- Oversaw government equipment and supplies valued in excess of $40K.

TEAM LEADER   2/2006 to 2/2008

U.S. Army, Carlisle Barracks, Carlisle, PA /Iraq

Led a specialized team in logistics patrol operations in support of military missions of international significance. Motivated a multifunctional team to achieve organizational directives through a collaborative leadership approach; maintained positive morale while driving peak performance.

Accomplishments:
- Facilitated value-added training programs for up to 132 personnel, instilling team and individual proficiency.
- Controlled more than $2M in essential military equipment, supplies, and assets.
- Commended for planning and leading 40+ successful combat logistical patrols.
- Lauded for leading a convoy of 200 individuals travelling throughout unstable regions in Iraq.
- Recognized as NCO of the Month for May 2006.

EDUCATION, TRAINING, AND DEVELOPMENT

University of Texas – Bachelor of Arts in Psychology (2011)]
Primary Leadership Development Course; Recruiting and Retention School; Basic NCO Course; Automated Logistical Specialist; Reception Battalion Attrition; Security Manager's Training

AWARDS AND HONORS

Bronze Star, Army Commendation Medal (2), Army Achievement Medal (5)

KATHLEEN P. MILLER

219 Broadway, New York, NY 10006
Home: (212) 555-1212 ~ Mobile: (212) 555-1234
prochef@mydomain.com

CULINARY MANAGEMENT/CATERING SERVICES

EXPERTISE
- Culinary Planning
- Inventory Management
- Staff Development
- Menu Creation
- Beverages & Wines
- Back-of-house Operations
- Catering/Banquet Management

EXECUTIVE LEADERSHIP
- Drive to succeed and excel
- Motivated by challenge
- Skilled in building teams
- Innovative culinary creations
- Customer service
- Seasoned negotiator
- Expert inventory planner

BUSINESS KNOWLEDGE
- Startup Operations
- Strategy and Planning
- Improvising
- Branding and Awareness
- Staff Development
- Safe Food Handling
- Growth Revenue/Enhancement

CULINARY MANAGEMENT
Directed a 24-person staff consisting of 2 sous chefs, 9 cooks, 6 prep cooks, 4 dishwashers, and 2 porters tasked with simultaneous preparation of food and beverage items for 500+ daily covers. Researched and recommend new wines and spirits to accompany menu items.

- Planned and directed $500K+ in kitchen enhancements for four geographically separate locations.
- Implemented a unified daily specials menu system that improved customer menu selection and increased average check totals by 12%.

BANQUET MANAGEMENT/CATERING SERVICES
Managed all aspects of catering functions of a 4-person crew for 120-seat establishment. Research competitor's menu items and recipes found in industry trade journals items. Create innovative menu themes and catering packages.

- Conducted test kitchen studies with customer focus groups to determine response to presentation and taste of proposed menu items.
- Led a startup establishment to achieve a Zagat rating of 20 within three years.

INVENTORY CONTROL/OPERATIONS
Created numerous back-of-the-house operating policies to improve food preparation and handling, inventory management, and customer service. Prepared and led kitchen operations to pass State Board of Health inspections.

- Negotiated bulk pricing and delivery agreements on fresh ingredients with up to 25 specialty vendors, reducing costs by 8%.
- Maintained a 93% accuracy rate in forecasting food and beverage needs.

PROFESSIONAL EXPERIENCE

Executive Chef, La'Italia, New York, NY 4/1995 to 12/2009
La'Italia is a $12M, four-location restaurant averaging 300+ daily covers.

Working Chef/Partner, The Silver Counter, New York, NY 4/1990 to 4/1995
Co-partner of a two-location, $2M-per-annum establishment consisting of 45 employees and averaging 500+ daily covers.

Chef, Two Brothers Café, New York, NY 10/1988 to 3/1990
A 150-seat, $1.5M-per-annum establishment/off-premises catering operation with approximately 300+ peak covers.

MILITARY EXPERIENCE

Line Cook, United States Navy
Manned sauté, broiler, vegetable, and sides stations. Spearheaded the ship's mess hall renovation.

EDUCATION/AFFILIATIONS

Associate Degree in Culinary Arts, Culinary Institute of America, Hyde Park, NY

Active Member, The American Institute of Food and Wine, New York, NY

STEPHANIE MAYERS

173 Pierce Avenue ♦ Macon, GA 31204
478-742-2442 ✉ info@careerprocenter.net

ELECTRONICS TECHNICIAN WITH 15 YEARS OF NETWORK ADMINISTRATION,
NETWORK SECURITY, AND MANAGEMENT EXPERIENCE.

AREAS OF EXPERTISE AND TECHNICAL SKILLS

♦ Leadership/Management	♦ Network Security	♦ Security Management
♦ Information Assurance	♦ Training/Instruction	♦ Electronics Inspection
♦ Miniature/Microminiature Repair	♦ Program/Project Management	♦ Communication Skills

PROFESSIONAL BACKGROUND

Miniature/Microminiature Electronics Repair Inspector   SECRET SECURITY CLEARANCE

U.S. Navy, Western Regional Maintenance Division, Los Angeles, CA   07/2010 - Present

Conducted detailed inspections of miniature and microminiature electronic repair sites aboard Navy ships and naval shore stations to verify functionality and compliance of all applicable regulations and technical specifications, leading to decreased downtime due to mechanical failure.

- Handpicked for the position of Miniature and Microminiature Electronics Repair Inspector by the Pacific Fleet Miniature/Microminiature Repair Coordinator.
- Provided technical support to 60 miniature/microminiature repair sites and 325 electronics repair technicians.
- Key player in the recertification of 125+ miniature/microminiature electronics repair technicians.
- Achieved certification as an Electronics Tester through successful completion of all United States Military Apprenticeship Program requirements.

Information System Security Technician/Field Service Technician

U.S. Navy, Naval Communications Station, Bahrain   12/2008 - 07/2010

Supervised 12 personnel providing Tier II technical support to 4,200 computer users spread across 3 critical military networks (classified and unclassified) in the Middle East region.

- Developed and implemented a process to create pre-imaged hard drives for field service technicians; increased trouble ticket resolutions by 75%, and improved field service technician efficiency by 68%.
- Responded to 204 network security alerts and network defense actions from the Cyber Defense Command; enabled Naval Communications Station, Bahrain to establish and maintain 100% compliance with Navy security requirements for information systems.
- Achieved certification as an Internetworking Technician through U.S. Military Apprenticeship Program.

NOTABLE EVALUATION COMMENTS: *"Trained junior sailors both personally and professionally. Petty Officer Mayers consistently delivers sustained, superior results."*

Stephanie Mayers
Page 2

Electronics Division Supervisor
U.S. Navy, *USS America*, San Diego, CA 12/2005 - 12/2008

Led a team of technicians in the systematic ship-wide verification of schematic drawings and diagrams, encompassing 3 radar systems, 8 electronic navigation systems, and 28 communications systems.

- Managed the inventory and organization of more than 3,000 individual electronic components and the installation of soldering stations and electronic Module Test and Repair equipment, resulting in the certification of the ship's miniature/microminiature circuit repair station.

NOTABLE EVALUATION COMMENTS: *"Demonstrates outstanding leadership and management."*

Network Administrator/Department Supervisor
U.S. Navy, Fleet Information Warfare Center, Cabala, CA 6/2002 - 12/2005

Delivered crucial software and message preparation training to 150 operators of the Defense Messaging System.

- Selected as the 2004 Sailor of the Year for Fleet Information Warfare Center; formally recognized by senior leadership as the organization's top performer.

NOTABLE EVALUATION COMMENTS: *"Combines dynamic management and communication skills with unrelenting energy, enthusiasm, and dedication."*

EDUCATION AND TRAINING

ASSOCIATE'S DEGREE IN SCIENCE, BUSINESS STUDIES, San Diego College, San Diego, CA

Professional Navy Training:
Miniature/Microminiature Electronic Repair Inspector
Primary Leadership Development Program
Microminiature Electronics Repair
First Line Leadership Development Program
Single Audio System Maintenance
Communications Security (COMSEC) Maintenance Technician
Fiber Optics Maintenance Technician

AWARDS

Navy and Marine Corps Achievement Medal (7)
Fleet Information Warfare Center Sailor of the Year
Letter of Commendation

ALLAN J. GILLIAM

EVENT MANAGER
ACTIVE TOP SECRET CLEARANCE

- Top-notch management skills to produce, schedule, and coordinate large-scale events, productions, meetings, and conferences with international dignitaries.
- Recognized interpersonal skills, working with diverse cultures and foreign leaders, providing a positive environment for negotiation and resolution.
- White House experience working with top staffs of top officials such as the Secretary of Defense and First Lady Michelle Obama.
- Provide expert advice and management for events to top United States (U.S.) government officials involving North Atlantic Treaty Organization (NATO) and foreign government leaders.

"Al's actions and many accomplishments have brought only the highest accolades."

~ EXCERPT FROM RECENT PERFORMANCE REVIEW

Career History

EVENT PRODUCER/PROTOCOL MANAGER   5/2009 to Present
United States Air Force (USAF), Washington, DC
Plan, organize, and execute protocol and public relations events for the Chairman and Vice Chairman of the Joint Chiefs of Staff (JCS) involving numerous Very Important Persons (VIPs) and Distinguished Visitors (DVs). Display cultural sensitivity and diversity awareness for foreign dignitaries and American officials of all backgrounds, providing proper dignity and respect. Train personnel on organization, time management, and interpersonal skills.

Accomplishments:
- Serve as White House Liaison interacting with staff of the President of the United States and the First Lady.
- Personally requested for advice and services by offices of Defense Secretaries Gates and Rumsfeld.
- Manage and created positive environment for U.S. bilateral defense talks involving 24 foreign government DVs.
- Manage and implement changes to $750K Operational Representational Fund budget with 100% accountability.
- Action Officer of the Month, 03/2011.

MAJOR DUTIES
- Lead 19 personnel to produce VIP itineraries and events such as parades involving more than 300 people.
- Manage scheduling, communications, transportation, tours, security, facilities, meals, and related requirements.
- Produce and advise on various ceremonies, parades, formal dinners, protocols, and flag and service etiquette.
- Coordinate with high-ranking members of the White House Cabinet, Congress, Senate, and U.S. military.
- Invite and organize media coverage from the Press, including television, radio, Internet, and print media.

173 Pierce Avenue • Macon, GA 31204 • 478-742-2442 • info@careerprocenter.net

ALLAN J. GILLIAM

EVENT MANAGER
ACTIVE TOP SECRET CLEARANCE
~ PAGE 2 ~

CHIEF OF INFORMATION/PROTOCOL   5/2005 to 5/2009
USAF, Fairford, England
Planned and produced all aspects of protocol activities at seven locations throughout the United Kingdom (UK) working with Royal Air Force (RAF) personnel. Managed VIP itineraries, travel, transportation, housing, communications, meals, and security arrangements. Maintained professional relations with senior leaders and dignitary staff members.

Accomplishments:
- Led support for more than 100 DV visits within one year, managing all arrangements.
- Represented the U.S. at international air show with 3,000 guests and 48 DVs from more than 30 countries.
- Produced the first-ever RAF Fairfield Hangar Ball attended by 730 guests.
- Developed and implemented community service events such as charity food pantry.

MAJOR DUTIES
- Personally handled all VIP special requests.

- Arranged for special briefings and tours.

- Maintained expertise on international customs, courtesies, and ceremonies to support international relations.

- Designed and produced various awards and recognition certificates.

Education & Training

Community College of the Air Force, Washington, DC
USAF Senior Non-Commissioned Officer (NCO) Academy

Awards & Special Accomplishments

Meritorious Service Medal
Joint Service Commendation Medal
Air Force Commendation Medal
Joint Service Achievement Medal
National Defense Service Medal
Global War on Terrorism Service Medal

173 Pierce Avenue • Macon, GA 31204 • 478-742-2442 • info@careerprocenter.net

Graham Whittaker

173 Pierce Avenue   Macon, GA 31204
☎ (478) 742-2442
info@careerprocenter.net
Secret Security Clearance

SENIOR FINANCIAL ANALYST

Offering eight years' experience in Financial Analysis and Business Operations, with an impending Bachelor of Science in Business Administration and Finance. Provide insightful and detailed analysis of business operations, finding opportunities for substantial cost reduction, improved productivity, and improved resource management. Mentor, train, and coach subordinates for top productivity and performance. Develop effective forecasting models for budget and investment analysis. Comfortable consulting with executive management and board members in support of financial presentations and justifications.

▶ Financial Analysis	▶ Resource Management
▶ Asset Management	▶ Financial Auditing
▶ Financial Planning	▶ Project Management
▶ Continuous Process Improvement	▶ Capital Budgeting & Expenditures
▶ Budget Preparation & Forecasting	▶ Workforce Optimization

COMPUTER PROFICIENCY:
Microsoft (MS) Windows; MS Office Suite; AF Financial Systems: General Accounting and Finance System; Integrated Automated Travel System; Integrated Accounts Payable System; Micro-based Budget Automated System; Commander's Resource Integration System; Automated Business Service System

PROFESSIONAL EXPERIENCE

UNITED STATES AIR FORCE   **2003 – Present**
Financial Analyst/Manager, MACON, GA   2008 – Present
Perform, supervise, manage, and direct financial management activities. Serve as financial advisor to senior management and resource managers, determine fund availability and propriety of claims, and present weekly Status of Funds briefings, keeping leadership abreast of current spending rate and budget execution. Prepare and execute financial plans. Perform audits and implement fraud prevention measures.

▶ Manage largest-funded program, revamping a $10.5M budget and reviving financial management infrastructure.
▶ Established financial Working Group/Financial Management Board, improving leadership insight.
▶ Validated $3M during review of prior year's program, reclaiming more than $70K in erroneous obligations.
▶ Devised plan to align Global War on Terrorism funding execution with Information Operations to avoid major work stoppage impact by reallocating funds to pay for procured contracts.
▶ Selected "Superior Performer" during 2009 Unit Compliance Inspection.

Customer Interface Manager/Financial Analyst, MACON, GA   2006 – 2008
Provided customer service to 9,000 active duty, Reserve, Air National Guard, and civilian personnel in the preparation, verification, computation and processing, and auditing of pay transactions and entitlements. Processed, verified, and audited all advance military pay and closure of members' pay-affecting issues.

Graham Whittaker, *Financial Analyst*   Page Two

▶ Improved key processes and efficiency to include standardizing military pay continuity binders and transforming customer service from traditional counter-assistance to innovative appointment-based service.
▶ Developed workload management procedures, streamlining customer-service operations.
▶ Initiated resolution of members' long-term pay concerns, reducing open case files by 45% in 30 days.

Manager, Liaison Operations, MACON, GA   2005 – 2006
Provided customer service and served as accounting liaison for installation-level organizations, vendors, and finance/accounting services.

▶ Cleared more than $1M in delinquencies, allowing for continued purchase of vital supplies.
▶ Certified more than 1,500 commitment documents in the accounting system, valued at $18M.
▶ Critical contributor during $25M Fiscal Year 2005 closeout deemed most successful in organizational history.

MACON, GA   2003 – 2005
Financial Analyst
Performed financial analysis of $1M in agency funding and $30M agency, tenants, and civilian payroll. Identified unfunded requirements, prepared status of funds updates, forecasted trend plans, prepared mid-year reviews, distributed funds, and prepared budget directives.

▶ Resolved errors in civilian pay projection program, saving the organization $1M+; continually researched civilian pay expenses incorrectly charged, saving an additional $113K.
▶ Justified more than $265K for Homeland Defense funding; proposal was approved and received 100% funding.
▶ Identified and researched $312K in erroneously charged contingency travel expenses; ensured 100% of reimbursable contingencies, resulting in subsequent reimbursement of $300K.

EDUCATION/TRAINING

Bachelor of Science in Business Administration (2011)
GEORGIA UNIVERSITY COLLEGE, MACON, GA
Associate in Applied Sciences in Financial Management
GEORGIA UNIVERSITY COLLEGE, MACON, GA

United States Air Force (USAF):
Financial Analyst Apprentice; Budget Analyst's Essential Guide to Formulation; Justification and Execution; Management Concepts; Defense Planning; Programming, Budgeting, and Execution; Fundamental Accounting Procedures in Federal Agencies; Basic Contracting Operations; Enhanced Defense Financial Management Training

AWARDS AND COMMENDATIONS

Air Force Commendation Medal; Air Force Achievement Medal
National Defense Service Medal; Global War on Terrorism Service Medal
Korean Defense Service Medal; Humanitarian Service Medal
Non-Commissioned Officer (NCO) of the Quarter of Air Mobility Command Level; Nominee
Stripes for Exceptional Performers; Nominee
1/12 AF Outstanding Airmen; NCO of the Year (2)

JOHN JONES, CF, RF, PLM

173 Pierce Avenue, Macon, GA 31204
☎ 478-742-2442
💻 info@careerprocenter.net

> ### FORESTRY & TIMBERLAND ADMINISTRATION

More than 10 years of diverse expertise in all aspects of Forestry Management and Timberland Administration. Innovative visionary leader, qualified to position portfolios for investment diversity and earn strategic gains by cumulative savings and expert management. Highlighted milestones include:

- ❑ *Expertise in identifying undervalued and hidden timberland/real estate asset conditions.*
- ❑ *Negotiated substantial contracts to save $17M.*
- ❑ *Establish and foster a large national and international network of colleagues and customers.*
- ❑ *Prepare economic investment analysis for growth and yield on a 9K-acre timber tract.*
- ❑ *Co-Chair, Mountain Chapter/Member GA Society of American Foresters Executive Teams.*

■ ■ ■

PROFESSIONAL EXPERIENCE

SENIOR RESOURCE FORESTER, ABC TIMBER COMPANY, Atlanta, GA   2004 – Present
Administrator of annual capital budget ranging from $250K to $400K and annual revenues ranging from $1.1M to $1.7M. Manage and implement resourceful and innovative silviculture, marketing, and real estate services spanning the Georgia region. Spearhead key business developments in real estate and non-timber income.

Accomplishments & Contributions:
- 🌲 Improved contractor performance 2005 to 2011 while accelerating TQM scores by 15%.
- 🌲 Authored a comprehensive web-based "Safety Action Plan" model, adopted corporate-wide.
- 🌲 Achieved the highest performance rating for two consecutive years.
- 🌲 Revised antiquated third-party document addressing tree-planting guidelines to ensure source integrity.
- 🌲 Introduced cost-saving guidelines to verify existing LTL data with corporate council and accounting.
- 🌲 Selected to attend the NCSFN Cooperative professional conferences.
- 🌲 Represented company interests in technical plenary sessions as a Forestry BMP Expert.
- 🌲 Increased ROI by 4-7% on HBU properties and 2-3% on core properties.
- 🌲 Facilitated new software improvements and acquisitions; Geographic Information System (GIS), Global Positioning System (GPS), Personal Digital Assistant (PDA), and Microsoft (MS) Office Suite.
- 🌲 Served as Communication Leader on the Safety Action Committee.

OWNER/REGISTERED FORESTER, FORESTRY & TIMBER SERVICES, INC., Augusta, GA 2001 – 2004
Launched a successful forestry and timberland management and mapping service providing expertise in timber sales, growth, and management. Achieved substantial business growth through exceptional customer service and expertise in forest investment economics.

Accomplishments & Contributions:
- 🌲 Analyzed individual timberland investments to ascertain a broader portfolio, summarize recent activity, and prepare comprehensive findings to meet customer investment objectives.

JOHN JONES, CF, RF, PLM

☎ 478-742-2442
🖳 info@careerprocenter.net

FORESTRY & TIMBERLAND ADMINISTRATION

(Continued)
- 🌲 *Displayed effective analysis, writing, and public-speaking attributes in technical and finance issues.*
- 🌲 *Accomplished many chip-mill, timber-lease, tax-assessment, seedling, and harvest analysis projects.*
- 🌲 *Built loyal and substantial client base, increasing bottom-line profitability three consecutive years.*
- 🌲 *Conducted compliance audits on wood chip facilities, preparing cost-analysis and feasibility studies.*
- 🌲 *Maximized opportunities for process improvements.*

HERBICIDE SPECIALIST/STAFF FORESTER,
FORESTRY RESOURCES, INC., *Macon, GA*   *1999 – 2001*

Accomplishments & Contributions:
Represented herbicide manufacturers in the sale of forestry herbicide applications. Provided technical sales, service, and support to manufacturers such as Dupont, Monsanto, American Cyanamid, and Dow Elanco.

- 🌲 Recognized for achieving the "Highest Sales Volume" in company for managed herbicide application.
- 🌲 Increased territorial sales by 21% over previous year.

MILITARY EXPERIENCE

LOGISTICS MANAGER, UNITED STATES ARMY, *U.S. and International Locations*   *1982 – 1997*

EDUCATION & SPECIALIZED TRAINING

Master's in Business Administration (MBA), UNIVERSITY OF GEORGIA
Bachelor of Science in Forest Management, GEORGIA UNIVERSITY COLLEGE

- 🌲 Specialized training in forest investments and project economic analysis
- 🌲 International Conference on Geospatial Information in Agricultural and Forestry
- 🌲 Distance Learning Courses in GIS Using NT
- 🌲 Applied Information Technology
- 🌲 GPS, GIS, & RS in Environmental Assessments
- 🌲 Super A.C.E. Inventory & Analysis Software
- 🌲 Threatened and Endangered Species seminar

CURRENT PROFESSIONAL AFFILIATIONS

Co-Chair, MOUNTAIN CHAPTER, SOCIETY OF AMERICAN FORESTERS

Member, GEORGIA FORESTRY ASSOCIATION/SOCIETY OF AMERICAN FORESTERS

JEAN KESSLER

173 Pierce Avenue
Macon, GA 31204
Phone: 478-742-2442
info@careerprocenter.net

~ Human Resources Generalist ~
(Active Secret Security Clearance)

Detail-oriented and results-driven professional with five+ years of honorable U.S. military experience, providing specialized expertise in administrative management and human resources. Adept at streamlining large-scale administrative processes to improve organizational efficiency and productivity. Distinguished record of facilitating value-added training and development programs for a diverse range of personnel. Motivating team leader, mentor, and advisor with a strong ability to build and maintain relationships with leaders, colleagues, and personnel. Highly effective oral and written communicator, providing clear and concise presentations, briefings, and correspondence.

AREAS OF EXPERTISE

- Administrative Management
- Counseling and Guidance
- Procedural Development
- Employee Relations
- Fiscal Management

- Human Resources
- Training and Development
- Relationship Building
- Communication and Coordination
- Operational Readiness and Support

- Workforce and Staffing Planning
- Regulatory Compliance
- Career Planning and Progression
- Performance Management
- Analysis, Evaluation, and Review

SELECT VALUE-OFFERED HIGHLIGHTS

⇨ Skillfully identified and corrected performance evaluation and recognition/awards program deficiencies; resolved more than 70 administrative discrepancies and reengineered programs to improve overall accuracy and effectiveness, garnering a 60% increase in annual recognition submissions and maintaining a 100% on-time evaluation rating.

⇨ Formally praised for outstanding organizational skills and project management abilities; planned and executed the conversion of more than 1,700 administrative records with an error rate of below 0.6%.

⇨ Well known as a "people-focused leader" and expert crisis manager; lauded for addressing and resolving difficult and sensitive employee relations issues utilizing superb interpersonal, problem-solving, and communication abilities.

⇨ Applied superior strategic planning capabilities to design and execute a $14M educational facility relocation plan.

PROFESSIONAL EXPERIENCE

UNITED STATES ARMY
Human Resources Manager/Advisor   02/2011 – 12/2011
U.S. Army, Bagdad, Iraq

⇨ Presided over a specialized team of 56 personnel supporting essential Human Resources (HR) and administrative programs for more than 8,500 personnel and dependants as well as 175K military retirees.

⇨ Offered expertise and guidance in personnel management and career development/progression for the entire Air Force Base (AFB) and eight geographically separated teams.

⇨ Established key directives and informational instructions for military base personnel; ensured consistent comprehension, assimilation, and practice of U.S. Air Force (USAF) and Department of Defense (DoD) procedures, regulations, and standards.

Jean Kessler | **Page 2**

Administrative Advisor | **05/2010 – 05/2011**
Mississippi National Guard, Grenada, MS

⇨ Provided leadership, direction, and guidance to an executive-level leader's support staff of 12 individuals to sustain six distinctive USAF and DoD educational institutions.
⇨ Acted as counselor, advisor, and mentor in the planning and execution of administrative; personnel management; disciplinary; morale, health, and welfare; and operational readiness activities.
⇨ Organized and maintained the Personnel Data System (PDS), championed personnel retention initiatives, provided career development and progression advice and assistance, and served as focal point for benefits administration.

Human Resources/Operations Specialist | **05/2010 – 05/2011**
U.S. Army, Camp Shelby, MS

⇨ Presided over a specialized team of 56 personnel supporting essential HR and administrative programs for more than 8,500 personnel and dependants as well as 175K military retirees.
⇨ Offered expertise and guidance in personnel management and career development/progression for the entire AFB and five geographically separated teams.

Team Leader | **01/2009 – 04/2010**
U.S. Army, Bagdad, Iraq

⇨ Expertly controlled personnel management activities, ensuring accuracy, integrity, and timeliness of processes.
⇨ Performed detailed assessments of personnel management procedures to ensure strict compliance with established regulations; continually reviewed discrepancy reporting to determine deficiencies and recommend corrective actions.
⇨ Produced and distributed vital military information to leaders and personnel; aided in obtaining passports and visas, coordinating transportation, acquiring pay entitlements, and managing personal affairs.
⇨ Provided oversight, direction, and support for more than 125 students enrolled in a highly technical military radar training program.
⇨ Coordinated and monitored the completion of prerequisite training courses for more than 300 students annually.
⇨ Generated essential administrative correspondence, including the editing and thorough examination of temporary duty assignments, training reports, and memoranda submitted for senior-level approval and signature.

EDUCATION

Bachelor of Arts in Banking and Finance
Mississippi State University, Biloxi, MS

Officer Candidate School Graduate
Alabama Military Academy, Mobile, AL

TRAINING AND DEVELOPMENT

Planning Objectives, Human Resource Management, Transition Processing, Military Personnel Data System, Evaluation Manager, Personnel Management, Airmen Support Files, Unit Personnel Record Group, Master Personnel Record Group, Air Force Policies & Procedures, Risk Management, Data Files Management, Customer Relations, Team Building, Maintenance Policies & Procedures, Training & Development

BRODY DAVIS

Active Top Secret/SCI (Sensitive Compartmented
Information) Security Clearance

478-742-2442 ■ info@careerprocenter.net
173 Pierce Avenue, Macon, GA 31204

INTELLIGENCE OPERATIONS

- Electronic surveillance, intelligence gathering, and analytical platforms
- SIGINT, HUMINT, and MASINT experience
- All-source intelligence product development
- Counterterrorism and counterinsurgency operations

> *"Polished ability to lead his peers and subordinates alike...demonstrates expertise traditionally displayed by officers far senior. His understanding of the integration of assets in a most difficult counterinsurgency combat environment proves his unlimited potential."*
>
> ~ LIEUTENANT COL. MARK DAVIES, Squadron Commander, U.S. Army

■ ■ ■

PROFESSIONAL EXPERIENCE & ACHIEVEMENTS

COMPANY COMMANDER, United States Army: Afghanistan & Iraq   3/2010 to Present

Commanded a military unit that performed reconnaissance, surveillance, and security operations in the Kandahar province of Afghanistan, an area of more than 500 square kilometers encompassing 50+ towns and villages. Managed 63 personnel, including a Fusion Cell of intelligence analysts assigned directly to the unit. Supervised the use of 16 vehicles and associated equipment worth more than $22M.

- Neutralized 26 Improvised Explosive Devices (IEDs), found 2 large caches of military equipment, and captured a High-Value Target as identified by administration.
- Secured the Weesh Border Crossing Point with Pakistan and closed smuggling routes in the Registan Desert, identified as two of the "Top 10 Keys to Success in Afghanistan" by General David Petraeus.
- Cultivated relationships with civilian population through development and humanitarian projects, which led to an increase in actionable intelligence from those sources.
- Managed 63 personnel, including a Fusion Cell of intelligence analysts assigned directly to the unit. Supervised the use of 16 vehicles and associated equipment worth more than $22M.
- Captured fingerprint, eye, and facial data on possible insurgents with the Biometric Automated Tool Set/Handheld Interagency Identity Detection Equipment system.
- Used the All-Source Analysis System (ASAS) and the Tactical Ground Reporting Network (TiGRNet) to evaluate data.
- Built partnerships with Afghan National Police, Border Police, and National Army leaders. Coordinated activities with British and Canadian units of the International Security Assistance Force.

ASSISTANT OPERATIONS OFFICER, Ft. Jackson, SC   9/2006 to 3/2010

Planned and executed training and deployment tasks for a surveillance and reconnaissance unit. Used information gained during previous service in Afghanistan to improve the training plans during pre-deployment exercises at Ft. Bragg and the National Training Center.

BRODY DAVIS

Active Top Secret/SCI (Sensitive Compartmented
Information) Security Clearance

478-742-2442 ■ info@careerprocenter.net
173 Pierce Avenue, Macon, GA 31204

{position continued}
- Served as the Operations and Liaison Officer during readiness training at the National Training Center (NTC). The unit had just been created and lacked an HQ department to handle interagency coordination and other liaison duties.

ASSISTANT OPERATIONS OFFICER, Ft. Jackson, SC   9/2006 to 3/2010

- Engaged in frequent interaction with local civilian and Islamic religious leaders to develop human intelligence data.
- Commanded Firebase Doa China, located only four kilometers from the Afghanistan-Pakistan border.
- Supervised the daily operations of 143 personnel. Managed the maintenance and readiness of 56 combat and support vehicles and other equipment valued at more than $10M.
- Coordinated fixed-wing aircraft and helicopter support for a quick-reaction military organization.

INTELLIGENCE ANALYST SPECIALIST, Ft. Jackson, SC   8/2002 to 9/2006

Prepared All-Source Intelligence products for unit leaders. Directly managed 120 security clearance submissions and assisted in an additional 1,200 evaluations. Operated the AN/MLQ-40 Prophet electronic warfare suite, ASAS-Lite analysis system, TiGR Net intelligence-sharing application, and other computerized tools to collect and evaluate data.

- Selected to attend Officer Candidate School (OCS) in 2005.

■ ■ ■

EDUCATION

Bachelor of Arts Degree in History
UNIVERSITY OF SOUTHERN CALIFORNIA, Los Angeles, CA

■ ■ ■

SELECTED AWARDS

Bronze Star Medal   Purple Heart   Army Commendation Medal   Army Achievement Medal
National Defense Service Medal   Afghanistan Campaign Medal   Global War on Terrorism Service Medal

FREDDIE PULEO
Active Top Secret Clearance

173 Pierce Avenue, Macon, GA 31204 ... Email: info@careerprocenter.net ... Phone: 478-742-2442

~ Research and Development ■ Intelligence ~

*More than 10 years of honorable U.S. military experience, providing specialized expertise
in intelligence, force protection, research and development, and team leadership.*

Adept at leading high-priority intelligence missions in support of military operations of international significance. Distinguished record of facilitating value-added training and development programs for a diverse range of personnel. Motivating team leader, mentor, and advisor with a strong ability to build and maintain relationships with leaders, colleagues, and personnel. Currently hold a "Top Secret" security clearance.

★ Displayed exceptional negotiation and diplomacy skills to broaden the U.S. Fifth Fleet program from 10 outdated systems to 14 state-of-the-art non-lethal systems with a $2M annual budget.

★ Formally praised for outstanding organizational skills and project management abilities; reported more than 1,600 high-priority real-time tactical reports during missions of critical importance to national security.

★ Lauded for creating intelligence collection training curriculum utilized across the entire U.S. Navy.

★ Spearheaded the expansion of the U.S. Fifth Fleet Psychological Operations (PSYOP) team from one individual to a joint operations unit of seven with an operating budget of $50K.

Demonstrated Strengths...

■ Electronic Intelligence	■ Analysis, Evaluation, and Assessment	■ Training and Development
■ Communication and Presentation	■ Negotiation and Collaboration	■ Procedural Development
■ Core Curriculum Design	■ Relationship Building	■ Strategic Planning
■ Employee Relations	■ Leadership and Management	■ Force Protection
■ Budget Control	■ Operational Readiness and Support	■ Administrative Support

Professional Experience

Assistant Targeting Officer   11/2010 –12/2011
U.S. Army, Baghdad, Iraq
Led the Joint Electronic Warfare Cell, providing oversight for operational coordination, consolidation, analysis, and execution of airborne Electronic Warfare (EW) throughout Iraq.

★ Devised and instituted comprehensive training program focused on Counter-Improvised Explosive Device; course instructed to more than 50K personnel deploying to Iraq.

★ Maintained the sensitive database, monitoring 60K+ line items and briefing 720+ post assignment reports to senior leaders, including the General's staff.

★ Developed and integrated strategic plans for 97 successful offensive assignments, garnering the capture of 115 individuals of potential threat and 250 weapons caches.

Psychological Operations (PSYOP) Distribution Manager   8/2009 – 9/2010
U.S. Navy, Manama, Bahrain
Specialized in the acquisition, testing, evaluation, distribution, and installation of a variety of PSYOP equipment and products in support of military operations of international significance.

★ Facilitated PSYOP and Force Protection (FP) training events and exercises, instilling proficiency in essential organizational operations; educated the crews of 60 large-scale U.S. and Coalition vessels.

★ Built alliances with local Bahrain, U.S., and international organizations to acquire 26 PSYOP products accepted by the U.S. Fifth Fleet; distributed approximately 10K PSYOP product units to U.S. and coalition forces.

FREDDIE PULEO (2)

Professional Experience Continued

★ Communicated with U.S. and coalition fleet commanders to provide products to serve the needs of 27 nations.

Electronic Intelligence Instructor   5/2006 – 8/2009
U.S. Navy, National and International Locations
Served as Subject Matter Expert (SME) in Electronic Intelligence (ELINT); conducted comprehensive training events for a diverse range of military and joint personnel.

★ Designed and administered the first-ever Information Assurance (IA) "Train the Trainer" program.
★ Hand-selected to analyze and update core curriculum for far-reaching ELINT training programs.
★ Represented the Navy as a Trusted Agent for critical Intel Programs supporting 27 special operations.
★ Facilitated 176 hours of training for 22 personnel, garnering 6 system IA certifications.
★ Prepared and certified 16 items of critical intelligence collection hardware for fleet utilization.
★ Praised for leading 3,600 man-hours of Cluster SNOOP training for 30 individuals as the Subsurface ELINT SME.

Electronic Intelligence/Electronic Support Supervisor   5/2000 – 5/2006
U.S. Navy, National and International Locations
Led and advised a highly specialized team of 13 personnel executing subsurface direct support ELINT/Electronic Support (ES); provided indications and warnings through real-time intelligence analysis and reporting.

★ Managed the inventory and disposition of more than 1,000 program-related publications, magnetic media, and technical references, achieving organization goals, objectives, and timelines.
★ Employed exceptional communication and presentation abilities to lead more than 90 man-hours of technical ELINT and Subsurface Direct Support Program training for 40+ participants.
★ Reported 1,600 high-priority real-time tactical reports during missions of critical importance to national security.

Education

Bachelor of Science in Criminal Justice, University of Maryland
Associate Degree in General Studies, University of Maryland

Training and Development

Direct Support Element Basic Operator ~ Subsurface Cryptologic Technician (CT) Augmentee Operator Pipeline
Battle Force ELINT Analyst ~ First Line Leadership Development Program
Primary Leadership Development Program ~ Armed Sentry/Security Reaction Force
Subsurface Augmentee ELINT Operator ~ Communication and Intelligence Specialist
Cryptologic Technician, Technical Instructor Course ~ IUSS Maintenance Technician
Department of Defense (DoD) Information Assurance Awareness ~ Introduction to LEAN Enterprise

Awards and Honors

Joint Meritorious Commendation Medal
Navy and Marine Corps Achievement Medal (10)
Navy and Marine Corps Commendation Medal (4)

John Smith

🖃 info@careerprocenter.net

📫 173 Pierce Avenue ■ Macon, GA 31204

☎ (C) 478.742.2442

Investigations Research ❏ Field Training ❏ Management

Eleven years of investigations experience specializing in research, field training, and management. Extensive field experience in addition to first-line management of up to 60 professional/technical staff. Maintain the highest level of security and discretion in interviewing and evaluating client responses.

QUALIFICATION HIGHLIGHTS

- Selected for early promotion, assuming investigative leadership position with Office of Personnel Management (OPM) contractor after only five months with the company.
- Skilled instructor, experienced in developing and delivering cutting-edge training to groups as large as 30 investigators.
- Supervisory excellence, with robust mentoring skills and a positive management style.
- Expert communicator experienced in interacting with other investigators, senior military leaders, law enforcement, corporate managers, and federal agency personnel.
- Current Top Secret Clearance (SCI); last investigation January 2014.

PROFESSIONAL EXPERIENCE

CACI, Chantilly, VA   **5/2003 - Present**
CACI is a major provider of homeland security solutions for knowledge management and information sharing, network services and information as-surance, systems integration, and intelligence and engineering.

Senior Field Supervisor/Mentor/Background Investigations Trainer
Promoted to this position following several years of successful case management and field investigations. Manage 60 investigators engaged in background investigations for government clearances. Evaluate performance and provide quality ratings based on employee productivity, reports and documentation, and overall case management. Trained 25-30 new investigators during two-week Background Investigator training course, addressing OPM guidelines and the OPM Investigators' Handbook.

- Monitor and manage investigator caseloads to ensure achievement of program objectives.
- Communicate weekly with investigators via teleconference, email, and one-on-ones, covering new policies and procedures and addressing problems or issues.
- Recommended software interface for use by OPM Program Management Office (PMO). Supported a remote employee input for inclusion in the program.
- Cited by management as "an excellent ambassador of CACI."

Case Manager
Coordinated with OPM Program Managers and PMO staff to review and recommend revised policies regarding CACI's OPM Contract. Provided training for and evaluated potential investigators, with focus on proper methods and procedures for conducting Personnel Security Investigations and generating required investigative reports.

- Developed and revised training guidelines, curriculum, and multimedia course materials for advanced investigators training required for OPM Contract.

John Smith, Page Two

"John has a high level of technical and professional knowledge regarding security background investigations..."

"...provides logical solutions to case problems that do not sacrifice the quality or timeliness of the work product."

"...takes interest in the individual growth of his team...."

"Provides sound guidance in a timely manner."

"John is an excellent ambassador of CACI and projects a positive image for the company."

CACI, cont'd...
* Promoted security awareness among investigators.

Investigator/Personnel Security Team Lead, RAF Crauhton, United Kingdom
Promoted after only five months of service with CACI. Primary operational contact and technical advisor/expert for CACI leadership and local client (Office of Special Investigations - OSI) on investigator processes. Ensured investigative unit exceeded contract requirements stipulated by the federal government.

* Demonstrated ability to interview, follow leads, research records, and prepare reports.
* Traveled throughout the UK conducting personnel security investigations.
* Expert collaboration with senior military leaders during sensitive investigative operations.

U.S. Investigations Services, Hyattsville, MD   2/2001 - 5/2003
The largest supplier of background investigations to the federal government and the preeminent source of background and drug-screening services to commercial institutions nationwide.

Special Investigator
Planned and executed specialized background investigations, including Top Secret/SCI and special access program clearances. Collaborated with other government organizations and federal agencies, including the Military Services, Departments of State, Energy, and Transportation, NASA, FAA, and DHS.

* Completed 323 investigations between 08/2001 and 03/2002, generating 270 reports with a 93.01% adequacy rating.
* Selected to support Federal Aviation Administration (FAA) Air Marshal hiring cycle in 2001. Managed nearly 1,800 investigations/interviews over a three-week cycle.
* Selected for detail to multiple Air Force Bases (AFBs) in Florida to support an overflow of urgent security/background investigations following 9/11.

EDUCATION/TRAINING

B.S., Sociology/*Criminal Justice Concentration*
THE OHIO STATE UNIVERSITY, Columbus, OH
Relevant Coursework: Research Methods; Theory; Criminal Justice

AWARDS

Certificate of Appreciation: For Outstanding Contributions to the Office of Personnel Management Federal Investigative Services Contracts Supporting Field Investigations and Support Services Operations

AFFILIATIONS

Volunteer, Veterans of Foreign Wars, 2004 - Present

DONALD LEE SIMMONS

CompTIA A+ Certified Professional • IT Technician Training

Information Technology Management

Systems Integration ... Policy Compliance/Audits ... Maintenance/Repair ...
Disaster Recovery & Contingency Planning

- Hallmark Information Technology (IT) Manager with six years' experience. Central advisor for overall IT goals, providing infrastructure, integrity, security, sensitive privacy programs, regulatory compliance, telecommunications, and management. Results- and accomplishment-oriented; influential director, manager, leader, and supervisor with high-level achievement and success at strategic thinking, problem solving, project rollout, cross-functional teams, and project deployment. Sought by command for recommendations based on superior performance.

- Exceptional supervisory experience with a proven ability to lead and coordinate with local IT staff and comply with Federal Desktop Core Configuration (FDCC) regulation contracts, strategic planning, systems engineering integration, and future emerging technology; monitor network security reports, hardware, and software to analyze, prevent, and defend against unauthorized access.

- Demonstrated capacity to plan, support, and oversee teams and customer support through various repairs, maintenance, upgrades, replenishment processes, policy guidance and development, consulting, Risk Assessment Plan, IT Contingency Plan, and Disaster Recovery Planning.

• TECHNOLOGY PROFILE •

Voice over Secure Internet Protocol (VoISP)	Windows NT, XP, Vista
Microsoft (MS) Office 2010	Windows Server 2000, 2003, 2007, 2010
Novell Network	CISCO Call Manager VoIP

PROFESSIONAL EXPERIENCE AND ACHIEVEMENTS

CLIENT SUPPORT TECHNICIAN, Macon Air Force Base (AFB), GA   4/2009 to Present

Provide level 1 computer support for 1.3K+ users. Establish new user accounts, distribution lists, organizational accounts, mailbox storage space allotment, and security groups for secure and non-secure networks. Maintain and initiate user account agreements and Information Awareness and Protection training for 7K active user network accounts.

- Hand-selected to stand up the AFB's first Client Support Team.
  - → Flawlessly manage hardware-related computer items, ensuring Service Level Agreements (SLAs), manufacturer warranties, and guarantees of more than $650K in equipment assets.
  - → Software License Monitor responsible for keeping copies of software license agreements and ensuring the agreements were enforced; provided 25 upgrades to enhance interoperability and systems integration.

WORK GROUP MANAGER, Royal Air Force (RAF) Brampton, United Kingdom   4/2008 to 4/2009

Client Support Technician responsible for providing Tier 1 technical support to 450+ geographically separated users. Developed and implemented training for work group managers and ensured proper documentation was filed, authorizing administrative rights.

DONALD LEE SIMMONS

CompTIA A+ Certified Professional • IT Technician Training

→ Provided direct technical support for command and staff. Software License Monitor and IT Asset Custodian responsible for maintaining Wing Staff agencies equipment and software license account.

→ Performed hands-on technical support for VoIP users and their IT equipment.

→ Created the initial Wing SharePoint page; responsible for maintaining new content and providing administrative support for permission issues.

→ Advised leadership on future IT requirements; procured new equipment to replace aging computers.

  • Maintained IT assets account and recruited to lead final construction phase of the Valley View Medical Center, a $144M, 325K-square-foot project.

  • Terminated fiber-optic cabling, connecting desktop capabilities for the Joint Analysis Center on RAF Upwood. Routinely installed Category 5 cable throughout facilities on RAF Brampton. Responsible for managing IT equipment and its accountability for entire organization. Hand-selected to stand up the 301st Combat Support Wing's first Client Support Team.

EDUCATION

Bachelor of Science, Management Information Systems (In Progress)
UNIVERSITY OF GEORGIA, Atlanta, GA
Certified Manager of Software Testing (CMST) (SMST 100M-1),
HyperText Markup Language (HTML), 2008
GEORGIA STATE UNIVERSITY, Macon, GA

PROFESSIONAL DEVELOPMENT

U.S. Air Force Training and Certifications
Squadron Information Assurance Officer Training
Air Force Client Support Administrator Course
Air Force Airman Leadership School
Government-wide Purchase Card Training
Records Management Familiarization Course
Information Manager Technical Training School
Dreamweaver Computer-Based Training (CBT)
CompTIA A+ Certified Professional
Air Force HTML Course
IT Technician Training

AWARDS AND SPECIAL ACCOMPLISHMENTS

Air Force Commendation Medal; Air Force Achievement Medal
Joint Service Achievement Medal; Iraq Campaign Medal
Commutations and Information Airman of the Year

BRYAN ADAMS
173 Pierce Avenue | Macon, GA 31204 | 478-742-2442| info@careerprocenter.net

INFORMATION TECHNOLOGY | HELP DESK | FIELD ENGINEER

"Energetic, loyal, and committed team player. Successfully accomplishes job requirements on own initiative. Stands for what is right. Strong sense of self-confidence and positive outlook; inspired her peers to develop a positive sense of job accomplishment. Demonstrated true 'esprit de corps' and set an excellent example for others by doing the job right the first time. Handled situations with a no-nonsense approach and stated opinion in a straightforward manner."
~ DONALD MCGUIRE, Department Head, Fort Dix Military Entrance Processing Station

PROFESSIONAL EXPERIENCE & ACHIEVEMENTS

UNITED STATES ARMY   **9/1992 to PRESENT**
INFORMATION SYSTEMS HELP DESK MANAGER: Manheim, Germany   4/2007 to Present
Managed 15-person Network Service Center (NSC) providing assistance for more than 120 high-level communications sites across Europe, providing customer support of the Local Area Network (LAN) and physical support of Wide Area Network (WAN) across Heidelberg, Manheim, and Kaiserslautern, Germany, sites.
- Established regulatory observance for 42 COMSEC accounts containing 3500+ line items.
- Managed team tasked with migration of 500+ personnel to Windows Vista Operating System (OS).
- Administered 80 hours of position-specific training as instructor of middle-management course.

Accomplishments:
√ Collaborated on KG-250 upgrades, enhancing Electronic Key Management System availability by 100%.
√ Provided IT and Help Desk support to more than 400 customers.
√ Administered LAN installation ahead of schedule with 99% reliability rate.
√ Maintained 100% accountability for sensitive COMSEC property and equipment valued at $2M.

OPERATIONS MANAGER: Atlanta, GA   2/2005 to 4/2007
Managed Information Systems Operations and Help Desk, providing worldwide support and providing en-route, initial entry, or early entry communications support for up to 1500 users. Directed information management issues for 119 personnel deployed on eight missions to six countries, providing support of incidents ranging from armed conflict to humanitarian relief issues.
- Performed 12 monthly and one annual rekey procedures, resulting in 99.3% Secure Internet Protocol Router Network (SIPRNet) uptime for 2007.
- Supervised maintenance of records and administration of actions for 100 personnel.
- Managed operations, maintenance, and configuration of 350+ LAN client system systems.

Accomplishments:
√ Held 100% accountability of $1.8M+ in enterprise networking equipment.
√ Oversaw maintenance and operation of $2.5M of communications equipment, with 100% accountability.
√ Recognized as subject matter expert on COMSEC and Information Technology (IT) Desktop Support.
√ Delivered, installed, and administered 348 computers to six teams over three-month period, reducing maintenance calls by 50%.

EDUCATION AND CERTIFICATIONS

BACHELOR'S DEGREE IN INFORMATION TECHNOLOGY, University of Phoenix Online Program

SECURITY PLUS CERTIFICATION

JASON PETERSON

Active Secret Security Clearance

173 Pierce Avenue, Macon, GA 31204
Phone: 478-742-2442
Email: info@careerprocenter.net

INFORMATION TECHNOLOGY PROJECT MANAGER
Databases ■ Multimedia ■ Training ■ Network Engineering ■ Customer Service

Information Technology (IT) expert with nearly two decades of experience designing, planning, developing, troubleshooting, and maintaining networks, email, servers, hardware, software, cabling, databases, and wireless connectivity. Strategic planner and manager, supervising teams of personnel and executing program budgets, providing Quality Assurance (QA) oversight to complete projects and achieve organizational goals on time and under budget. Multimedia expert developing enhanced audiovisual materials for the web.

Professional Experience & Achievements

Defense Information Systems Agency (DISA), Falls Church, VA
SENIOR KNOWLEDGE MANAGER/FIELD ENGINEER II, 2/2004 to Present
Led development of software and enterprise application systems, including testing and rollout. Maintain Information Security, Intrusion Detection, and Prevention to safeguard confidential and classified data. Taught Adobe Photoshop, Illustrator, and Flash. Earlier positions include Content Manager/System Administrator and Multimedia Developer.
- Outstanding Academic/Technical Achievement, 2007 and Outstanding Customer Service Team, 2006 awards.
- Conceived and created video training library that reduced help desk calls by 50% using TechSmith Camtasia.
- Decreased system footprint and lab costs by 30% by integrating programs into a single suite.
- Implemented weekly virtual meetings with senior staff and clients to reduce travel costs by 40%.

Department of the Navy (DON), Washington, DC
NETWORK ADMINISTRATOR/TEAM LEAD, 6/2001 to 2/2004
Directed a team of system administrators supporting the operations of 450 local and remote users in 10 states. Trained and mentored new technical support personnel. Researched emerging technologies to achieve goals, solve problems, and expand existing architecture.
- Awarded Top Network Administrator within Naval Reserve Recruiting Command for 2001 and 2002.
- Developed and installed data retrieval system as part of Continuity of Operations Plan (COOP).
- Configured LAN Protocols (TCP/IP, IPX, FTP, DHCP, HTTP) and centrally managed security patches/backups.
- Planned enterprise rollout of Xerox Document Centers with network scanning, reducing downtime by 40%.
- Set up virtual capability to enable offsite users to telecommute, saving $100K+ in annual travel and office leases.
- Led Tiger Team to integrate site users and legacy applications to Navy/Marine Corps Intranet (NMCI).

Certifications

Microsoft Certified Systems Administrator (MCSA) Charter Member ■ Microsoft Certified Professional (MCP)
Microsoft Certified Systems Engineer (MCSE) Windows 2000 ■ Network Engineering & Management Diploma
The Customer Service Agent in Action ■ Defense Collaboration Tool Suite Macromedia Director II Certificate of
Training ■ Defense Messaging System (DMS) User Training

Education

MASTER'S DEGREE IN COMPUTER INFORMATION SYSTEMS (2010)
BACHELOR'S DEGREE IN COMPUTER NETWORKING (2007)
George Washington University, Washington, DC

EDWARD PHILLIPS

info@careerprocenter.net

173 Pierce Avenue, Macon, GA 31204   ☎ (478) 742-2442

AREAS OF EXPERTISE
- Security Operations
- Law Enforcement
- Leadership and Training
- File Management
- Safety Initiatives
- Vehicle Maintenance
- Operational Support

QUALIFICATIONS
- Planning and Scheduling
- Policies, Systems, and Procedures
- Multitasking
- Secret Security Clearance
- CDL-A Driver's License

MILITARY SERVICE
U.S. Army
(06/2007 – 12/2011)
U.S. Marine Corps
(01/1995 – 01/2005)

AWARDS
Army Commendation Medal; Army Achievement Medal; Meritorious Unit Commendation; Nat'l Defense Service Medal; Iraq Campaign Medal; Army Service Ribbon; NATO Medal; Army Lapel Button; Non-Commissioned Officer Professional Citation; Armed Forces Service Medal; Rife Expert Badge; Pistol Expert Badge

CAREER PROFILE

Highly motivated professional offering expertise in **security management, law enforcement, emergency response, logistics, inventory, leadership, team building, customer service, and technology**. Utilize oral and written communication skills to clearly interact with staff on multiple organizational levels, effectively identifying problems, providing intuitive analyses, and developing innovative solutions. Achieve excellence independently and as a team player. Thrive and excel in a multitasking, high-paced environment.

CAREER HIGHLIGHTS

- Forecasted, facilitated, and maintained ammunition inventory for 800+ personnel.
- Planned, developed, and implemented a complex warehouse safety and security program.
- Successfully coordinated and tracked 500+ security assignments.

EXPERIENCE

United States (U.S.) Army, Fort Sill, OK   06/2007 – 12/20110
Ammunitions Manager
- Planned and implemented critical security policies, procedures, and methods of operation.
- Performed risk assessment to prevent security threats, theft, or damage.
- Supervised 20 personnel, ensuring optimal and effective training.
- Directed operations within the Tactical Command Center, utilizing encrypted radios, setting patrol routes, and performing emergency evacuations.
- Managed inventory and ammunitions for the operation center valued at more than $225K.
- Maintained an extensive filing system of confidential records.

Swift Transportation, North Syracuse, NY   04/2006 – 11/2006
Vehicle Operator
- Operated an 18-wheeled vehicle to pick up and deliver goods.
- Performed vehicle repairs and preventative maintenance.

Engineering Assignments, West Palm Beach, FL   09/2005 – 02/2006
Target Maintenance Technician
- Performed maintenance and repair to ensure safe operational conditions of computerized targets.
- Analyzed equipment malfunctions and demonstrated expertise in troubleshooting and repair.
- Provided technical advice to managerial staff regarding maintenance requirements, financial impact, and resource capabilities.

U.S. Marine Corps (USMC), Oceanside, CA   05/1995 – 01/2005
Abatement Manager/Operational Manager/Trainer
- Directed all Hazardous Material (HAZMAT) handling and disposal operations.
- Conducted law enforcement, security, and force protection tasks, including the utilization of surveillance patrols, suspicious activity investigation, and screening methods.
- Developed and provided optimal inventory control standards.
- Supervised subordinate personnel, ensuring appropriate training and setting work schedules.
- Developed and enforced policies, procedures, security directives, and safety regulations.
- Managed the compilation and analysis of technical source data for executive utilization.
- Responded to emergency sites, offering expertise and experience for successful resolution.

EDUCATION & TRAINING

State University of New York, New York, NY, B.S., Corporate Homeland Security (expected completion 2012)

Coursework and Additional Training:
Investigative Techniques and Reporting; Environmental Science; Homeland Security; Foundations of Risk Management; Political Power in America; Vehicle Crew Evaluator Training; Improvised Explosive Device Defect, Train the Trainer; Hazardous Waste Worker's Course; First Responder, Operations Level Health and Safety Training; Environmental Quality Sampling; Supervisor's Health and Safety Training; Defense Hazardous Materials/Waster Handling; New Equipment Training

TECHNOLOGY

Microsoft (MS) Windows Operating System; MS Office (Word, Access, Excel, PowerPoint, Outlook); Internet Explorer; General Office Equipment

GAIL RODGERS

info@careerprocenter.net

173 Pierce Avenue, Macon, GA 31204

☎ (478) 742-2442

AREAS OF EXPERTISE
- Client Services
- Clinical Therapy
- Patient Assessment
- Administrative Management
- Supervision and Training
- Team Building and Motivation
- Innovative Strategies
- Organizational Management
- Procedural Analysis
- Problem Resolution
- Communication and Technology
- Budgetary Management and Compliance

CERTIFICATIONS
- Certified Alcohol and Drug Counselor (2005 to 2011)

MILITARY SERVICE
United States Army (09/26/1990 to 10/30/2011)

AWARDS
Accommodation Medal (2); Achievement Medal; National Defense Medal (2)

PROFESSIONAL PROFILE

Mental Health professional offering expertise in clinical therapy, substance abuse programs, and administration with additional high-level skills in leadership, training, and technology. Utilize oral and written communication skills to clearly define expectations and mentor subordinates, effectively identifying problems, providing intuitive analyses.

CAREER HIGHLIGHTS

- Forecasted, facilitated, and maintained ammunition inventory for 800+ personnel.
- Increased care services, saving the facility $167K+ in care costs and $50K in travel expenses.
- Designed a Mental Health Insurance Portability and Accountability Database to enable disclosure tracking with zero errors.
- Authored articles for military personnel facing lifestyle changes and geographical isolation.
- Researched and developed a tobacco cessation program.
- Maintained a leadership role during a $2.3M facility move.
- Designed and implemented a Basic Transitional Program for 2K+ trainees.

PROFESSIONAL EXPERIENCE

U.S. Army   1990 – 2011
Mental Health Services Technician (07/2008 – 10/2011)

- Provided mental health, substance abuse, and family advocacy program services for 9K+ beneficiaries.
- Monitored and facilitated 3,500+ annual patient visits and a 23-bed unit.
- Directed the activities, training, and schedules of nine subordinate staff members.
- Managed an annual operating budget of $25K+.
- Analyzed patient requirements, developed treatment plans, and led group therapy sessions.

Mental Health Element Manager (05/2006 – 07/2008)

- Provided managerial guidance and scheduling for 10 staff members.
- Delivered training/program support to 15 suicide prevention and violence awareness instructors.
- Developed operating instructions for procedures for overall efficiency improvements.

Alcohol and Drug Prevention and Treatment Program Supervisor (02/2000 – 09/2004)

- Delivered optimal instruction for all clinical students.
- Directed all administrative program planning processes.
- Managed a $20K program budget and $15K in equipment and inventory.
- Developed and implemented the Airman Basic Transitional Program, assisting 2K trainees.
- Provided suicide prevention and sexual assault briefings to 3,200 personnel.

ADDITIONAL PROFESSIONAL EXPERIENCE

1999-2000 – Family Advocacy Program Supervisor (USAF); 1999-2000 – Exceptional Family Member Program Manager (U.S. Army); 1990-1999

EDUCATION AND TRAINING

University of Texas, El Paso, TX, B.S. in Social Psychology
Government Purchase Care Course; Supply and Inventory Custodian Training; Operational Problems in Behavioral Science; Income Tax Advisor Training; Mental Health Abuse Control; Security Manager's Training; Investment Seminar; Advanced Customer Service Training for Management; Motivational Enhancement Interviewing; Smoking Cessation Facilitator Course; Train the Trainer

JOHN MONROE

173 Pierce Avenue | Macon, GA 31210 | 478-742-2442 | info@careerprocenter.net

MAINTENANCE MANAGEMENT SPECIALIST WITH 20 YEARS OF HONORABLE U.S. AIR FORCE EXPERIENCE, LEADING INNOVATIVE PROJECT AND PROGRAM MANAGEMENT STRATEGIES

- *Maintenance Operations*
- *Inventory Control*
- *Training and Development*
- *Building Relationships*
- *Supply Procurement*
- *Communication and Coordination*
- *Analysis and Evaluation*
- *Strategic Planning*

Maintenance and Management: Led an expert team of 20 Aerospace Ground Equipment mechanics to execute major maintenance, servicing, pickup, and delivery of 200+ items of support equipment valued at $5M+.

Quality Assurance: Led more than 700 personnel from 14 career fields in major line item inspection preparations; garnered the best pass rate in eight years at 93% and achieved an overall "Excellent" rating.

Personnel Management: Led five teams comprised of 130 specialized maintenance technicians in two operating locations; ensured operational readiness, productivity, and efficiency.

CAREER PROGRESSION

PRODUCTION SUPPORT SUPERVISOR   11/2008 to Present
United States Air Force (USAF), Macon, GA

Oversee Air Force (AF) equipment maintenance directives in support of high-priority military missions; provide leadership to 12 production support personnel.

☑ Organize and confer maintenance requirement schedules and workforce plans for Aerospace Ground Equipment assets valued at more than $30M.

☑ Maintain accountability for up to 650 Technical Orders (TOs).

☑ Lead the Hazardous Material (HAZMAT) handling program to ensure proper storage, labeling, and usage; ensure Material Safety Data Sheet availability.

☑ Lead in-depth self-inspection program efforts in preparation for Inspector General evaluations; systematically regulate 2,000+ specialized tools and diagnostic equipment valued at $250K.

☑ Facilitated equipment and procurement, storage, and disposal programs for 850+ stock items. Authorize Government Purchase Card requests for up to 50 suppliers on a monthly basis.

☑ Serve as Training Coordinator, fostering a positive personnel development culture; assess the proficiency of personnel, make determinations for training requirements, and establish milestones.

☑ Continually update the Training Business Area system to document training plans, completion, and proficiency of personnel.

Accomplishments:
o Lauded for securing a 95% on-time repair cycle turn in with zero delinquencies.
o Oversaw 160 tons of high-priority cargo.
o Saved more than $275K by effectively negotiating an aircraft replacement contract.
o Achieved 100% training requirement completion for a team of 12 personnel.

PRODUCTION SUPERVISOR   04/2006 to 11/2008
USAF, Macon, GA

Oversaw maintenance, servicing, pickup, and delivery of essential Air Force (AF) ground equipment; consistently met organization requirements by establishing effective priorities and duties for personnel.

JOHN MONROE
478-742-2442   info@careerprocenter.net

☑ Led five teams comprised of 130 specialized maintenance technicians in two operating locations; ensured operational readiness, productivity, and efficiency.

☑ Managed accountability for Aerospace Ground Equipment assets valued at more than $20M.

☑ Integrated knowledge in accounting, microeconomics, and macroeconomics to support financial activities associated with service orders, budget management, and billing.

Accomplishments:

o Recognized for accomplishing a 95% mission capability rate and Quality Assurance evaluation pass rate.

o Commended for managing execution of more than 29K equipment dispatches in support of vital flying operations; enabled more than 17k flying hours.

o Key contributor to the organization earning the 2007 Air Force Meritorious Unit Award by overseeing equipment preparations for Headquarters directives for multiple flying operations.

EQUIPMENT CONTROL MANAGER   07/2002 to 04/2006
USAF, Macon, GA

Directly supported a multifunctional USAF team by overseeing essential equipment maintenance operations.

☑ Led an expert team of 20 Aerospace Ground Equipment mechanics to execute major maintenance, servicing, pickup, and delivery of 200+ items of support equipment valued at $5M+.

☑ Served as technical advisor for highly specialized maintenance activities.

Accomplishments:

o Assisted with the recovery of more than 500 Hurricane Katrina/Rita survivors.

o Performed in-depth analysis and inspection of assigned equipment; garnered the highest equipment reliability rate within the department at 95%.

o Achieved an "Outstanding" rating for environmental compliance assessments and inspections.

o Lauded for maintenance operations productivity; key contributor to the organization being nominated for the 2004 Maintenance Effectiveness Award.

EDUCATION

Georgia State University, Atlanta, GA – Bachelor's Degree in Business Management (2011)

AWARDS AND HONORS

Meritorious Service Medal (2)
AF Commendation Medal (2)
AF Achievement Medal (2)
Meritorious Unit Award (2)
AF Outstanding Unit Award (7)
National Defense Service Medal (2)
Global War on Terrorism Expeditionary Medal

Karen Murphy

🖅 info@careerprocenter.net

📧 173 Pierce Avenue, Macon, GA 31204

☎ (478) 742-2442

AREAS OF EXPERTISE

LEADERSHIP
- Skill Set Evaluations
- Performance Evaluations
- Mentoring and Counseling
- Manage teams up to 100

TECHNICAL
- Knowledge of Building Design and Planning
- Installation Operations and Maintenance
- Facility Management
- Wheeled Vehicle and Heavy Equipment Maintenance
- Logistics

COMPUTER SKILLS
- Microsoft (MS) Windows, Office Suite
- Unit Level Logistics System
- Standard Army Maintenance/Retail Systems
- Automated Fund Control Order System (AFCOS)
- Budget Organization and Tracking System (BOATS)
- Jetforms/Formflow
- Adobe Systems

COMMUNICATIONS
- Instruction/Training
- Technical Communications
- Reports and Documentation

LAWS, REGULATIONS
- OSHA Directives
- Financial Guidance
- Federal Acquisition Regulations (FARs)

SECURITY CLEARANCE
- Secret (current)

MAINTENANCE MANAGEMENT • RESOURCE MANAGEMENT

Professional Manager with 20+ years' experience managing complex technical environments employing skilled workforces, evaluating resource requirements, and supervising both operations and staff. Expert-level skills in planning, requirements evaluation, acquisition, and quality assessment. In-depth ability to manage technical staff engaged in complex tasks in fast-paced or intense environments. Excellent communicator who interacts with senior executives, administrative staff, technical workers, and professionals in such fields as engineering, architecture, logistics, and maintenance. Hold government Secret security clearance.

Resource Manager, Construction and Facilities Management Office (CFMO)

Headquarters, Washington, DC   10/2004 – Present

Manage comprehensive resource management for the Construction and Facilities Management Office (CFMO), including staff, materiel, funding, and contracts management. Plan, organize, and oversee execution of multiple construction programs and facilities management projects dictated by National Guard priorities. Evaluate funding needs and develop budgets to support projects valued at $4.3M. Defend funding projections and push projects to completion, ensuring effective allocation during project execution.

- Oversee four accounts totaling $7M in annual funds and one military construction account totaling $11.5M.
- Collaborate with Director of Engineering in planning Areas of Responsibility detailed in cooperative agreements for services and facility leasing between the DC National Guard, DC government, and commercial properties.
- Manage four federal Government Charge Card accounts with unlimited purchase authority.
- Led CFMO engineering and facilities divisions in planning for 24 major projects (2004-2005) exceeding $3.5M.
- Improved quality of purchasing and contracting documents submitted for review and action.
- Executed 99.2% of the $3.2M annual budget for Fiscal Year (FY) 2009.
- Analyzed/funded 310+ job orders in FY 2008, sustaining critical levels of maintenance for the Guard.

Maintenance Director

Maintenance Shop, Army National Guard, Macon, GA   09/2002 – 10/2004

Coordinated organization's response to maintenance needs for all National Guard elements throughout Georgia. Directed and oversaw work of 22 staff, including subordinate supervisors and technical employees. Acted as Subject Matter Expert (SME), offering technical advice and assistance to subordinate managers and line staff. Provided full administrative and supervisory oversight to four maintenance shops performing maintenance on complex equipment used by Georgia National Guard.

- Competitively selected for promotion to Resource Manager.
- Prepared and reviewed plans for all four maintenance shops, scheduling work to ensure quality, quantity, and deadlines were managed effectively.
- Rated as "Outstanding" on 2003 Performance Evaluation
- Oversaw work processes and products for organic equipment used by various business units: Humvees, 2 ½- to 10-ton cargo trucks, 5- and 10-ton recovery vehicles, generators, pumps, 5,000-gallon fuel tankers, 1,200-gallon tank and pump units, 22-ton stake and platform trailers, 10K-ton forklifts, and other equipment.
- Provided quality assurance inspections for work in process. Corrected deficiencies noted on safety inspections of both Material Safety Data Sheets (MSDS) and shelf-life management.
- Planned and conducted periodic safety, occupational health, and Hazardous Materials (HAZMAT) training for shop employees. Ensured employees observed all applicable safety regulations, including Occupational Safety and Health Administration (OSHA) directives and wearing of personal protective clothing and equipment. Corrected stock inventory of repair parts, developing a new system for organizing and centrally locating parts.

Karen Murphy

✆info@careerprocenter.net

✉ 173 Pierce Avenue, Macon, GA 31204   ☎ (478) 742-2442

Automotive Worker Supervisor

Maintenance Shop, Army National Guard, Macon, GA	12/1999 – 09/2002

Supervised up to seven staff, including automotive workers and tool and parts attendants, in accomplishing maintenance and repair of more than 700 pieces of Georgia National Guard equipment, including wheeled vehicles, communications equipment, weapons, protective masks, and food services equipment.

- Monitored maintenance reports, logbooks, oil sample procedures, job orders, and Materiel Condition Status Reports to meet all internal reporting requirements and federal, state, local, and National Guard standards.
- Ensured all OSHA standards were met, including the use of safety equipment and protective clothing. Participated in Organizational Maintenance Safety programs.

SELECTED MILITARY EXPERIENCE:
Army National Guard
Maintenance Manager

Maintenance Shop, Army National Guard, Macon, GA	12/1999 – Present

Oversaw organizational maintenance operations of 5 military police organizations comprised of more than 400 staff within the Georgia Army National Guard.

- Monitored and tracked ordering/receipt of all required repair parts ordered by administrative staff.
- Oversaw scheduled maintenance, including annual and special services, and performed quality checks of work in progress. Provided technical guidance to maintenance staff and assisted with troubleshooting, complex problem solving, and recovery operations for all vehicles and equipment.

Deployed to Baghdad from 12/2005-12/2006 in support of the Global War on Terrorism (GWOT) Maintained quality assurance standards for combat and support vehicle maintenance and repairs in 11 separate military police groups throughout Iraq, ensuring 90%+ readiness rate during high-intensity combat operations.

- Coordinated training for 14 mid-line supervisors, 32 equipment records specialists, and more than 50 line mechanics performing vehicle repairs.
- Provided oversight for civilian contractors in country providing maintenance to 52 specialized vehicles.

U.S. Army, National Guard	**12/1999 – Present**
U.S. Army Service:	**09/1979 – 12/1999**

LEADERSHIP TRAINING

Leadership Development Course; Managing Difficult Employees and Federal Labor Relations, Supervisor Development; Senior Supervisor Course; Strength Management, Advanced Supervisory Leadership School

SELECTED TECHNICAL TRAINING

Government Services Administration "Smart Pay" Travel Card: Charting the Course; Chemical/Waster Management and HAZWOPER Training; Environmental Compliance

AWARDS

Bronze Star Medal   Iraqi Campaign Medal   Global War on Terrorism Service Medal   Army Commendation Award   Army Achievement Awards (2)   Civilian Performance Evaluations: "Outstanding" Ratings

RANDAL L. ASTRO

173 Pierce Avenue
Macon, GA 31204
Home Phone: 478-742-2442
Email: info@careerprocenter.net

PROGRAM AND PROJECT ADMINISTRATION

MANAGEMENT PROFILE

TOP SECRET/SBI
CLEARANCE (Current)
Strategic Planning
Test & Evaluation
Program Management
Cost Control/Budgets
Operations Management
Negotiations/Partnering
Executive Communications
Human Capital Management
Innovative Engineering Designs
Cross-Functional Collaborations
Quality Systems, including
Lean Six Sigma/Root Cause
Analysis

❑ **Experienced Program Manager with an outstanding record of leadership** in sophisticated technical programs for the Department of Defense (DoD). Test & Evaluation expertise applied to complex systems, both developmental and operational. Front-line performer in high-tech, multibillion-dollar programs.

❑ **Achieved unmatched levels of efficiency,** applying 15 years' experience in Earned Value Management (EVM) to implement the best solutions; balance cost, schedule, and performance to produce optimum results.

❑ **Adaptable and versatile,** with practical knowledge and experience across multiple fields, including space, aircraft, missile, and submarine programs (e.g., Tomahawk TTL, National Space Systems) and international weapons sales.

❑ **Accomplished Team Builder and Leader,** with successful engagements directing both technical and support staff in complex projects and programs with expansive budgets, aggressive timelines, and high expectations for success. Build effective partnerships with state and federal agencies, DoD managers, and private enterprises, including the defense industry.

CAREER CHRONICLE

UNITED STATES NAVY   **1985 – Present**
NATIONAL RECONNAISSANCE OFFICE, *Chantilly, VA*
Deputy Director, Reconnaissance Systems Officer   *(08/2009 – 07/2010)*
Direct and manage spacecraft production for a $13B+ national imagery satellite, including end-to-end design, integration, test, and launch. Maintain accountability and authority for cost, schedule, and performance, and supervise the program office comprising 40 government employees and 120 support contractors.

- **Led interface with contractor base** of more than 2,000 individuals.
- **Developed annual budget forecasts** and execution plans for inclusion in U.S. President's Budget Submissions to Congress.

Division Chief, Vehicle Engineering Division, Reconnaissance Systems Office   *(04/2008 – 07/2009)*
Deputy Program Manager for spacecraft production. Administered cost and performance of $13B+ national imagery satellite and performance of 15 government/30 support contractors collaborating with 1,500+ contractors.

- **Orchestrated stellar program peformance and cost control,** harvesting 60+ days of margin and reducing schedule erosion from 10+ days per month to less than 1 day per month.
- **Drove completion of a complex system thermal vacuum test,** reducing test window from 125 to 116 days and yielding 108% efficiency.

DEFENSE SECURITY COOPERATION AGENCY (DSCA), *Arlington, VA*
Executive Military Assistant to the Director/Deputy Director   *(10/2006 – 04/2008)*
Selected from among a group of 24 peers as primary advisor to senior agency executives, providing daily and long-range acquisition support and coordination of $21B in new foreign military sales executed by 450 personnel to 200+ countries.

RANDAL L. ASTRO —   Home Phone: 478-742-2442 • Email: info@careerprocenter.net

- **Authored sensitive correspondence** between agency executives and senior military/government leaders, including Joint Staff, Congress, and foreign governments. Coordinated meetings to promote coalitions between senior U.S. government and foreign officials.

PMA-280, Patuxent River, MD
Deputy Program Manager, Tomahawk Program Office   *(02/2004 – 03/2006)*
Deputy Program Manager for Tomahawk Advanced Projects and Tactical Tomahawk Torpedo Tube Launched Program, managing development of the nation's most advanced precision weapons system, with a combined value of $300M.

- **Led and directed a 32-member team** in design, development, and testing, overseeing cost, schedule, and performance for a $45M annual budget and values of $100M+ in R&D (production value = $38M annually).
- **Talented negotiator,** instrumental in preserving the UK's commitment to purchase 65 weapons, protecting the $1.6B multiyear procurement supporting the program.

Selected as a United States Naval Candidate for the NASA Manned Space Program (2003).

ACADEMIC ACHIEVEMENTS

Engineer's Degree, Aeronautical & Astronautical Engineering
NAVAL POSTGRADUATE SCHOOL – Monterey, CA

M.S., Aeronautical Engineering
NAVAL POSTGRADUATE SCHOOL – Monterey, CA

Outstanding Thesis Award, Engineer's Program, NAVAL POSTGRADUATE SCHOOL
   Exploration of Fibre Channel as an Avionics Interconnect for the 21st Century Military Aircraft

B.S., Systems Engineering, *Distinguished Graduate; Designated Faculty Candidate*
U.S. NAVAL ACADEMY – Annapolis, MD

ENGINEERING & ACQUISITION ACHIEVEMENTS

Designated Engineering Test Naval Flight Officer
USN Test Pilot School – Patuxent River, MD
Final Project – "Flight Test of F-4G Wild Weasel Aircraft"

Specialty Training
Program Manager Course (PMT 401); Defense Acquisition University (DAU)
U.S. Government Executive and Defense Industry Course (SAM-E)
International Program Security Requirements Course (IPSR)
Missile Technology and Control Regime (MTCR)

Acquisition Certifications/Affiliations
DAWIA Level III: Program Management; Test & Evaluation
DAWIA Level I: Business, Cost Estimating, and Financial Management; Information Technology; Systems Planning, Research, Development, & Engineering
Level I: International Affairs Certification

AWARDS

Defense Meritorious Service Award (2);
Meritorious Service Award; Navy Commendation Award (2)
Navy Achievement Award (4)
Awarded NRO Silver Medal by Director, National Reconnaissance Office
Order of the Daedalians & Edward Heinemann Award

JENNIFER MCMAHON
173 Pierce Avenue ▪ Macon, GA 31204
Mobile: 478-742-2442 ▪ Home: 478-742-2442
info@careerprocenter.net

SECURITY/LAW ENFORCEMENT/MEDIA RELATIONS

Leadership & Management	Crisis/Emergency Management	Operational/Physical Security
Proactive Crime Reduction	Public Relations/Reputation Management	Press Relations/Public Speaking
Performance Improvement	Training and Motivation	Multimedia Campaigns
Financial Management	Business Process Reengineering	Relationship Development

OPERATIONS MANAGEMENT: Administer the busiest military police station in the U.S. Army. Provide quality customer service, emergency response, and crisis management. Increase efficiency by consolidating redundant operations, streamlining report processing, restructuring, and expanding training programs.

LAW ENFORCEMENT: Recognized as the most progressive law enforcement professional in the Department of Army, contributing to Fort Bragg earning the Army Community of Excellence for four years, and recognition as the "Army Times Best Installation." Earned the International Association of Chiefs of Police Award for Innovative Technology and the National Crime Watch Council Award for National Night Out.

PHYSICAL SECURITY: Spearheaded comprehensive advances in force protection programs to effectively expose and deter criminal, terrorist, or hostile activities. Execute installation access control program. Partner with security specialists in the development and upgrade of high-tech access control points, contributing to Fort Bragg earning the Army's Force Protection/Antiterrorism award for three consecutive years.

COMMUNICATION/NETWORKING: Initiate proactive law enforcement campaigns, personal involvement with key community leaders, and community outreach events to garner public trust/support. Conduct liaison and share intelligence with multiple local, state, and federal agencies. Advise high-ranking officials on projects, plans, and operations.

PUBLIC/MEDIA RELATIONS: Qualified spokesperson; address scheduled audiences and professionally manage unanticipated events and emergencies. Establish trust and rapport with local and international media to further develop credibility with public and internal audiences. Respond to media queries with authority and official presence, applying calm, thoughtful, and sincere approach to managing sensitive, confidential, crisis, and controversial issues.

PROFESSIONAL EXPERIENCE/ACCOMPLISHMENTS

UNITED STATES (U.S) ARMY *(Secret Clearance)*   **1997 – Present**

Sheriff, DIRECTORATE OF EMERGENCY SERVICES, Macon, GA   (2006 – Present)

Supervise full-service law enforcement agency of approximately 215 sworn officers and 16 narcotic and explosive dog teams in the law enforcement, security, and protection of 40K military members, families, and civilians living and working on 150K-acre installation. Contracting Officer's Technical Representative (COTR) for 220-person, $15M security contract. Train and supervise a rotating installation guard force of 775+ per year.
➤ *Executed post-9/11 Installation Access Control Program; developed plans and procedures implemented Army-wide.*
➤ *Reengineered the organizational structure to meet current and future operational requirements.*

Public Information Officer, 8TH U.S. ARMY, Macon, GA   (2004 – 2006)

Supervised information gathering and distribution to U.S. and Korean soldiers and civilians in a global information environment. Oversaw content of multiple local and national publications and broadcasts; published biweekly newspaper, numerous information pamphlets, and a monthly full-color joint service magazine. Advised general officers on media matters; served as spokesperson for military organizations.
➤ *Pursued commercial contract for division's biweekly newspaper, requiring less military manpower at a lower cost.*
➤ *Contributed articles to the Indianhead newspaper, Warrior Radio, and public access channel via various media.*

JENNIFER MCMAHON, PAGE 2

> *Coordinated more than 40 print and broadcast interviews, conducting media escorts throughout the peninsula.*

Assistant Operations Officer, XVIII AIRBORNE CORPS, Macon, GA   (2003 – 2004)
Advised Secretary of the General Staff, 3 directors, 17 division/branch chiefs, 6 principal staff sections, and 12 units to ensure major staff actions, projects, and operations were conducted efficiently in support of organizational vision.
> *Managed $2M+ budget and the annual $30K International Merchant Purchase Authorization Card program.*

Chief of Protocol, XVIII AIRBORNE CORPS,, Macon, GA   (2002 – 2003)
Advised Corps Commanding General and staff of the most visited post in the Army on matters pertaining to protocol, customs, and courtesies of the Army, other services, and other countries.
> *Planned and executed 250 visits involving more than 800 visitors during a four-month period, including two visits by the Chief of Staff of the Army, two visits by the Commanding General, U.S. Army Forces Command, three congressional delegations (including a congressional field hearing), and three Chiefs of Staff of three foreign armies.*

Chief Deputy Sheriff, DIRECTORATE OF EMERGENCY SERVICES, Macon, GA   (2000 – 2002)
Assisted in the coordination of law enforcement support, security, and crime-prevention activities for the largest military police station in the U.S. Army. Supervised the daily operations of more than 100 law enforcement officers. Served as Incident Commander during crises. Assumed full responsibility in the absence of the primary officer.
> *Developed force protection plans to increase security in the event of a natural disaster, civil unrest, or national crisis.*
> *Effectively planned and coordinated support activities to include the establishment of school security, implementation of traffic study surveys, and development of a domestic violence awareness taskforce.*

Chief of Plans, 16TH MILITARY POLICE BRIGADE (AIRBORNE), Macon, GA   (1999 – 2000)
Advised the Corps Commander on military police employment in support of combat operations during exercises and contingency operations. Planned and executed training exercises. Developed plans for global and domestic deployments.
> *As Senior Observer/Controller, trained reserve component military police units to support operations in Bosnia.*
> *Represented Brigade and the Military Police Corps Regiment in joint and Major Command-level exercises.*

Assistant Operations Officer, 1ST CORPS SUPPORT COMMAND, Macon, GA   (1997 – 1999)
Administered Support Command Emergency Operations Center and Combat Service Support Operations Center. Coordinated among five subsidiary units; other major support units; Headquarters (HQ); and local, state, and federal emergency operations centers.
> *Analyzed and simplified reporting methods into streamlined process to ensure accurate reporting of shortfalls.*
> *Managed Emergency Operations Center, Command Post, and Service Support Operations Center during Hurricane Fran disaster relief operations; coordinated support to Ft. Bragg, the local community, and the state.*
> *Arranged critical briefings to the Command Group and Federal Emergency Management Agency (FEMA) personnel.*
> *Revised and published Standard Operating Procedures (SOPs).*

EDUCATION/TRAINING
> **Master of Arts Degree in Industrial Education,** University College, Macon, GA, 2007
> **Bachelor of Science Degree in Child Psychology w/Departmental Distinction in Journalism,** University College, Macon, GA, 1997
> **U.S. Army Military Education:** Command and General Staff College; Combined Arms and Services Staff School; Public Affairs Officer Course; Basic and Advanced Military Police Officer
> **U.S. Army Training:** Court Decisions and Legal Update; Damage Control; WMD: Incident Management/Unified Command; Hate Crimes Training for Law Enforcement Professionals; Counterintelligence Agent Sustainment (Assistant Trainer); Domestic Violence; Protective Services Training; Post Critical Incident; First Police Survival

AWARDS AND COMMENDATIONS
Bronze Star Medal; Meritorious Service Medal (3); Army Commendation Medal (3); Army Achievement Medal; National Defense Service Medal; Southwest Asia with Bronze Star; Global War on Terrorism (GWOT); Korea Defense Service Medal; Humanitarian Service Medal; Army Service Ribbon; Overseas Service Ribbon (2)

BRETT JOSEPH DANIELS

173 Pierce Avenue • Macon, GA 31204
H: 478-742-2442 • C: 478-742-2882
Email: info@careerprocenter.net

SECRET SECURITY CLEARANCE

SUMMARY OF QUALIFICATIONS

Multidimensional professional offering 20+ years of specialized expertise in leading teams, recruiting, marketing, operations, and security management. Rapidly advanced through increasingly challenging responsibilities, achieving fast-track promotions throughout tenure in the United States Air Force (USAF). Led 250+ personnel over three states to goal-exceeding accomplishments in recruitment. Successfully upheld law and order in area populated by almost 10K, developing strong no-tolerance drug enforcement team and extinguishing theft and larceny rings. Intuitive and effective training techniques routinely resulted in 100% pass rate for subordinates. Engineered protocols that reduced processing errors by 99% and decreased excess work by 50%.

PROFICIENCIES SYNOPSIS

- Leadership, Supervision, and Training
- Sales, Marketing, and Recruiting
- Personnel Management
- Public Safety and Security Management
- Operations Management
- Risk and Crisis Management

CAREER OVERVIEW AND HIGHLIGHTED ACCOMPLISHMENTS

UNITED STATES AIR FORCE USAF)   **1984 TO 2010**

RECRUITING SUPERVISOR New York, NY   (06/2008 – 08/2010)
MEDICAL RECRUITER, Oralndo, FL   (08/2004 – 06/2008)
RECRUITING SUPERVISOR, Little Rock, AR   (08/2000 – 08/2004)
RECRUITER, Biloxi, MS   (10/1996 – 08/2000)

LEADERSHIP AND PERSONNEL MANAGEMENT:
- Directed operations and managed 250+ personnel in 55K-square-mile area covering three states.
- Served as Interim Operations Flight Chief, sustaining operations' functions at full capacity for 10 recruiters.
- Inspired recruiting team while developing strong training platforms for subordinate recruiters to emulate.
- Administered operational risk management for applicants, winning Top Safety Award and Overall Top Squadron Award, 2006.
- Created spreadsheet to monitor applications flow, facilitating 10-day decrease in resolving management deadlines.
- Received Meritorious Service Medal, 03/2010.

RECRUITMENT MANAGEMENT:
- Represented USAF at events, community outreach programs, colleges, universities, and high schools; enlisted new recruits.
- Achieved 72% six-year contract rate for 2nd Quarter, 2009, 22% over goal.
- Doubled organization medical recruit quota with 100% selection rate, earning 2nd Personal Senior Recruiter Badge.
- Processed 250+ personnel in 2008 with 100% accuracy, leading organization to win "Standard of Excellence Award."
- Performed 600+ credit checks and waivers, ensuring success for management program and securing flow of qualified applicants.
- Placed 1,900+ phone calls to potential applicants during 1998, resulting in 28 additional recruits toward organization goal.

OPERATIONS MANAGEMENT:
- Authored training plan for specialized officer recruiters, garnering 700% increase in Officer Training School recruitment.
- Cross-trained unit management in entrance processing, decreasing returned case files by 50% and saving $300 per returned file.
- Educated seven recruiters on correct entrance processing procedures, alleviating 95% of errors.
- Developed entrance processing system error protocol, increasing recruiters' efficiencies and reducing errors by 99%.
- Revised quality review standards and improved processing turnaround, enabling attainment of 114% of 2008 goals.

BRETT JOSEPH DANIELS	PAGE 2

ACHIEVEMENTS:
√ Obtained 80% of organization's 2005 recruitment goal, achieving a 144% increase over 2004.
√ Achieved 125% of Medical Corps scholarship program goal with retention of five new recruits.
√ Earned "Top D Flight Recruiter" Award in 1998 and 2000 for meeting 200% of recruitment goal and in 1999 for 150% of goal.
√ Admitted to "Superintendent's Club" in 1998 for beating organization quota by 100%.
√ Booked 56% of 1999 recruits into critical Mechanical-Electronics jobs, 16% over quota.

LAW ENFORCEMENT OFFICER, Las Vegas, NV	(12/1993 – 10/1996)
LAW ENFORCEMENT PATROLMAN/OFFICER, Osan, Korea	(10/1992 – 12/1993)
SECURITY SUPERVISOR, Belleville, IL	(07/1989 – 10/1992)
LAW ENFORCEMENT PATROLMAN, Belleville, IL	(07/1988 – 07/1989)
LAW ENFORCEMENT PATROLMAN/SUPERVISOR, Berlin, Germany	(07/1984 – 07/1998)

LAW ENFORCEMENT AND SECURITY MANAGMENT:
- Spearheaded the creation of Security Police Joint Drug Enforcement Team, increasing detection rate 80% over previous period.
- Obstructed entry of illegal narcotics by an additional 30% while leveraging Source Management Course material.
- Investigated use of cocaine by personnel responsible for security of nuclear weapons area, leading to confinement and discharge.

PUBLIC SAFETY AND CRISIS MANAGEMENT:
- Handpicked for Operation Gatekeeper of surveillance team working to reduce larcenies; reduced crime by 60%.
- Assisted in protection of 700+ personnel and $983M of equipment/transport in Iraq during Operation Desert Storm/Shield.
- Ensured safe passage of $2M+ to regional finance office without incident.

LEADERSHIP AND PERSONNEL MANAGEMENT:
- Ensured physical and mental fitness of personnel, providing training, equipment, and briefings.
- Developed study material and provided needed training, resulting in a 100% pass rate during standardized evaluations.
- Led 44-man defense team deployed to Iraq in support of Operation Desert Storm.
- Participated in Operation Warmheart charity softball tournament that raised $11K+ for 150 local families at Christmas.

ACHIEVEMENTS:
√ Achieved Non-Commissioned Officer (NCO) of the Year Award for 1990.
√ Scored consistent 95-97% on annual Quality Control Evaluations.
√ Handpicked by director to conduct briefings for incoming personnel at two newly established bases.

EDUCATION

ASSOCIATE'S DEGREE – HUMAN RESOURCE MANAGEMENT, Community College of the Air Force, 2010
Management and Leadership, Confrontation Management, Managerial Communications, and Investigative Principles

SPECIALIZED TRAINING

Law Enforcement Specialist Course	Management Preparatory Course
Law Enforcement Agencies Data System	Standardized Field Sobriety Testing
DWI Detection and Standardization Field Sobriety Testing Course	Equal Opportunity and Treatment Education
Professional Selling Skills Core Course	Professional Selling Skills Applications Course
Air Force NCO Academy Diploma	Officer Accessions Workshop
Information Assurance Awareness	Recruiter Course

AWARDS

Meritorious Service Medal	Air Force Commendation Medal (6)
Air Force Achievement Medal (2)	Joint Service Achievement Medal

PHILIP M. BRYANT

173 Pierce Avenue,
Macon, GA 31204
478-742-2442
| info@careerprocenter.net

Subject Matter Expert (SME) Weapons Systems Integration Engineer, offering 12+ years of experience specializing in Information Technology (IT), electronics design, Electronic Warfare (EW) and Radio Frequency (RF) systems, systems lifecycle design and testing, new business development, technical writing, operational testing, systems integration, delivery, and support for multi-segmented and multifaceted electronic defense systems. Uniquely diversified research, development, test, and evaluation technician with robust experience in network design, problem solving, and systems troubleshooting. Astute team leader with substantial experience working within Naval Air Warfare Center Weapons Division IT policies.

- Systems Design & Testing
- RF & Microwave Systems
- Program Development
- Electronic Warfare Systems
- Network Design & Implementation
- Policy Development & Compliance
- Project Team Leadership
- Process Analysis
- Teaching & Mentoring

SELECT ACCOMPLISHMENTS

- Achieved long-term reputation as top troubleshooter and problem solver for highly complex networking and electronic systems deployed in military and related system platforms and environments.

- Shaped the ALM-268 Countermeasures Receiving Set Test Set, providing the de facto industry test bed platform for the AN/ALR-676(V)3 RWR System, used worldwide by U.S. Forces.

- Designed the Advanced Digital Processor for the APR-39A(V)1 Radar Warning Receiver, resulting in $110M contract.

- Developed Infrared Countermeasures Assessment System "Test Events Module."

- Fostered the development of the Electronic Warfare Integration Laboratory at Silver Lake, resulting in a superior laboratory environment for investigation and correction of system anomalies observed in combat.

- Designed and developed the very first solid-state disk drive (Extended Memory Unit) as a replacement for the DEC RFRS-11 magnetic disk system; this solid-state drive was used in U.S. Navy Destroyer Class Close In Weapons Systems (CIWS) for cruise missile defense and led to widespread, worldwide commercial applications.

PROFESSIONAL EXPERIENCE

Senior Systems Engineer, RIVERS TECHNOLOGY, LTD., ATLANTA, GA   2009 to 2011

Rivers Technology is an advanced technology and engineering provider for U.S. government agencies and military services. Conducted project management analysis, scheduling, development, fabrication, test, calibration, repair, and deployment of AIM-9M, AIM-9X, and CATM-9M missiles and DATM Guidance Control System Test Sets.

- Procured and deployed branch engineering workstation based on Raid-0, dual 64-bit architecture for new system designs, finite element analysis, Pro/E solids modeling tools, and state-of-the-art rapid prototyping methods to produce low-cost prototypes and engineering models intended for toolbox environment.
- Supported Information Assurance (IA) activities through design, development, test, integration, and hardening of systems in accordance with Defense Acquisition Workforce Improvement Act (DAWIA) requirements for all WSE Branch Information Systems, as directed by the customer.
- Prepared and authored new business proposals for Rivers Technology and prospective customers. Provided technical guidance and oversight of personnel; trained and mentored less-experienced team members.
- Migrated work facilities from Pt. Moon to Silver Lake in accordance with directives from Base Realignment and Closure (BRAC) office; prepared shop tooling, layout, production facilities, and program documentation.

PHILIP M. BRYANT   Page 2

Senior Systems Analyst, ELECTRONIC WARFARE CORPORATION, (EWC), ATLANTA, GA   2006 to 2009

EWC provides a range of diverse technical, engineering, and computer solutions to U.S. military and government agencies. Developed solution papers, white papers, AOAs, and Test Event Modules (TEMs) for one-of-a-kind, classified Infrared Countermeasures Assessment System (ICAS). Prepared and developed proposals and performed design, fabrication, calibration, testing, and integration of test instrumentation for Directed Energy project utilizing microwave and pulsed RF systems.

- Developed and documented High Power Microwave (HPM) test process, including full-cycle test procedure, data capture, analysis, and lessons-learned process flow, overcoming undocumented features of test system software.
- Findings yielded $150K in company revenue and received official recognition.
- Researched and designed TEMs using advanced virtual computing clusters such as Beowulf and VMware for virtual
- High Performance Computer (HPC) to enable the ICAS development center concept as a preamble to anticipated funding for the ICAS at Silver Lake.
- Designed and integrated HPM test instrumentation and analysis of pulsed RF systems in the time domain; designed instrumentation systems and managed fabrication, deployment, calibration, test, integration, and data reduction.
- Authored systems documentation and solutions and crafted new business proposals for potential customers. Conducted engineering analysis in digital, analog, RF, and Information Warfare domains/contexts.

Senior Group Engineer, COMPUTER TECHNOLOGY INCORPORATED (CTI), MACON, GA   1998 to 2006

CTI provides robust skills and services to systems engineering, security, networks, hardware, software, embedded applications, and human factors affecting government and business IT needs. Served in multiple capacities, including Technical Director, Group Engineer, Senior Systems Architect, Hardware Development Manager, and Lead Engineer. Developed and implemented complete EW integration laboratory and test bed for diverse military EW systems in U.S. Navy combat aircraft. Lead Technical and Administrative Engineer on multiple systems and projects valued at up to $12M.

- Developed engineering solutions to troublesome issues affecting test teams; provided electronic workarounds integrated into and stabilizing aircraft flight systems and laboratory tests.
- Managed interdisciplinary relations with the advanced systems development team leader for the F/A-18 IPT.
- Designed and administered Windows Internet Name Service, Domain Name System, Dynamic Host Configuration Protocol, Point-to-Point Protocol, and Transmission Control Protocol/Internet Protocol.
- Provided 24/7 support for troubleshooting; liaison to systems end-users, developers, and program managers.
- Delivered unique and original solutions and diagnostic tools at the operational systems and detailed component level.
- Developed and integrated testing of classified flight hardware and EW systems for U.S. Navy aircraft.

EDUCATION AND TRAINING

- *Bachelor of Science, Information Technology, University of Georgia, Atlanta, GA*
- *Professional Certifications: CompTIA Security+ Certified, 2011; CompTIA A+ Certified, 2011; CompTIA Network+ Certified, 2011*

TECHNICAL QUALIFICATIONS

- Information Technology (IT) design, setup, maintenance, and hardening of complex and highly distributed information systems to DAWIA requirements
- ALR-62 (V) ALR-69 (V), AVR 2. APR-39 (V) 1, APR-39-XE2, & ALR-67 (V) 3 RWR; TACAN, ALQ-126B, ALQ-162, ASPJ, IBUs, ALE-47, ALE-50/55, GPS, and ad-hoc equipment, including NVS, Telemetry, Flight Qualified Memory, Data Collection/Reduction Equipment
- ECP, ECR, Deviations, Waivers, MIL-STD-1553 A/B, IEEE 802, RS-232, RS-422, RS-485, and Multipoint
- Data Bus Structures and Instrumentation: ATM, PCA, ISA, EISA
- Project/Program Management, MIL-STD-1521 & 2167, MIL-STD-881, and technical team management
- International project management and systems implementation and support
- Quality Control, MIL-Q-9858, ISO-9000

TONY CRAFT

✉ info@careerprocenter.net

📪 173 Pierce Avenue, Macon, GA 31204　　　　　☎ (478) 742-2442

~ MANAGEMENT~

*Seeking a position with a company in need of a highly qualified professional with demonstrated success
in project management, optimizing business efficiency, and exceeding corporate objectives*

Focused and self-motivated professional with proven track record in operations management, employee supervision, organizational management, and activity coordination. Strong leadership and motivational skills; proven ability to quickly build rapport, establish trust, and train and motivate people of all levels. Adept in establishing solid business relationships to ensure continuity in operations and optimal learning and support. Excellent problem solver with strong communication, team player, and interpersonal skills. Able to handle multiple projects and meet deadlines under pressure. Recognized for professionalism, positive mental attitude, and commitment to excellence.

- **Personnel and Human Resources:** Adept in managing technical personnel, conducting training and client negotiation, and managing personnel information systems, motivating, developing, and directing people as they work.
- **Problem Solver:** Respond rapidly and appropriately to changing circumstances. Evaluate problems, make astute decisions to effect positive change, and refocus on new priorities.
- **Project Management:** Train and motivate high-performance teams, and identify and mitigate risks. Employ solutions to increase communication while using time efficiently to track progress and meet goals.

───── AREAS OF EXPERTISE ─────

- Business Development
- Coordination and Management
- Staff and Team Management
- Operations Management
- Task Delegation
- Client and Public Relations
- Team Building and Leadership
- Training and Development

───── PROFESSIONAL EXPERIENCE ─────

ADMINISTRATION MANAGEMENT SPECIALIST, FEDERAL AVIATION ADMINISTRATION (FAA)　1995 - PRESENT
- Manage and direct day-to-day operations while supervising employees; highly involved in strategic planning, team leading, and people coordination
- Solely manage and supervise 27 specialists and perform scheduling, employee motivation, and monitoring performance levels to improve quality of work
- Manage delegation of duties and lead schedule management while overseeing facilities to ensure organization of operation and business functions
- Conduct extensive trainings and implement corrective actions to develop employee improvement plans
- Perform public relations duties and functions, including facility tours and contact briefings

ORGANIZATIONAL SKILLS
- Organize and orchestrate caseloads/workloads such as approving and disapproving vacation leaves to ensure all tasks are attended and staff are performing at their optimum potential
- Record and update daily, monthly, and yearly traffic totals to ensure future references
- Maintain confidentiality and facility security by securing visitors and their proper credentials and computer passwords, and monitoring implementation of policies and regulations
- Arrange all schedules and coordinate tasks to comply with facility procedures and union contract and policies

OPERATIONS MANAGEMENT
- Coordinate with Service Area Manager, Human Recourses Director, and Facility Manager to monitor and observe employee performance and facility performance measures
- Skilled in working and coordinating with various offices and personnel, including Flight Standards District Office, Regional Communications Center, and Facility Manager
- Proficient in computer operations and possess working knowledge in developing schedules , facility rotations, facility logs, and forms utilizing Microsoft (MS) Word and Excel
- Deliver weather and system information to pilots, operators, and general public in a timely manner; advise operators and pilots of hazardous conditions and provide alternatives to complete mission requirements

AIR TRAFFIC CONTROLLER	Federal Aviation Administration	Lansing, MI	1988–1995
AIR TRAFFIC CONTROLLER	Federal Aviation Administration	Bangor, ME	1987–1988
AIR TRAFFIC CONTROLLER	Federal Aviation Administration	Augusta, ME	1986–1987

───── EDUCATION AND TRAINING ─────

B.S. IN BUSINESS ADMINISTRATION • CONCENTRATION IN MANAGEMENT (Undergraduate)
Colorado Technical University Online • Colorado Springs, CO　　　　　　　　　　　**2006**

Air Traffic Control • *Federal Aviation Administration Academy* • Oklahoma City, OK
Supervisors in the FAA • *Leadership Development and Labor Relations* • Palm Coast, FL
Air Traffic Control Operational Workshop • Fort Worth, TX

Resume Notes

RANDAL L. ASTRO

173 Pierce Avenue
Macon, GA 31204
Home Phone: 478-742-2442
Email: info@careerprocenter.net

Aeronautical & Astronautical Engineering

MANAGEMENT PROFILE

TOP SECRET/SSBI CLEARANCE (Current)
Strategic Planning
Test & Evaluation
Program Management
Cost Control/Budgets
Operations Management
Negotiations/Partnering
Executive Communications
Human Capital Management
Innovative Engineering Designs
Cross-Functional Collaborations
Quality Systems, including
Lean Six Sigma/Root Cause
Analysis

❑ **Experienced Program Manager with an outstanding record of leadership** in sophisticated technical programs for the Department of Defense (DoD). Test & Evaluation expertise applied to complex systems, both developmental and operational. Front-line performer in high-tech, multibillion-dollar programs.

❑ **Achieved unmatched levels of efficiency,** applying 15 years' experience in Earned Value Management (EVM) to implement the best solutions; balance cost, schedule, and performance to produce optimum results.

❑ **Adaptable and versatile,** with practical knowledge and experience across multiple fields, including space, aircraft, missile, and submarine programs (e.g., Tomahawk TTL, National Space Systems) and international weapons sales.

❑ **Accomplished Team Builder and Leader,** with successful engagements directing both technical and support staff in complex projects and programs with expansive budgets, aggressive timelines, and high expectations for success. Build effective partnerships with state and federal agencies, DoD managers, and private enterprises, including the defense industry.

CAREER CHRONICLE

UNITED STATES NAVY   **1985 – Present**
NATIONAL RECONNAISSANCE OFFICE, *Chantilly, VA*
Deputy Director, Reconnaissance Systems Officer   *(08/2009 – 07/2010)*
Direct and manage spacecraft production for a $13B+ national imagery satellite, including end-to-end design, integration, test, and launch. Maintain accountability and authority for cost, schedule, and performance, and supervise the program office comprising 40 government employees and 120 support contractors.
- **Led interface with contractor base** of more than 2,000 individuals.
- **Developed annual budget forecasts** and execution plans for inclusion in U.S. President's Budget Submissions to Congress.

Division Chief, Vehicle Engineering Division, Reconnaissance Systems Office   *(04/2008 – 07/2009)*
Deputy Program Manager for spacecraft production. Administered cost and performance of $13B+ national imagery satellite and performance of 15 government/30 support contractors collaborating with 1,500+ contractors.
- **Orchestrated stellar program performance and cost control,** harvesting 60+ days of margin and reducing schedule erosion from 10+ days per month to less than 1 day per month.
- **Drove completion of a complex system thermal vacuum test,** reducing test window from 125 to 116 days and yielding 108% efficiency.

DEFENSE SECURITY COOPERATION AGENCY (DSCA), *Arlington, VA*
Executive Military Assistant to the Director/Deputy Director   *(10/2006 – 04/2008)*
Selected from among a group of 24 peers as primary advisor to senior agency executives, providing daily and long-range acquisition support and coordination of $21B in new foreign military sales executed by 450 personnel to 200+ countries.

RANDAL L. ASTRO —   Home Phone: 478-742-2442 • Email: info@careerprocenter.net

- **Authored sensitive correspondence** between agency executives and senior military/government leaders, including Joint Staff, Congress, and foreign governments. Coordinated meetings to promote coalitions between senior U.S. government and foreign officials.

PMA-280, Patuxent River, MD
Deputy Program Manager, Tomahawk Program Office *(02/2004 – 03/2006)*
Deputy Program Manager for Tomahawk Advanced Projects and Tactical Tomahawk Torpedo Tube Launched Program, managing development of the nation's most advanced precision weapons system, with a combined value of $300M.

- **Led and directed a 32-member team** in design, development, and testing, overseeing cost, schedule, and performance for a $45M annual budget and values of $100M+ in R&D (production value = $38M annually).
- **Talented negotiator,** instrumental in preserving the UK's commitment to purchase 65 weapons, protecting the $1.6B multiyear procurement supporting the program.

Selected as a United States Naval Candidate for the NASA Manned Space Program (2003).

ACADEMIC ACHIEVEMENTS

Engineer's Degree, Aeronautical & Astronautical Engineering
NAVAL POSTGRADUATE SCHOOL – Monterey, CA

M.S., Aeronautical Engineering
NAVAL POSTGRADUATE SCHOOL – Monterey, CA

Outstanding Thesis Award, Engineer's Program, NAVAL POSTGRADUATE SCHOOL
    Exploration of Fibre Channel as an Avionics Interconnect for the 21st Century Military Aircraft

B.S., Systems Engineering, *Distinguished Graduate; Designated Faculty Candidate*
U.S. NAVAL ACADEMY – Annapolis, MD

ENGINEERING & ACQUISITION ACHIEVEMENTS

Designated Engineering Test Naval Flight Officer
USN Test Pilot School – Patuxent River, MD
Final Project – "Flight Test of F-4G Wild Weasel Aircraft"

Specialty Training
Program Manager Course (PMT 401); Defense Acquisition University (DAU)
U.S. Government Executive and Defense Industry Course (SAM-E)
International Program Security Requirements Course (IPSR)
Missile Technology and Control Regime (MTCR)

Acquisition Certifications/Affiliations
DAWIA Level III: Program Management; Test & Evaluation
DAWIA Level I: Business, Cost Estimating, and Financial Management; Information Technology; Systems Planning, Research, Development, & Engineering
Level I: International Affairs Certification

AWARDS

Defense Meritorious Service Award (2);
Meritorious Service Award; Navy Commendation Award (2)
Navy Achievement Award (4)
Awarded NRO Silver Medal by Director, National Reconnaissance Office
Order of the Daedalians & Edward Heinemann Award

JAMES HELWIG

SAFETY ■ OPERATIONS ■ PROGRAM MANAGER
Inspecting and Reporting ... Decision Making ... Process Improvement

■ Active Top Secret/SCI Clearance ■

Meticulous program and safety management professional with 20 years' experience improving processes and procedures while ensuring compliance with quality and safety requirements.

- **Safety Management:** Directed group's safety program, identifying and mitigating risk to more than 700 personnel, 7 organizations, and $416M in assets.

- **Planning and Coordination:** Developed air refueling plan for continuous air coverage for the President of the United States and 11 other Heads of State.

- **Operations Management:** Led 75-person planning group in improving program performance and accomplishing 100% of mission objectives.

"[James is a] phenomenal officer; #1 officer of all I have worked with in my 15 years in the Air Force."
~ HAROLD ADAMS, Major USAF, Operations Planning Director

PROFESSIONAL EXPERIENCE

U.S. AIR FORCE (USAF), 08/1991 to Present
Government Flight Representative, Defense Contract Management Agency, Lake Charles, LA   04/2011 to Present
Develop safety program to identify hazards and mitigate risk during depot-level maintenance, repairs, and test flights for KC-10 Extender and E-8C Joint Surveillance Target Attack Radar System (STARS) aircraft. Analyze and evaluate the effectiveness of program operations for two contracts worth $4.9B. Inspect and evaluate activities to determine compliance with contract regulations, procedures, and sound management and quality practices. Complete mishap and accident summaries and issue corrective action reports, as required, to inform contractors of needed safety improvements.

Accomplishments:
- Adapted quickly to new role, creating procedures to reduce risk to personnel and aircraft and leading to the safe delivery of 14 KC-10 and 10E-8C aircraft per year.
- Identified need for new lightening safety procedures; coordinated with contractor to initiate necessary improvements.

Delivery Control Manager, Ramstein Air Base (AB), Germany   06/2008 to 04/2011
Planned and coordinated the delivery of aircraft to exercises and contingency operations throughout Europe, the Middle East, and Africa. Planned mission route and handled all airspace and diplomatic clearances. Adapted plans to meet unexpected delays or problems, including aircraft at divert sites, severe weather, and maintenance issues. Led short-notice movements vital for combat aircraft maintenance. Demonstrated outstanding oral communication skills and ability to handle sensitive, high-visibility operations with officials from 16 foreign countries.

Accomplishments:
- Directed movement of 406 aircraft on 58 assignments, supporting operations in Iraq and Afghanistan.
- Delivered F-16 Block 50 aircraft to Pakistan, handling sensitive diplomatic issues.
- Adapted to unexpected contingencies such as providing tanker support to six F-16 aircraft at three divert sites or twelve F-18s needed for operations in Afghanistan.
- Provided executive-level briefings and written reports for Special Forces leaders, improving situational awareness.

173 Pierce Avenue | Macon, GA 31204 | 478-742-2442| info@careerprocenter.net

JAMES HELWIG

Operations Manager, Ramstein AB, Germany   5/2005 to 6/2008

Managed aerial refueling operations in Europe, directing the utilization of 15 aerial refueling aircraft worth more than $840M. Tasked high-priority missions to ensure national security objectives, prioritizing air refueling, airlift, and operational support missions. Identified resources, including staff, funding, and equipment required to support varied levels of program operations. Developed air refueling policy and procedures for European operations, gathering and integrating input from 12 agencies. Streamlined processes, improving aircrew alert times and Command and Control (C2) scheduling.

Accomplishments:

- Directed 4.1K KC-135 aerial refueling flights, ensuring the ability of U.S. aircraft to meet all objectives.
- Orchestrated short-notice refueling of MC-130 aircraft, evacuating 140 U.S. citizens during Noncombatant Evacuation Operations (NEO) from Lebanon.
- Planned and scheduled refueling operations, enabling the movement of medical teams throughout Tanzania and Liberia for a six-location Presidential tour in Africa.
- Developed air refueling plan for continuous air coverage for the President of the United States and 11 other Heads of State.

Safety Manager, 85th Group, Keflavik, Iceland   5/2001 to 5/2005

Directed group's safety program, identifying and mitigating risk to more than 700 personnel, 7 organizations, and $416M in assets. Conducted various safety inspections, ensuring compliance with Department of Defense (DoD), Occupational Safety and Health Administration (OSHA), and Air Force (AF) requirements for F-15, KC-135, MC-130, and HH-60 aircraft operations.

Accomplishments:

- Led group to a zero percent ground mishap rate—the best in the AF.
- Oversaw 2.2K HH-60 hours, 1.5K F-15 flights, and 679 KC-135 aerial refuelings with zero class A or B mishaps.
- Analyzed HH-60 mishap, identifying fleet-wide problem and initiating appropriate technical fix.
- Coordinated with civil aviation; devised air-collision avoidance procedures, improving awareness of AF flights nationwide.
- Rewrote Mishap Response Plan, adapting the plan to organizational, staffing, and manning changes.

EDUCATION

Master's Degree in Aeronautical Science (2004)
EMBRY-RIDDLE AERONAUTICAL UNIVERSITY, Daytona Beach, FL, GPA: 3.8

Bachelor's Degree in Political Science (1991)
UNIVERSITY OF TEXAS, Austin, TX

AWARDS & SPECIAL ACCOMPLISHMENTS

Meritorious Service Medal (4) ■ Air Medal ■ Aerial Achievement Medal (3) ■ AF Commendation Medal (3)
Joint Service Achievement Medal ■ AF Achievement Medal ■ AF Organizational Excellence Award
National Defense Service Medal (2) ■ Global War on Terrorism Service Medal
Department of the Navy Safety Excellence Award, 2004 ■ USAF Flying Safety Plaque, 2004
SAF Europe Safety Outstanding Unit Award, 2003 ■ USAFE Tactical Deception Officer of the Year, 2003

---

173 Pierce Avenue | Macon, GA 31204 | 478-742-2442 | info@careerprocenter.net

ANDRE FIAMMETTA

173 Pierce Avenue | Macon, GA 31024 | 478-742-2442 | info@careerprocenter.net

DETAIL-ORIENTED AND RESULTS-DRIVEN LEADER WITH 15+ YEARS OF AIRCRAFT MAINTENANCE , 7 YEARS OF AIRCRAFT LOGISTICS MANAGEMENT, AND 8+ YEARS OF NETWORK ADMINISTRATION/INFORMATION TECHNOLOGY IMPLEMENTATION AND CUSTOMER SUPPORT/HELP-DESK EXPERIENCE.

AIRCRAFT MAINTENANCE

TS/SCI Security Clearance valid through 07/2013 (SSBI)

- Strategic Planning
- Program Management
- Aircraft Maintenance
- Communication and Coordination
- Analysis and Evaluation
- Inspection and Assessment
- System Integration
- Avionics Equipment
- Subject Matter Expert

- **Aircraft Maintenance Operations:** Experienced in aircraft maintenance and testing operations, utilizing budgets of up to $77M. Hands-on maintenance experience with F-16A-D (7 years), F-15A-E (7 years), RQ-4 Global Hawk (4 years), and U-2S Dragonlady (1 year) airframes.

- **Program Management:** Recognized for developing a complex aircraft test plan; successfully supported a congressionally mandated $4.5B Acquisition Category (ACAT) I program that encompassed 222 C-130 Hercules aircraft.

- **Problem Solving:** Revealed an RQ-4A Global Hawk explosive/fire hazard at a Forward Operating Base (FOB); developed solution within a 12-hour timeframe, allowed resumption of worldwide USAF RQ-4A Global Hawk flight operations.

- **Analysis and Evaluation:** Lauded for leading and directing vital compliance program inspection preparations; garnered an overall "Excellent" rating from Headquarters' (HQ) inspection team.

PROFESSIONAL EXPERIENCE & ACHIEVEMENTS

TEST AIRCRAFT SUPPORT CHIEF   11/2010 to Present
United States Air Force (USAF), Buckley Air Force Base (AFB), CO

Provide broad-scope oversight production activities for 60 uniquely configured test aircraft fleet valued at $16.9B. Lead and mentor 485 civilian personnel executing maintenance operations for USAF, Department of Defense (DoD), and Joint Service flight testing and evaluation support objectives.

- Manage an operating budget of $54M in support of high-priority USAF assignments.
- Serve as primary advisor to four distinct aircraft maintenance teams.
- Reinforce 150 sustainment and developmental testing programs; mentored personnel and provided informal On the Job (OJT) training and development.

Accomplishments:
- → Led logistics compliance program inspection preparations; garnered an overall "Excellent" rating from inspection team.
- → Recognized for maintaining a 94% QA pass rate by creating Technical Order usage enforcement structures.

AIRCRAFT MAINTENANCE LEAD   10/2009 to 11/2010
USAF, King Khalid Air Base (AB), Saudi Arabia

Provided leadership to, and enforced maintenance discipline for, 186 Airmen and 30 contract personnel serving in 20 unique USAF career specialties to sustain a $1.5B U-2S Dragonlady fleet, sensors, and related equipment. Managed execution for the removal and replacement of components, composite parts, and assemblies; upkeep of aircraft systems; and maintenance of support equipment.

- Conducted periodic inspections and overhauled and updated systems as defined by engineering partners.
- Maintained engineering drawings, schematics, specifications, technical guides, and manuals.
- Performed detailed analysis and evaluation of QA maintenance directives with follow-up corrective actions.

ANDRE FIAMMETTA, AIRCRAFT MAINTENANCE CHIEF, PAGE 2
(478) 742-2442 | info@careerprocenter.net

Accomplishments:
- → Provided quality maintenance leadership to subordinates; unit passed 720 of 767 quality maintenance inspections; sustained "Excellent" 93.9% QA pass rate.
- → Led mid-level managers in personnel and equipment resource management; reduced deferred aircraft discrepancies by 25%, lowest in worldwide U-2S Dragonlady fleet.

AIRCRAFT TEST & EVALUATION DIRECTOR   04/2006 to 10/2009
UNITED STATES AIR FORCE (USAF), Bolling AFB, Washington, DC

Led high-priority Operational Test and Evaluation (OT&E) activities utilizing the specialized skills of 229 military and civilian personnel. Expertly planned test preparations for 15 DoD acquisition programs valued at $29B.

- • Provided subject matter expertise to Air Mobility Command (AMC) personnel on logistic suitability supporting USAF and Joint Forces testing for a $77M evaluation program.

Accomplishments:
- → Reviewed and validated unit-level manpower utilization; eliminated six excess duty positions.
- → Developed a complex C-130 Hercules Avionics Modernization Program test plan; successfully supported a congressionally mandated $4.5B Acquisition Category (ACAT) I program that encompassed 222 aircraft.

UNMANNED TEST DIVISION MANAGER   10/2004 to 04/2006
USAF, Andrews AFB, MD

Oversaw a multiorganizational team of 75 specialized personnel executing test activities on Unmanned Aerial Vehicle (UAV) programs. Created and incorporated methodology utilized to assess operational supportability, maintainability, reliability, and availability of a variety of unmanned aircraft.

- • Led congressionally mandated RQ-4 Global Hawk and MQ-9 Reaper acquisition efforts valued at $7.7B+.
- • Led Avionics Modernization Program recovery effort; enabled $204M acquisition program to resume.
- • Provided oversight of contractor Technical Order validations; supported an $11B acquisition decision.

Accomplishments:
- → Revealed an RQ-4A Global Hawk explosive/fire hazard at FOB; developed a solution within a 12-hour timeframe; efforts allowed resumption of worldwide Global Hawk flight operations.
- → Saved $500K asset; identified RQ-4 Global Hawk ground station design flaw, leading to emergency Time Compliant Technical Order distribution and implementation.
- → Eliminated 720 flight test hours and 11K man-hours. Efforts saved $14M in maintenance costs.

EDUCATION AND PROFESSIONAL DEVELOPMENT

Gotham University – Bachelor's Degree in Engineering Management (12/2003)

Community College of the Air Force – Associate Degree in Avionic Technologies (5/1996)

Acquisition Profession Development Program Certifications: Level I and Level II Test & Evaluation (T&E); Level I Flight Test; Level I Life Cycle Logistics; Level I Program Management; Level I Systems Planning, Research, Development, & Engineering

Computer Software: Expert in Microsoft Word, Excel, PowerPoint, Outlook, Project, and SharePoint.

AWARDS AND HONORS

Air Force Achievement Medal (1st and 2nd oak leaf clusters)
Air Force Commendation Medal (1st oak leaf cluster)
Meritorious Service Medal (1st, 2nd, and 3rd oak leaf clusters)

HENRY JOSELIO

173 Pierce Avenue | Macon, GA 31042 | 478-742-2442 | info@careerprocenter.net

AIRCRAFT MAINTENANCE OPERATIONS & MANAGMENT

- Strategic Planning
- Work Process Analysis
- Heavy and Corrective Maintenance
- Contracting and Acquisitions
- Inventory Schedules
- Personnel Management

- Aircraft Maintenance Management professional with four years of experience in industrial property management and aircraft/equipment maintenance.

- Active Secret Security Clearance.

- Completed four lifecycle phases of project management, as specified by Project Management Institute, and certified to work on all air frames, both rotary and fixed wing.

- Senior technical expert for quality assurance, safety, and risk management.

PROFESSIONAL EXPERIENCE & ACHIEVEMENTS

AIRCRAFT MECHANIC, UNITED STATES ARMY   **09/2007 to Present**

Assist in implementing and ensuring compliance with preventive and corrective maintenance programs for UH-60 Blackhawk helicopters. Have provided additional support by overseeing management and maintenance of ground support equipment, which entailed supervising and directing 100+ personnel.

MAINTENANCE

- Troubleshoot and maintain aircraft structures, subsystems, and components.
- Utilize solid understanding of electrical/mechanical/hydraulic/pneumatic systems and knowledge of safety and security regulations, practices, and procedures.
- Ensure physical/mechanical integrity, complete functionality, and operational readiness of billion-dollar aircraft and aerospace ground equipment; implement and manage preventive and corrective maintenance programs.
- Assist with special inspections, and conduct pre-flight, through-flight, post-flight, and isochronal inspections.
- Remove and install aircraft subsystem assemblies, such as engines, transmissions, gear boxes, rotor hubs and blades, and mechanical flight controls, and their components. Service and lubricate aircraft and subsystems.
- Perform backline repairs and operational checks on flight control surfaces, cockpit control leavers, including flap/slat, main landing gear, spoiler handles, cargo doors, and main landing gear components.
- Adjust, align, rig, and calibrate aircraft systems; make engine throttle adjustments; and service aircraft with fuel, lox, and nitrogen.

QUALITY CONTROL AND ADMINISTRATION

- Prepare forms and records related to aircraft maintenance, serve as air crewmember, and provide technical guidance to subordinate personnel.
- Alter or modify material according to approved modification work orders.
- Requisition and maintain inventory of shop and bench stock for repairing aircraft avionics equipment.
- Planned and organized work assignments by determining resources, materials, number of subordinates, and types of skills required to maintain balanced workload, accomplish goals, and meet long-range work schedules.
- Facilitated changes that ensured work proceeded in accordance with regulatory requirements, organizational standards, and performance plans.

EDUCATION & PROFESSIONAL DEVELOPMENT

Diploma, McLoud High School, McLoud, OK
UH-60 Helicopter Repairer, 04/2008; HAZMAT Familiarization and Safety in Transportation, 08/2008

AWARDS & SPECIAL ACCOMPLISHMENTS

Army Commendation Medal, Army Good Conduct Medal, National Defense Service Medal, Kuwait Defense Service Medal, Global War on Terrorism Service Medal, Army Service Ribbon, Overseas Service Ribbon

JOHN V. SANTOS

COMMUNICATIONS SYSTEMS SPECIALIST

173 Pierce Avenue, Macon, GA 31204
478-742-2442
info@careerprocenter.net

*Results-oriented professional with active Secret Security Clearance and hands-on experience
in communication technology, evaluating, analyzing, maintaining, and repairing
communications systems and expertise in electronics training.*

■

- ☑ **Perform installation, operation, and maintenance of multifunctional/multiuser communications and information processing systems,** providing support for critical Command and Control (C2) systems and peripheral equipment.

- ☑ **Led and developed teams with innovative ideas and drive to succeed;** hands-on, extensive experience in testing, maintaining, troubleshooting, and repairing avionic, electronic communications, and network systems; experience includes various radio and radiotelephone systems.

- ☑ **Demonstrated knowledge of current developments and trends in communications, concepts, and technology;** hands-on experience with analog and digital logic and circuits; DC, AC, and solid state theory; computer and network systems, and satellite, telephone, and radio communications systems.

CAREER HISTORY AND ACHIEVEMENTS

AVIONICS/ELECTRONICS INSTRUCTOR, United States Army, Fort Gordon, GA   **04/2009 to Present**
Implement training program to train electronics professionals on the installation, operation, and maintenance of aircraft electronic equipment and systems; provide training to address combining of air and ground elements. Plan and manage training activities, ensuring adherence to the training budget, monitoring the use of training materials and supplies, and initiating procurement to ensure sufficient quantities.

- ☑ Ensure the availability of training resources and participate in developing training curriculum to improve training capabilities and reduce training costs.
- ☑ Use a variety of techniques and methods, such as classroom lectures, hands-on activities in a laboratory environment, and field work-based learning, to ensure trainees understand the material.
- ☑ Lecture trainees on electronics theories and application techniques used in the field.
- ☑ Secure funding for the preparation of training and provided justification for the procurement of training materials.
- ☑ Establish policies, procedures, and objectives for training plans, developed and maintained information, issued status reports, and initiated activities to improve operation effectiveness.

COMMUNICATIONS SYSTEM REPAIRER, United States Army, Fort Gordon, GA   **06/2007 to 02/2009**
Deployed to Iraq as an Avionics Communications Equipment Repairer, performing electronics system installation, maintenance, and repair, ensuring the highest level of communications support for 152 helicopters. Supervised the activities of four personnel and provided technical guidance to subordinates performing maintenance/repair of aircraft comm. equipment.

- ☑ Maintained communications systems, verified maintenance forms and records, monitored and enforced shop safety, and accounted for more than $700K worth of technical equipment.
- ☑ Supervised team throughout all aspects of Aviation Intermediate Maintenance, increasing in the section's overall productivity rate by 10%; ensured the integrity of communications security systems.

EDUCATION AND TRAINING

New York State University of Georgia/Business, South, Georgia, 1998
*Leadership Development Course; Electronics Maintenance Advanced Leader Course;
Avionics Communication Repairer Course; General Radiophone Operator License*

AWARDS AND RECOGNITION

Army Achievement Medal (3); Army Commendation Medal (3);
Global War on Terrorism (GWOT) Expeditionary Medal; GWOT Service Medal

---

JAMES D. VICTORY, SR., COLONEL, USA

173 Pierce Avenue ■ Macon, GA 31204
Cell: 478-742-2442
Email: info@careerprocenter.net

Senior Executive: COO / CAO / CKO

Quality Assurance ■ Change Management ■ Operational Efficiency ■ Strategic Planning ■ International Liaisons

Dynamic, pragmatic, results-oriented executive leading demanding and complex organizations. Catalyst for change management and process improvement with current posting in the Department of Defense (DoD) Inspector General's office. Demonstrate strong bias for action and aggressively drive development of vision statements, strategic plans, recruiting and training programs, quality control, and marketing initiatives to reinforce organizational growth and performance.

Administrative excellence and quality focused...background in regulatory and government affairs as well as facilities and human capital management. Facile communicator with direct experience at the Cabinet and Executive Branch level. Flexible and adaptive with cross-cultural expertise...**international engagements** include projects in Baghdad, Kosovo, Bosnia, and Saudi Arabia and long-term assignments to Japan, Italy, and Saudi Arabia. Fast-track promotions to Colonel in the U.S. Army. Currently hold Top Secret/SCI security clearance.

SELECTED EXPERIENCE AND ACHIEVEMENTS

Department of the Army Inspector General (IG), Maryland Military Department, Baltimore, MD, 12/2007 to Present
Advise National Guard CEO on business performance of a department that fulfills state and federal missions as part of nation's "citizen-soldier" corps.

CHIEF QUALITY ASSURANCE INSPECTOR (INSPECTOR GENERAL/IG)
Operational Audits | Investigations Coordination | Evaluation & Process Improvement | Regulatory Compliance
Lead independent fact-finding investigations, inquiries, and inspections for all of the organization's operations, including areas of policy compliance; fraud, waste, and abuse; human capital resources; and overall operational efficiency. Expertly analyze inefficiencies or process failures and develop strategic recommendations for senior leaders to mitigate outstanding issues.

- Performed physical security inspections for major Army commands. Identified inefficiencies and obstacles, and provided sample tactics, techniques, and procedures to divisional CEOs for inclusion in security programs.
- Overhauled two key human resources systems: Individual Personnel Management Records System and an internal Headquarters (HQ) system processing military service members qualifying for pay/compensation due to injury or illness.
- Achieved certification as DoD, Army, and Air Force Inspector General (IG) via executive-level IG training.
- Orchestrated organizational audits and provided report findings and recommendations for improving recruiting, training, retention, information assurance, suicide prevention, and readiness and emergency management procedures.
- Created a multimedia after-action review of the organization's support to the 2009 Presidential Inauguration.

Multi-National Forces – Iraq, Baghdad (Operation Iraqi Freedom)   Baghdad, Iraq, 06/2007 to 10/2007
Coalition Forces operating in the Global War on Terrorism

CHIEF OF OPERATIONS
Analysis & Advisement | Planning & Training | Policy Development
Executed supervision of 85-person Strategic Operations Center in Baghdad during deployment. In a demanding and high-intensity environment, directed the integration of all operational divisions for Multi-National Forces – Iraq (Coalition Forces).

JAMES D. VICTORY, SR.   Cell: 478-742-2442 ▪ info@careerprocenter.net

- Drove critical process improvements. Built new set of Standard Operating Procedures (SOPs) detailing 17 separate potential threat scenarios and outlining response strategies. Created synergy between operational divisions and a framework for knowledge management that would transcend frequent personnel changes in a war theater.

United States Forces, Japan   **Yokota AB, Japan, 04/2004 to 04/2007**
U.S. Armed Forces tasked with defending Japan in close cooperation with the Japan Self-Defense forces – maritime defense, ballistic missile defense, domestic air control, communications security, and disaster response operations.

DEPUTY DIRECTOR, OPERATIONS
International Responses and Coordination | Operational Efficiency | Quality Control | Training Plans
Led central coordination for military projects/operations and Joint Operations Center branches for U.S. Forces Japan. Expertly liaised with U.S. and Japanese government agencies and organizations (e.g., Office of the Secretary of Defense, Joint Staff, American Embassy, Japanese Staff Office, and others) to manage high-profile military exercises, events, and exigent circumstances within the Pacific Region. Developed and supervised business processes to bolster performance. Executive responsibility for the Directorate's $300K budget. Acted as Director in his absence.

- Formed Operational Planning Team to develop Emergency Action Plans that became the operational foundation for U.S. Forces Japan's responses to crises/events. Vetted plan during the 2006 real-world North Korean missile threats.
- Revitalized training curricula, tying instructional objectives to real-world missions. Directed successful bilateral senior-leader weapons defense seminar currently being emulated by Office of the Secretary of Defense leaders.
- Designed U.S. humanitarian responses to both major Japanese earthquake and Asian Tsunami, securing approval for crisis action plan from the Secretary of Defense within 36 hours of the event. Results: Tremendously positive response from Japanese citizens.

U.S. Army Recruiting Organization (3rd Recruiting Brigade)   **Fort Knox, MI, 04/2002 to 04/2004**
Tasked with building a population of new recruits for active duty Army service.

RECRUITING BATTALION COMMANDER (CEO)
Sales & Marketing | Operations & Logistics | Building Coalitions | Diversity
Led 300 Army employees, including Department of the Army civilians, throughout 7 sub-organizations and 57 recruiting stations effectively organized across the state of Michigan.

- Expertly managed $2.1M organizational budget; obtained 60% of the DoD market share of recruits with 40% fewer recruiters than other military services.
- Directed operations/maintenance of 67 facilities and 250 vehicles in harsh environment. Oversaw logistical functions associated with recruiting sales, including vehicle provisioning, gas cards, technology, and multimedia equipment.

EDUCATION   **MA,** LOUISIANA STATE UNIVERSITY, Baton Rouge, LA
                         BA, History, THOMAS E. EDISON STATE COLLEGE, Trenton, NJ

PROFESSIONAL DEVELOPMENT   **2008** – DOD Combatant Command and Joint Inspector General Course; Air Force Installation Inspector General Training Course; **2007** – US. Army Inspector General's Course; **1997** – Senior Strategic Management Course

AWARDS   Defense Superior Service Award; Meritorious Service Award (7); Army Commendation Award (3); Army Achievement Award (4); Army Superior Unit Award; Joint Meritorious Unit Award; Global War on Terrorism Award; Humanitarian Service Award

DEREK SANTIAGO, COLONEL, USA

173 Pierce Ave ▪ Macon, GA 31204
Cell (478) 742-2442 ▪ Work (478) 742-2882
info@careerprocenter.net

EXECUTIVE MANAGEMENT/CHIEF OPERATING OFFICER/PROGRAMS AND PROJECT LEADER

Executive manager offering 29+ years experience across diverse operational venues. Project-oriented, visualizing results to create dynamic strategic plans. Adroitly manage resources and balance human capital alignments. Experience with budgets exceeding $15B. Superior oral and written communication skills, tailoring presentations for senior executives, middle managers, and employees at all levels. Expert collaborator with ability to take charge, build consensus, and inspire cooperation across disparate groups. Top Secret Clearance/SCI.

Human Capital Management	Strategic Planning	Quality Assurance
Plans and Programs	Operations Management	Communications Skills
Budgeting	Coalition Building	Training Initiatives

"Provided the leadership and guidance required to move his team to the next level ... a year marked by significant improvements and above standard performance."

2009 Performance Evaluation, Brigadier General William M. Buckler, Jr.

PROFESSIONAL EXPERIENCE/CAREER HIGHLIGHTS

UNITED STATES ARMY RESERVE – ACTIVE DUTY ASSIGNMENTS	**02/1994 – Present**
UNITED STATES ARMY– ACTIVE DUTY	**11/1981 – 08/1992**

DIRECTOR, *Army Reserve Installation Management (USARIM),* Fort McPherson, GA   03/2010 – Present
Advise the Army Reserve Command Group on coordinating and managing six Army Reserve Installations comprising 264K acres and 140K cross-functional employees required to support the functions and performance of 27K reserve military personnel. Directly coordinate with subordinate managers to oversee activities of up to 1,900 military, 3,300 civilian, and 2,700 contracted personnel. Manage an annual budget of $231M+ and installation assets totaling $2.6B.*

- ▶ Directed development of Training Support Systems, a standardized automated reporting tool, to enable key resourcing decisions affecting reserve training.
- ▶ Monitored and made key recommendations on diverse funding streams supporting Army Reserve Installations.
- ▶ Strengthened communication/coordination between senior installation executives and the Army Reserve staff to resolve operational issues and resourcing decisions.

EXECUTIVE MANAGER (COMMANDER), *412th Engineer Command,* Yongsan, Seoul, Korea   05/2008 – 02/2010
Guided and directed a geographically separated organization providing multidisciplinary engineering services (e.g., construction, infrastructure repair, transportation hub maintenance) for Army assets located in the Pacific region. Adroitly integrated guidance from multiple senior executives to consolidate and enhance administration and management systems. Dual-hatted as Lead Engineer (manager) for the Eighth U.S. Army (EUSA) for ~four months. Accountable to the CEO/Commanding General for analyzing military operations on the Korean peninsula and for planning, coordinating, and overseeing construction projects pivotal to humanitarian/civic action projects throughout the Pacific realm.

- ▶ Managed via subordinate leaders a group of 14 multidisciplinary engineers across the 412th TEC and EUSA, with additional responsibility for approximately 50-75 staff during semiannual military exercises.
- ▶ Employed innovative recruiting methods to staff essential skills sets using expat personnel as well as Korean-American engineering professionals.
- ▶ Implemented Composite Risk Management processes to identify hazards, reduce risk, and prevent both accidental and tactical loss.
- ▶ Implemented training on cutting-edge technologies available from the Army's Engineering Research & Development Center to ensure the highest levels of team readiness.

DEREK SANTIAGO, COLONEL, USA (2)

INSTALLATION CEO (COMMANDER), Fort McCoy, WI   06/2005 – 04/2008
Managed the only U.S. Army Installation in Wisconsin, encompassing 60K+ acres valued at $50M. Executed an annual budget exceeding $231M and managed physical plant valued at $1.3B+ and cross-functional staff of 1,660 civilian employees and 45 permanently assigned military staff working across 18 cross-disciplinary business units.

▶ Led the military equivalent of a small city engaged in training events conducted in a four-season climate for 150K cross-service personnel to support and ensure readiness for military operations worldwide.

▶ Directed the operations, maintenance, and performance of modern rail and air capabilities, equipment storage sites, and materiel maintenance capabilities. Stewarded 46K acres of federal maneuver and training land.

▶ Spearheaded the mobilization/demobilization of 215 military units and more than 13K personnel to support the Global War on Terrorism (GWOT) being prosecuted in Iraq and Afghanistan.

▶ Optimized resources to drive multimillion-dollar infrastructure renovations to rehab aging WWII-era facilities.

Sr. USAR Program Manager, Headquarters, U.S. Army Corps of Engineers, Washington, DC   06/2004 – 06/2005
Directed the effective use of U.S. Army Reserve personnel in their support role to the U.S. Army Corps of Engineers (USACE) mission, particularly in construction projects related to the GWOT.

▶ Ensured mobilized personnel received appropriate authorizations, documentation, and resources to allow smooth transit to overseas contingency operational areas (both combat and support bases).

▶ Built collaborative networks with the Army Engineer School, Office of Chief Engineers – Pentagon, Office of Command, Army Reserves, and USACE/ENCOM to enhance approaches to engineering problems and issues.

CEO (Commander), 448th Engineer Battalion, Fort Buchanan, Puerto Rico   08/2001 – 07/2003
Led activities and performance of an 876-member engineer organization capable of constructing, rehabilitating, repairing, maintaining, or modifying diverse infrastructure elements. Managed organic maintenance capabilities valued at more than $2B. Directed training of up to 7 units focused primarily on construction and tactical engineering support. Enhanced human resource management via targeted programs to recruit, retain, and build staff performance.

▶ Reduced employee attrition from 14.7% to an average of 6.9%—the lowest rate within the Puerto Rican Regional Support Command. Increased overall personnel strength by 10% and improved the recovery rate of Potential-No-Show soldiers to 45%.

▶ Reduced the number of late performance evaluations for management personnel from 17 to 2.

EDUCATION

MS in Strategic Studies, U.S. Army War College, *Carlisle, PA (competitively selected for the 10-month program)*
BBA in Management, North Georgia College and State University, *Dahlonega,* GA

ADDITIONAL GRADUATE STUDIES AND LEADERSHIP TRAINING
University of Alaska, *Fairbanks, AK:* Accounting for Engineers
Murray State University, *Murray, KY:* Materials Management; Plant Layout and Materials Handling
U.S. Army: Strategic Management Course, including Quantitative Decision Making; Engineer Manager's Advanced Course; Junior Manager's Maintenance Course
U.S. Army Corps of Engineers: Computer Applications for Engineers/Engineer Managers; Economic Analysis for Military Construction Projects; General Construction Inspection; Economic Studies: Principles and Practices for Civil Engineering and Applications

---

AWARDS AND COMMENDATIONS

Legion of Merit; Meritorious Service Awards (6); Army Commendation Medal (6); Army Achievement Medal
Awards recognized superior performance as a leader and manager, including service overseas

---

GINA MARBURY, COLONEL, USA (RETIRED)

(478) 742-2442

123 Pierce Ave., Macon, GA 31210

gina.marbury@careerprocenter.net

~ HUMAN CAPITAL MANAGEMENT ~

**Strategic Planning & Vision | Human Capital Management | Process Innovation
Collaboration & Negotiation | Crisis & Action Planning
Resource Management | Executive Coalition Building
Top Secret/SCI Clearance, valid until June 2011**

Legislative Savvy

Recognized leadership in creating the most sweeping legislative changes since World War II to enhance educational benefits, promote retention, and improve quality of life for military personnel/families.

Human Capital Programs

Sophisticated knowledge of planning and managing human capital initiatives, assessing staff requirements, planning benefits, and gaining executive support for cutting-edge decisions.

Innovative Management

MA in Management, with record of accomplishment as a change catalyst, experienced across all organizational levels. Proven success in diverse environments, including combat theaters.

"... Outstanding leadership, knowledge, and tenacity were instrumental in transforming the Army's officer personnel management system." 2009 Performance Evaluation

SELECTED PROFESSIONAL HIGHLIGHTS

UNITED STATES ARMY, RETIRED as Colonel/O-6 (12/2011)   1977 – 2011

☑ 21 years of Continual Leadership within the U.S. Army, providing human capital policy and programs expertise to support the Army's robust organizational and personnel goals. Direct experience in planning, coordinating, and publishing key policies and regulatory guidance for the Department of Defense (DoD) to guide staffing, recruiting, retention, and benefits planning for the U.S. Army and Army Reserve Components.

ASSISTANT LEAD, Human Capital Core Enterprise, Office of the Chief, Army Reserve, Pentagon, DC   2010 – 2011

Hand-selected to manage Army Reserve Family Programs, which serve 205K full- and part-time personnel in 4,000+ locations worldwide. Conceived, built, and implemented suites of focused Human Resources (HR) programs that enriched and supported the health and welfare of military personnel and families.

❖ Led organizational change to reorient Family Programs to a customer-focused, field-based organization.
❖ Coordinated complex, sophisticated Management Decision Packages budgeted at $15M+ to ensure appropriate resource allocation for HR program execution.
❖ Implemented process improvements to increase personnel levels from 45% to 60% within four months. Saved significant monies by completing an initial phase to in-source personnel, converting contractor positions to Army civilian slots in only 90 days.

DIRECTOR, Defense Intelligence Support Office-Iraq, Office of Chief, Army Reserve, Washington, DC 2009 – 2010
In a deployed capacity, **supervised, directed, and controlled 200 Defense Intelligence Agency (DIA) personnel** serving in a combat area with U.S. Forces-Iraq and Multi-National Forces-Iraq. Coordinated with British and Australian partners to enhance intelligence support to military decision makers. Managed diverse functions to ensure intelligence personnel successfully transited in and out of the war theater.

GINA MARBURY	gina.marbury@careerprocenter.net	(478) 742-2442	Page 2

❖ Built an internal database personnel management system to track and account for 200+ personnel. System selected for use as DIA personnel management system-of-record to track and account for deployed staff.

❖ Tracked and accounted for hundreds of military, civilian, and contractor personnel to realize a 90% fill rate for intelligence roles in the combat theater.

❖ Awarded the **Bronze Star Medal** in recognition of expert human capital program management, including superior strategic planning processes and outstanding executive leadership.

ASS'T HR DIRECTOR (MILITARY), Office of the Ass't Secretary of Defense for Reserve Affairs, Washington, DC   2007 – 2009
Technical HR Expert providing legislative and statutory guidance related to National Guard and Reserve Educational Assistance Programs (e.g., Student Loan Repayment Program, ROTC, and voluntary education programs), incentive pay programs, and other initiatives designed to enhance recruiting and retention within the Army Reserve and National Guard.

❖ Successfully advocated to reengineer Montgomery GI Bill-Selected Reserve and Reserve Education Assistance Program, preparing testimony, correspondence, metrics, and other supporting data for congressional review.

❖ Provided critical input to 2008 National Defense Authorization Act, addressing military personnel planning, tuition assistance, and transfer of critical education issues affecting Army reservists to Department of Veterans Affairs.

DIRECTOR, Officer Career Policy Branch, HR Directorate (Military Personnel), Washington, DC   2004 – 2007
Led an elite group of Army HR specialists in planning, developing, and/or updating HR policy to align management systems with current requirements and the evolving Army mission, which included ongoing responses to overseas contingency operations.

❖ Planned, wrote, and updated policy, processes, and career progression guidance for building and retaining the military officer corps.

❖ Developed and submitted pioneering legislative changes relating to military officer career policy that optimized conditions for Army Reserve Officers, creating greater parity for these mid- and upper-level managers. **Created more legislative and policy changes in 12 months than in the previous 10 years.**

❖ Developed recruiting strategies that commissioned 10K+ new military officers. Built the "Blue to Green" program to transition officers leaving the Navy or Air Force for the Army, commissioning 71 officers from sister services at a cost savings of more than $14M.

HR STRATEGIC PLANS MANAGER, Strategic HR Readiness and Transformation Group, Washington, DC   2003 – 2004
Analyzed HR programs and offered technical advice on building, developing, and coordinating new strategies for transforming the Army's personnel system. Researched, analyzed, and coordinated HR initiatives that met the personal and professional needs of military personnel and families.

❖ Developed measures and metrics for the Army Reserve's Balanced Scorecard.

❖ Represented the Army as a liaison to the DoD Defense Advisory Council on Women in the Service.

Mobilization Officer, Office of the Deputy Chief of Staff for Personnel, Operations, Washington, DC   2001 – 2003
Additional International Experience: **Army HR Specialist:** Bosnia, Hungary, Germany   1996 – 1997

EDUCATION	MA, Management, St. Louis University, St. Louis, MO BA, Sociology, State University of Louisiana, Natchitoches, LA
EXECUTIVE TRAINING & CERTIFICATION	Human Resource Management Certificate, George Mason University Human Resource Management Qualification Course, Army HR Management School Lean Six Sigma White Belt Training
AFFILIATIONS	Society for Human Resource Management (SHRM), Member Military Officers Association of American (MOAA), Lifetime Member Reserve Officers Association (ROA), Lifetime Member Association of the United States Army (AUSA), Lifetime Member Council of College and Military Educators (CCME)
RECOGNITION	Bronze Star Medal (2010); Defense Meritorious Service Medal; Office of the Secretary of Defense Staff Identification Badge; Meritorious Service Medal (3); Army Commendation Medal (3); Global War on Terrorism Service Medal

GABRIELLA SANTOS, COLONEL, USA (RETIRED)   (478) 742-2442

123 Pierce Ave., Macon, GA 31210   gina.marbury@careerprocenter.net

~ HUMAN RESOURCES PROGRAMS MANAGER ~

**Strategic Planning & Vision | Human Capital Management | Process Innovation
Collaboration & Negotiation | Crisis & Action Planning
Resource Management | Executive Coalition Building
Top Secret/SCI Clearance, current**

Legislative Savvy

Recognized leadership in creating the most sweeping legislative changes since World War II to enhance educational benefits, promote retention, and improve quality of life for military personnel/families.

Human Capital Programs

Sophisticated knowledge of planning and managing human capital initiatives, assessing staff requirements, planning benefits, and gaining executive support for cutting-edge decisions.

Innovative Management

MA in Management, with record of accomplishment as a change catalyst; experience across all organizational levels. Proven success in diverse environments, including combat theaters.

"... Outstanding leadership, knowledge, and tenacity were instrumental in transforming the Army's officer personnel management system." 2009 Performance Evaluation

SELECTED PROFESSIONAL HIGHLIGHTS

UNITED STATES ARMY, RETIRED as Colonel/O-6 (12/2011)   1977 – 2011

☑ ***21 years of Continual Leadership*** *within the U.S. Army, providing human capital policy and programs expertise to support the Army's robust organizational and personnel goals. Direct experience in planning, coordinating, and publishing key policies and regulatory guidance for the Department of Defense (DoD) to guide staffing, recruiting, retention, and benefits planning for the U.S. Army and Army Reserve Components.*

ASSISTANT LEAD, Human Capital Enterprise, Army Reserve Headquarters, Hampton, VA   2010 – 2011

Hand-selected to manage Army Reserve Family Programs, which serve 200K+ full- and part-time personnel in 4,500+ locations worldwide. Conceived, built, and implemented suites of focused Human Resources (HR) programs that enriched and supported the health and welfare of military personnel and families.

❖ Led organizational change to reorient Family Support Programs to become customer-focused.
❖ Coordinated complex, sophisticated Management Packages budgeted at $17M+ to ensure appropriate resource allocation for HR program execution.
❖ Implemented process improvements to increase personnel levels from 50% to 65% within four months. Saved significant monies by completing an initial phase to in-source personnel, converting contractor positions to Army civilian slots in only 60 days.

DIRECTOR, Defense Intelligence Support Office-Iraq, Army Reserve, Washington, DC   2009 – 2010
In a deployed capacity, **supervised, directed, and controlled 250 Intelligence Agency personnel** serving in a combat area with U.S. Forces-Iraq and Multi-National Forces-Iraq. Coordinated with Coalition partners to enhance intelligence support to military decision makers. Managed diverse functions to ensure intelligence personnel successfully transited in and out of the war theater.

| **GABRIELLA SANTOS** | info@careerprocenter.net | ☎ (478) 742-2442 | **Page 2** |

- ❖ Built an internal personnel management system to track and account for 300+ personnel. System selected for use as Intelligence Agency personnel management system-of-record to track and account for deployed staff.
- ❖ Tracked and accounted for hundreds of military, civilian, and contractor personnel to realize a 95% fill rate for intelligence roles in the combat theater.
- ❖ Awarded the **Bronze Star Medal** in recognition of expert human capital program management, including superior strategic planning processes and outstanding executive leadership.

ASS'T HR DIRECTOR, Office of the Ass't Secretary of Defense for Reserve Affairs, Washington, DC   2007 – 2009
Technical HR Expert providing legislative and statutory guidance related to National Guard and Reserve Educational Assistance Programs (e.g., Student Loan Repayment Program, ROTC, and voluntary education programs), incentive pay programs, and other initiatives designed to enhance recruiting and retention within the Army Reserve and National Guard.
- ❖ Successfully advocated to reengineer Montgomery GI Bill, preparing testimony, correspondence, metrics, and other supporting data for congressional review.
- ❖ Provided critical input to 2008 Defense Authorization Act, addressing military personnel planning, tuition assistance, and transfer of critical education issues affecting Army reservists.

DIRECTOR, Officer Career Policy Branch, Washington, DC   2004 – 2007
Led an elite group of Army HR specialists in **planning, developing, and/or updating HR policy** to align management systems with current requirements and the evolving Army mission, which included ongoing responses to overseas contingency operations.
- ❖ Developed and submitted pioneering legislative changes relating to military officer career policy that optimized conditions for Army Reserve Officers, creating greater parity for mid- and upper-level managers. **Created more legislative and policy changes in 2 years than in the previous 10 years.**
- ❖ Developed recruiting strategies that commissioned 10,500+ new military officers. Built transfer program to transition officers leaving the Navy or Air Force for the Army, commissioning 71 officers from sister services at a cost savings of more than $14M.

HR STRATEGIC PLANS MANAGER, Readiness and Transformation Division, Washington, DC   2003 – 2004
Analyzed HR programs and offered technical advice on building, developing, and coordinating new strategies for transforming the Army's personnel system.
- ❖ Developed measures and metrics for the Army Reserve's Balanced Scorecard.
- ❖ Represented the Army as a liaison to the DoD Defense Advisory Council on Women in the Service.

EDUCATION	**MA, Management,** University of Pittsburgh, Pittsburgh, PA **BA, Sociology,** University of Memphis, Memphis, TN
EXECUTIVE TRAINING & CERTIFICATION	Human Resource Management Certificate, Washington and Jefferson College Human Resource Management Qualification Course, Army Management School Lean Six Sigma White Belt Training
AFFILIATIONS	Society for Human Resource Management, Member Military Officers Association of American, Lifetime Member Reserve Officers Association, Lifetime Member Association of the United States Army, Lifetime Member
RECOGNITION	Bronze Star Medal Defense Meritorious Service Medal Meritorious Service Medal (4) Army Commendation Medal (3) Global War on Terrorism Service Medal

Robin T. Jacobs

173 Pierce AvenuecMacon, GA 31204

Top Secret Security Clearance   H: 478-742-2442 ■ C: 555-123-4567 ■ Email: info@careerprocenter.net

HUMAN RESOURCES SPECIALIST

"Versatile and proactive mentor whose leadership spans departmental lines....
A relentless and dedicated leader!"

**A meticulous and articulate Personnel Management Specialist with expertise in policy
and regulation implementation, recruiting, staffing, training, problem resolution,
team building, and time management. Utilize computer technology such as Microsoft Word,
Excel, and PowerPoint to develop correspondence and presentations.**

- Performed a pre-deployment Quality Assurance (QA) Audit on 1,000 personnel and pay records, resulting in an $80K savings in unauthorized payments, crediting crewmembers with more than $20K in underpayments.
- Ensured career development, counseling, and mentoring of 75 personnel.
- Excellent administrative, managerial, and technical abilities, leading to 99% document accuracy rate.
- Implemented in-rate training for all personnel, resulting in 100% retention for first-term personnel.
- Established the first active Pass Liaison Representative (PLR) program, representing 18.5K constituents.

Professional Experience

UNITED STATES NAVY 1986 – 2011
Senior Personnel Manager, Atlanta, GA   2006 – 2011

Oversaw the personal growth and development of 13 military and civilian personnel and the interviewing and job placement of applicants into the Navy and Navy Reserve. Supervised, monitored, and evaluated local operations; managed workloads.

Leadership

- Analyzed trends and forecasts; conducted human needs assessments; assessed legal issues for service and civilian personnel.
- Supervised the classifier team and monitored the overall placement of recruits in their ratings.
- Developed a comprehensive training plan; cross-trained classifiers and recruiters, reducing attrition by 50%.
- Managed the personal and professional growth of eight classifiers.

Personnel Administration

- Implemented vast knowledge of recruiting procedures, resulting in significant reduction in processing times.
- Dedicated extensive mentoring to applicants, resulting in highly trained, educated, and fully prepared individuals.
- Designed, compiled, delivered, and administered curriculum and testing.
- Counseled applicants on Navy options available based on personal qualifications.
- Wrote directives and instructions; prepared written staff studies.

Recruitment and Classification

- Interviewed potential enlistees to determine aptitudes and interests for military assignments.
- Determined educational and occupational background, hobbies, abilities, and personnel interests.
- Administered and scored basic battery and other classification tests.
- Coordinated placement of applicants in various enlistment programs to meet objectives.

Robin T. Jacobs   **Page 2**

Personnel Manager, Normandy   2001 – 2006
Provided enlisted individuals with information and counseling related to occupations, opportunities for general education and job training, requirements for promotion, and rights/benefits. Assisted personnel with problems or personal hardships.

Human Resources (HR) and Supervision

- Made recommendations on the allocation of positions and recommended basic staffing patterns.
- Collected and computed wage and fringe benefit data and assisted in developing compensation plans.
- Validated employment exams to ensure compliance with legal and professional standards.
- Reviewed proposed personnel actions for conformity to budget amounts, personnel policies, and merit system regulations.
- Investigated complaints or grievances; recorded facts regarding events; made recommendations on grievance resolution.

Staffing and Recruitment

- Evaluated applicants' education and work experience to established standards for admission to the Navy.
- Conducted specialized recruitment efforts for hard-to-fill positions.
- Identified job class categories and wrote class specifications, including classification standards.

Career Development and Counseling

- Ensured career development, counseling, and mentoring of 75 personnel.
- Applied Navy regulations in computation of pay, deductions, and reimbursement.
- Developed basic training courses and course evaluation techniques.

Regulatory Compliance

- Reviewed and edited policy statements for conformance to established guidelines, regulations, and laws.
- Knowledgeable of the personnel administration principles and practices, including the merit system rules and regulations.
- Applied federal and state laws, rules, and regulations on Equal Employment Opportunity (EEO) and Affirmative Action.

Education and Training

Associate in Arts, Georgia University College, Atlanta, GA
Graduate, John Henderson High School

Awards

Navy and Marine Corps Achievement Medal (4)
Navy and Marine Corps Commendation Medal (2)
Navy Achievement Medal (2)
Certificate of Designation, Navy Passport Agent

GEORGE E. RITTER

173 Pierce Avenue, Macon, GA 31204 | 478-742-2242 | info@careerprocenter.net

INTELLIGENCE COLLECTION/ANALYSIS

Top Secret/SCI Security Clearance

Dedicated and experienced professional with direct experience in security operations and intelligence collection, analysis, and reporting, consistently delivering results while displaying strength of character and professionalism.

- Intelligence Collection
- Analysis/Reporting
- Coordination/Management
- Planning/Scheduling
- Security/Safety
- Training/Development
- Linguistic Support

- Led intelligence teams performing intelligence collection and analysis; currently deployed to Iraq. Administered the tactical operation of 23 electronic warfare systems in support of more than 4,000 personnel.
- Linguist Manager: Led Iraqi interpreters in forward movements, interpreting and analyzing foreign intelligence information.
- Computer Expertise: Microsoft (MS) Windows Operating Systems; MS Office (Word, Excel, PowerPoint, Access, Outlook, and Internet Explorer); Combined Information Data Network Exchange; Biometric Automated Toolset; Source Operations Management Matrix; HOT-R; Tactical Ground Reporting System; Multi Media Messenger (M3); QueryTree; FalconView; Google Earth

EXPERIENCE

Intelligence Specialist, UNITED STATES ARMY   11/2008 – 1/2012

Intelligence Operations and Support:
⇨ Provided intelligence and linguistics support, managed 6 local national intelligence assets, and supported the military installation, consisting of more than 4,000 personnel.
⇨ Analyzed and evaluated intelligence holdings to determine changes in enemy capabilities, vulnerabilities, and probable courses of action, and identified and filled gaps in current intelligence information.
⇨ Performed diagnostics on each system to ensure 100% capabilities.

Intelligence Documentation and Reporting:
⇨ Prepared all-source intelligence products, established and maintained systematic, cross-referenced intelligence records and files, and developed and maintained the situation map.
⇨ Drafted reports on captured enemy material and special intelligence reports, plans, and briefings.
⇨ Provided intelligence reports and support for the Battalion Sniper Section and for the Private Security Detail.
⇨ Developed a concise, well-articulated synopsis for use in briefings to company senior personnel.

Leadership and Guidance:
⇨ Supervised the receipt, analysis, dissemination, and storage of intelligence information and provided guidance to subordinate personnel, implementing quality controls and enforcing standards for intelligence products.
⇨ Supervised the use of electromagnetic systems to prevent hostile use of the electromagnetic spectrum; oversaw the operation, maintenance, and updating of software for 23 vehicles.
⇨ Managed Iraqi interpreter escorts during movement and encounters requiring travel documentation.

Team Development:
⇨ Conducted classes in database search techniques to facilitate entity-based searches versus geography-based searches and classes in the Intelligence, Surveillance, and Reconnaissance (ISR) assets used.
⇨ Applied operational experience and understanding of the relevance and importance of information to intelligence training, development of enemy courses of action, and development of intelligence requirements.

EDUCATION

Master of Science in Intelligence Management, San Francisco State University, San Francisco, CA
Bachelor of Arts in History, San Francisco State University, San Francisco, CA

AWARDS

Army Commendation Medal; Army Achievement Medal

Mark Zyggat

✉ info@careerprocenter.net

173 Pierce Avenue ♦ Macon, GA 31204 ♦ 478-742-2442

Intelligence Operations and Management
Security Clearance: Top Secret

AREAS OF EXPERTISE AND TECHNICAL SKILLS

- Leadership/Supervision
- Intelligence Oversight/Management
- Operational Planning
- Signals Intelligence (SIGINT)
- Personnel Management
- Policy Implementation
- Planning and Coordination
- Written/Verbal Communications
- Communication/Coordination

PROFESSIONAL BACKGROUND

Signals Intelligence Team Leader, Army National Guard, Overseas   **02/2004-Present**

Signals Intelligence Team Leader and Baghdad Fusion Cell Liaison Officer for Colorado National Guard Unit currently deployed in support of Operation Iraqi Freedom (OIF). Deliver timely, accurate, and synchronized Intelligence, Surveillance, and Reconnaissance (ISR) support to the Maneuver Units of Action (MUA), senior military leadership, staff, and subordinates during the planning, preparation, and execution of multiple, simultaneous decision actions.

- Coordinate with Headquarters (HQ)-level intelligence teams to effectively increase intelligence production quality by more than 50%
- Prepare, validate, and submit time-sensitive collection requirements for SIGINT
- Develop, coordinate, and manage sensitive SIGINT operations and coordinate special intelligence.
- Manage and prioritize the daily activities of 17 SIGINT personnel in a broad range of intelligence matters
- Develop complex analytical approaches to confidential situations and provide a complete assessment of the local population and influence key leaders within the area
- Consistently establish and maintain direct communication and coordination with operations personnel, ensuring intelligence collection and production requirements are complete
- Established and implemented Standard Operating Procedures (SOPs) for Signals Intelligence (SIGINT) procedures that directly increased the production of intelligence reliability and enhanced collection capabilities

Pharmacy Technician, PharmaPlus, Macon, GA   **05/2001-01/2004**

Provided technical and clerical support to the pharmacists in the processing of medication orders and the monitoring of drug therapy.

EDUCATION AND TRAINING

Bachelor of Arts/Psychology, University College, Macon, GA

Associate of Arts/Social Science, University College, Macon, GA

United States Army Training
Basic Officer Leader Course, 2009; Military Intelligence Officer Basic Course,
Human Intelligence (HUMINT) Collection Team Course, HUMINT Debrief School

COMPUTER EXPERTISE

Microsoft (MS) Windows; MS Office (Word, Excel, Access, Outlook); Internet browsers; ArcGIS 9; ArcMap; ArcCatalog; Analyst Notebook; National Security Agency (NSA) Databases

MARK MCGUIRE

173 Pierce Avenue
Macon, GA 31204

(C) 478-742-2442
info@careerprocenter.net

Intelligence Program Management | Policy Analyst | Security | Internal Investigations

Strategic Planning ◆ Quality Control ◆ Compliance Oversight ◆ Investigation Interviewing Skills
Crisis Management ◆ Problem Solving ◆ Budgets ◆ Confidentiality ◆ Contracting Management

Security/Intelligence Professional: Twenty-five years' professional experience and expertise in criminal and national security investigations, including 20 years of leadership within the Federal Bureau of Investigation (FBI). Apply broad law enforcement skills, including interview and interrogation, intelligence operations, crisis planning/response/communications, counterterrorism/counterintelligence operations, contract/resource management, security operations, and policy development and implementation. Maintain Current Top Secret/SCI Clearance. (Last investigation and polygraph – March 2005.)

▶ **Strategist** – Develop detailed plans to lead decisive action. Implement strategic responses to urgent intelligence concerns or evolving crises.

▶ **Quality Assessment** – Measure performance against organizational objectives, providing the highest standards of intelligence gathering, processing, and evaluation.

▶ **Communications** – Interface with agency executives, federal/state/local authorities, media, private-sector security specialists, and the public. Polished speaker experienced in training and public venues.

▶ **Ethics** – Observe a high degree of ethical conduct, openness, and sensitivity with victims, suspects, families, the media, and other law enforcement and intelligence partners.

FEDERAL BUREAU OF INVESTIGATION (FBI)   1990 – 2012

UNIT CHIEF/ASSISTANT SECTION CHIEF   2008 – 2012
Directorate of Intelligence, Washington, D.C.

Challenges: Team Leader for FBI's Strategic Execution Team (SET): **Develop and implement new field and Headquarters (HQ) intelligence functions, practices, and processes** amid a climate of critical oversight, public scrutiny, shifting priorities, and evolving FBI national goals. Blend program and project management skills, intelligence background, training flair, and internal Quality Control (QC) expertise to enhance performance across agency field offices.

Actions: **Standardized and realigned FBI field intelligence structure, responsibilities, and output.** Led expanded reorganization, promoting leaner performance and proactive responses to present or potential security threats across broad geographic territories. Assessed SET field offices' performance and conducted Quality Assurance checks against new objectives; documented performance and conducted training to build or expand competencies against new and aggressive agency goals.

Results: **Recognized by executive management** for driving the new **"What Good Looks Like"** standard, now used in SET field office onsite visits. Widely recognized by superiors, peers, and subordinates as Subject Matter Expert (SME). Received FBI incentive award and nominated for the Director's Award.

FBI SUPERVISORY SPECIAL AGENT   1998 – 2008
Multiple locations throughout the United States

Team Supervisor/Assistant Special Agent in Charge, Dallas FBI Field Intelligence (2005-2008)
* Managed Intelligence Program resources, capabilities, and outputs. Created and executed new standards and objectives for collection, strategic/tactical analysis, reporting, dissemination, and operations integration.

Counterterrorism Team Leader, Counterterrorism Division (2002-2005)
* Led the FBI's Counterterrorism Division Fly Team, a small, highly trained cadre of terrorism first responders comprising agents and analysts prepared to respond with virtually no notice to counterterrorism crises and security contingency events anywhere in the world.

Crisis-Hostage Negotiator, Critical Incident Response Group (CIRG) (1998-2002)
* Led the FBI's international kidnapping negotiation program.

Challenges: **Developed negotiation and investigative operational strategies and plans** to respond to emerging security threats or developing crises, including kidnapping/hostage scenarios or counterterrorism. Organized and led teams, both onsite and from Tactical Operations Centers (TOCs).

Actions: **Led multiple responses to high-intensity, usually short-notice hostage/barricade and kidnapping events.** Analyzed exigent circumstances and coordinated with on-scene commanders and federal, state, and local authorities to develop effective solutions, minimize violence, and preserve life. Analyzed intelligence, evaluated threats to hostages, and identified tactical or negotiated resolutions.

Results: **2005: Formed/led five-member combined agent and analyst team** to investigate attack on American Consulate at Jeddah, Saudi Arabia. Developed operational plans; prioritized critical actions, including physical evidence review and timeline; interviewed witnesses to secure statements; and reviewed security videotapes and procedures. Investigated/evaluated potential conspirators or accomplices, and investigated links to the U.S. Developed credible picture of events and established connections to previously unknown co-conspirators. Informed U.S. Ambassador and FBI HQ on the "big picture."

2001-2002: Organized and led negotiation teams to the Philippines in response to major international terrorism cases, including events during 9/11. **Deployed six times** during protracted kidnapping of an American missionary couple by Abu Sayyaf Group, a designated terrorist organization. Supported ongoing negotiations and strategic tactical responses. Hostage successfully rescued after 376 days in captivity. **Recognized by the agency** with substantial cash award in recognition of outstanding performance.

EDUCATION:
♦ **M.A., Applied Behavioral Science,** WASHINGTON UNIVERSITY, Fairfax, VA
♦ **B.A., Political Science,** ILLINOIS STATE UNIVERSITY, DeKalb, IL

MILITARY SERVICE:
♦ United States Marine Corps (USMC); Executive Officer/Logistics Manager

AWARDS/HONORS:
♦ Recommended for the **Director's Award;** Directorate of Intelligence; Incentive Awards (2)
♦ Office of the Director of National Intelligence **Meritorious Unit Citation**

XAVIER PHILLIPS
173 Pierce Avenue I Macon, GA 31204 I 478-742-2442 I info@careerprocenter.net

RESULTS-DRIVEN PROGRAM MANAGEMENT PROFESSIONAL WITH
28 YEARS' EXPERIENCE PLANNING AND EXECUTING INCREASINGLY COMPLEX
PROGRAMS FOR THE U.S. ARMY AND CIVILIAN SECTOR

PROGRAM MANAGER

- *Logistics Planning*
- *Project Management*
- *Problem Solving*
- *Supply Chain Management*
- *Team Leadership*
- *Oral Communications*
- *Active Secret Clearance*

- **Project Management:** Proven ability to determine requirements, define scope, develop goals, create timelines, assign work, allocate resources, and meet objectives as shown in setting up Left Behind Equipment (LBE) program in 30 days while saving $21.4M in first year.

- **Planning and Coordination:** Skilled planner capable of successfully designing, coordinating, and safely executing all aspects of the redeployment of equipment for 18K-person organization.

- **Supply Chain Management:** Able to manage all aspects of ensuring the right piece of equipment reached the right location at the right time for maintenance.

"David is a dynamic performer with unlimited ability."
~ PAUL HABHAB, Chief Warrant Officer 5, U.S. Army, 1st Cavalry Division

PROFESSIONAL EXPERIENCE AND ACHIEVEMENTS

PROGRAM MANAGER   08/2008 to Present
Fort Hood, TX

Manage LBE program for the Communications Equipment Command, ensuring proper maintenance and upkeep for all equipment not needed by Army forces when they deploy. Plan, direct, evaluate, and coordinate logistics support for complex electronics computer equipment. Identify maintenance needs, conduct quarterly inspections, and ensure the right equipment reaches the right location at the right time.
- Manage manning and budget requirements to meet program objectives within allotted resources; ensure sufficient personnel with proper skill sets at each location.
- Conduct all aspects of personnel management for 35 personnel to include hiring, payroll, assigning tasks, and monitoring and evaluating performance.
- Solve supply chain problems associated with getting the equipment back into inventory.

Accomplishments:
⇨ Created program from conception to implementation within 30 days; met 100% of milestones and deadlines.
⇨ Developed procedures and policies to manage excess equipment; saved $21.4M in first year and $56.1M to date.
⇨ Successfully managed equipment and personnel at 13 sites over 7 states; maintained up to 210K pieces of equipment in one year.

SENIOR LOGISTICS ANALYST   06/2007 to 08/2008
Lockheed Martin; Fort Hood, TX

Directed the post-deployment outfitting of a 5K-person U.S. Army organization. Coordinated with internal and external stakeholders across agencies to ensure synchronized resupply effort and to provide material readiness reporting. Developed equipment strategy, determining which individual pieces of equipment would be maintained at which locations and by whom.
- Managed field operations to eliminate performance risk for new Army organization.
- Coordinated regional- and national-level maintenance and rebuild programs.
- Directed maintenance, supply, transportation, property accountability, and related logistical activities.

XAVIER PHILLIPS, PAGE 2

173 Pierce Avenue | Macon, GA 31204 | 478-742-2442 | info@careerprocenter.net

Accomplishments:
⇨ Established all procedures for operations on new contract; ensured 100% of requirements were met.
⇨ Built cohesive team from 13 new liaisons; trained and mentored staff across 13 sites to ensure mission success.

SENIOR LOGISTICS PLANNER   07/2006 to 06/2007
U.S. Army; Fort Hood, TX

Designed and implemented logistics plan to bring deployed Army units back to the Continental U.S. (CONUS), to include the integration of deployed equipment and Equipment Left Behind (LBE) while ensuring proper accountability and maintenance. Planned and coordinated supply chain, maintenance, transportation, and accountability for each piece of equipment.

Accomplishments:
⇨ Established redeployment logistics plan to bring Army units home; subsequently implemented Army-wide due to its success.
⇨ Managed maintenance and supply projects across all functions and echelons; determined requirements, established timelines, met suspense dates, and achieved results.
⇨ Ensured proper maintenance of all equipment for 18K-person organization to include trucks, tanks, infantry fighting vehicles, Humvees, communications equipment, night-vision goggles, and more than 16K weapons.

LOGISTICS MANAGEMENT SPECIALIST   06/2005 to 07/2008
Anteon Corporation; Fort Hood, TX

Managed project to transform the 1st Cavalry Division into a modular, self-supporting organization. Provided logistics subject matter expertise, coordinating the modernization, resource management, outfitting, and training to enable the complete restructuring of the organization in time for upcoming deployment. Coordinated local and national return of equipment, resolving supply shortage issues created by the reorganization.

Accomplishments:
⇨ Directed 23K lateral property transfers to reconfigure the division; completed 18-month process in 10 months.
⇨ Identified opportunities for inventory reduction; removed 10K pieces of excess equipment.
⇨ Took excess items from storage and allowed them to be reissued; saved an estimated $18.2M and solved supply shortage problems.

MAINTENANCE SENIOR ADVISOR   01/2000 to **06/2005 to 07/2008**
U.S. Army, 1st Cavalry Division, Fort Hood, TX

Advised CEO on supply and ground equipment maintenance issues for 18K-person Department of Defense (DoD) organization. Oversaw supply chain and maintenance processes, automation, readiness, and reporting. Directed transportation, motor pool operations, barracks utilization, food services, inventory, property management, and all aspects of logistics. Supervised military, contractor, and government personnel and managed $250K-per-month government credit card.

Accomplishments:
⇨ Identified, negotiated for, and purchased off-the-shelf replacements for equipment shortages.
⇨ Determined lifecycle maintenance requirements for complex equipment prior to long-term storage.
⇨ Created, justified, and earned approval for $84.2M maintenance plan; plan adapted throughout the Army

EDUCATION

Bachelor's Degree in Business Management (2005); NEW YORK STATE UNIVERSITY; New York, NY; GPA 3.69

PROFESSIONAL DEVELOPMENT

Bradley Fighting Vehicle Systems Mechanic Course 85 ▪ Primary Leadership Development Course 88 ▪ Non-Commissioned Officer (NCO) Basic Course 92 ▪ NCO Advanced Course 99

AWARDS & SPECIAL ACCOMPLISHMENTS

Meritorious Service Medal (2) ▪ Army Commendation Medal (5) ▪ Army Achievement Medal (5)

MICHAEL EDWARDS

173 Pierce Avenue | Macon, GA 31204| 478-742-2442 | info@careerprocenter.net

SKILLED MEDICAL OPERATIONS MANAGER WITH THE EXPERIENCE AND ENERGY TO LEAD TEAMS TO NEW LEVELS OF PERFORMANCE

- Program Management
- Process Improvement
- Leadership
- Customer Service
- Communication

Consistently promoted to positions of greater responsibility due to leadership, technical expertise, and problem-solving abilities.

Capable of managing multiple projects simultaneously, with staff working in many different locations under hazardous or challenging conditions.

Top Secret – Sensitive Compartmented Information (TS-SCI) clearance.

Record of success in supervising medical, training, logistics, and technical operations.

*"His commitment to excellence, dedication to duty, and attention to detail consistently produced superior results….his particular strength is the ability to quickly and accurately identify important information, develop solutions, and implement actions." –*EXCERPT FROM A RECENT PERFORMANCE APPRAISAL

PROFESSIONAL EXPERIENCE & ACHIEVEMENTS

CHIEF OF MEDICAL OPERATIONS   05/2010 to Present
United States (U.S.) Army: Heidelberg, Germany

Lead operations for a medical organization consisting of 850+ personnel, organized in three distinct departments: a Headquarters (HQ) group; a Combat Support Hospital; and a multifunctional group that provides logistical, veterinary, preventative medicine, dental, optometry, and other services.
- Plan and coordinate more than 25 medical missions to Iraq, Afghanistan, Romania, Bulgaria, Germany, Poland, Tanzania, Cameroon, and the Republic of Georgia. Ensure mission teams, consisting of as many as 400 personnel, possess all the equipment, supplies, information, and support needed to succeed.
- Deploy classified and unclassified Microsoft (MS) SharePoint Portals to significantly improve coordination and communication between departments. Develop SharePoint Web Parts to provide customized functionality.
- Selected as unit's Knowledge Manager due to operational expertise and technical skills with MS SharePoint and other information applications.
- Managed the "reset" process for five subordinate units, during which they returned from overseas deployment and entered a downtime/training phase. Ensured these units met 100% of equipment, supply, personnel, and other requirements at or before scheduled deadlines.

INTELLIGENCE AND SECURITY PROGRAM MANAGER   05/2009 to 05/2010
U.S. Army: Heidelberg, Germany

Advised senior leaders on issues such as security, training, secret clearances, and potential threats to personnel deployed outside of Germany as part of humanitarian assistance or medical support missions.
- Managed security clearance review for more than 800 members of 13 separate departments.
- Restructured the unit to increase medical capabilities without reducing commitment to existing missions.
- Conducted monthly oral status briefings for the unit's Chief of Staff, representatives of the parent Medical Command organization, and senior leaders of the U.S. Army – Europe.
- Reduced the average time needed to perform a security investigation by 50%.
- Planned and supervised the deployment of two Forward Surgical Teams to Iraq and Afghanistan.

MICHAEL EDWARDS

173 Pierce Avenue | Macon, GA 31204| 478-742-2442 | info@careerprocenter.net

PROFESSIONAL EXPERIENCE & ACHIEVEMENTS

- Converted a field ambulance group to an Area Support Medical Company, adding physician assistants; behavioral health professionals; patient holding capabilities; and radiology, dentistry, and laboratory services.

MEDICAL OPERATIONS MANAGER   07/2008 to 05/2009
Heidelberg, Germany

Directed the operations of 400+ members of a medical services unit that combined Preventive Medicine, Veterinary, Dental, Optometry, Ground Ambulance, Combat Operational Stress Control, and Medical Logistics functions.
- Oversaw the successful completion of a continuous stream of 150+ separate projects, including the deployment of units, inspection programs, readiness exercises at firing ranges and training events, and evaluation visits by senior military leaders.
- Created a classified MS SharePoint Portal to improve the flow of data throughout the organization and allow dispersed personnel to collaborate on documents.
- Organized a staff of 3 personnel to perform the duties previously handled by 37.
- Supervised the certification and deployment of a medical logistics group (80 personnel), a veterinary and food safety detachment (60 personnel), and an HQ department (80 personnel).
- Implemented the unit's first classified SharePoint Portal.
- Reduced the time needed to collect and submit Unit Status Reports from 4.5 to .5 days.

TRAINING AND EXERCISE DIRECTOR   05/2007 to 07/2008
U.S. Army: Heidelberg, Germany

Managed all training, exercises, and schools for 850+ members of medical services unit. Planned and supervised training exercises to improve the unit's ability to provide medical services.
- Assigned personnel specializing in 130+ separate disciplines to 90+ schools and training courses.
- Controlled annual training and education budget of $645K.
- Created or contributed to four separate training exercises that upgraded the unit's skills at working under austere conditions with minimal logistical, technical, and administrative support.
- Implemented two new management systems for tracking training and school assignments.

EDUCATION

Bachelor of Arts Degree in Political Science
UNIVERSITY OF GEORGIA: Athens, GA

AWARDS & SPECIAL ACCOMPLISHMENTS

Bronze Star Medal • Meritorious Service Medal • Army Commendation Medal • Army Achievement Medal • National Defense Service Medal • Iraq Campaign Medal • Global War on Terrorism Service Medal

EDWARD M. AUSTIN

- Licensed Clinical Social Worker
- Licensed Master Social Worker, State of Georgia, No. 12345

173 Pierce Avenue, Macon, GA 12345
Email: info@careerprocenter.net
Phone: 478-742-2442

SOCIAL WORK PROGRAM DIRECTOR

Expertise in developing and leading proactive mental health programs that assist transitioning veterans with achieving quality and productive post-military lifestyles.

► Develop proactive programs and learning objectives designed to assist patients with regaining control and overcoming social and emotional problems.

► Coordinate human services, provide counseling and risk assessment, and conduct investigations using a plethora of client-management techniques.

► Collaborate with psychiatrists to make clinical psychiatric diagnoses and develop psychotherapeutic intervention plans to influence and change patient behaviors.

► Diagnose emotional dysfunction in patients and dependants with specialization in Post-Traumatic Stress Disorder (PTSD) as found in combat veterans. Implement a system of therapeutic intervention to relieve stress and assist the patient in achieving full independence. Provide family assistance and counseling, referral and follow-up services, group and individual assessment and treatment strategies, and client-support service referrals.

► Establish strategic coalitions with community organizations to expand clinics' network of services.

Areas of Expertise...

►Diagnosis & Assessment	►Program Development	►Patient Services
►Case Management	►Individual/Group Therapy	►Recordkeeping
►System Support	►Community Outreach	►Patient Privacy
►Federal & State Compliance	►Team Building	►Reporting

PROFESSIONAL PERFORMANCE OVERVIEW

ARMY RESERVES PSYCHOLOGICAL HEALTH PROGRAM (PHP), MACON, GA   1/11 to Present
Director of Psychological Health
Provide proactive support and strategic direction for all organizational public health and wellness programs, including the supervision and delivery of mental health programs and services such as assessments, individual and group therapy, crisis intervention, consultation, and educational/preventative outreach programming for military veterans.

► Conduct site visits to various local military units to observe and collect firsthand data on morale and mental health issues affecting assigned personnel. Counsel unit leadership on crisis intervention and morale boosters.

► Built a key referral relationship with a Veterans Center that has assisted members challenged by deployment issues.

► Develop and oversee training programs to help familiarize new service providers in their understanding of the unique challenges faced by military members, and assist with crafting programs that address these unique needs.

► Coordinate the Community Action Information Board activities, and report findings, psychological health statistics, and updates to the state, as required by law.

► Serve as the Point of Contact (POC) for follow-up and treatment, tracking of members with Traumatic Brain Injury (TBI).

► Orchestrated the launch of a field Joint Health and Wellness Center.

► Provided psycho-educational briefings on various topics to include stress management, anger management, post-deployment reintegration, self-care strategies, and a general introduction to PHP services.

VETERANS HEALTH ADMINISTRATION, ATLANTA, GA   11/09 to 12/10
Social Worker
Delivered targeted psychosocial treatments to a wide variety of veterans from various socioeconomic, cultural, ethnic, educational, and other diverse backgrounds with a focus on identifying rehabilitation and personal enhancement opportunities to help patients overcome physical and mental disabilities.

► Accurately documented patient care and progress as prescribed by the Mental Health Intensive Case Management and Medical Center Directives.

EDWARD M. AUSTIN

- Licensed Clinical Social Worker
- Licensed Master Social Worker, State of Georgia, No. 12345

173 Pierce Avenue, Macon, GA 12345
Email: info@careerprocenter.net
Phone: 478-742-2442

▶ Screened veterans to determine eligibility for certain outpatient programs.
▶ Applied knowledge of medical and mental health diagnoses, disabilities, and treatment procedures to assess acute, chronic, and traumatic illnesses/injuries.
▶ Referred and coordinated adult chronically mentally ill veterans with applicable outpatient programs.
▶ Provided support services and education to patient families as part of patient treatment plans.

MACON VET CENTER, MACON, GA   9/08 to 10/09
Readjustment Counselor/Clinical Social Worker
Simultaneously managed unique patient treatment cases involving military veterans and their dependants adversely affected by combat or other social influences. Identified eligible veterans in need of readjustment counseling through the utilization of assessment tools, interviews, observations, and background reviews.
▶ Monitored, evaluated, and recorded client progress according to measurable goals described in treatment and care plan.
▶ Developed comprehensive treatment plans to include psychiatric and medical care to help veterans diagnosed with PTSD readjust to society.
▶ Provided crisis intervention and stabilization to veterans and dependants; completed follow-up counseling sessions to ensure patients' physical safety.
▶ Established a relationship with the local Red Cross by meeting with its local Executive Director and Military Veterans Relations to build a referral system.
▶ Fostered relationships with Operations Enduring and Iraqi Freedom program personnel to establish assistance for eligible clients in need of additional treatment or resources to expedite their recoveries.
▶ Represented the organization at Jefferson County Mental Health coalition meetings; gathered key information on critical issues and newly available resources; briefed center management on findings.
▶ Collaborated with the Advisory Board at the University of Georgia in the development of a master's-level program for the Macon, GA location.

MENTAL HEALTH ASSOCIATION OF CALIFORNIA, SACRAMENTO, CA   4/08 to 8/08
Veterans Outreach Consultant
Gathered relevant information about available resources and treatment services for veterans diagnosed with PTSD. Created numerous community conduits to expand existing network of services and programs designed to assist veterans with managing their conditions.

ACTIVE MILITARY EXPERIENCE

United States Army   11/99 to 4/04
Bioenvironmental Engineering Technician

EDUCATION AND DEVELOPMENT

Master of Social Work (MSW), University of Georgia, Atlanta, GA
Bachelor of Arts in Psychology, University of Maryland, College Park, MD
Anxiety Disorders: Diagnosis and Treatment ~ Crisis Management ~ Disaster Mental Health Intervention~
Introduction to Dialectical Behavior Therapy ~ Legal and Ethical Issues for Mental Health Professionals
Overview of Psychopharmacology ~ PTSD ~ Psychosocial Rehabilitation and Recovery ~ Veterans and PTSD

AWARDS & PRESENTATIONS

Army Achievement Medal; National Defense Service Medal; Armed Forces Expeditionary Medal

Presenter, Brain Injury Association of Georgia, "Working with Veterans with Traumatic Brain Injury," 2009
Moderator, James L. Stone Legislative Policy Symposium (Justice for Returning Veterans), 2007
Panel Member, "Mental Illness as a Disability," University of Georgia, 2006
Attendee, "Bridges Out of Poverty Seminar," University of Georgia, 2006

ROBERT HATHAWAY

173 Pierce Avenue | Macon, GA 31204 | 478-742-2442 | info@careerprocenter.net

"Robert excels in leadership. He saved our company over 15% in production costs by streamlining procedures. I recommend him highly."

-- JAMES RENFREW, Engineering Director, Mesa Medical Center

TECHNICAL ADVISOR

- Gas Turbine Engines
- Maintenance/Repair
- Project Coordination
- Project Inspections
- Team Leadership
- Budget Administration

- **Experienced technical advisor and hands-on gas turbine field engineer and maintenance manager with 20+ years** of experience leading onsite maintenance, troubleshooting, and repair on gas turbines and their associated compressors and generators.

- **Exceptional supervisory experience with a proven ability to lead engineering** teams and the customer through various inspections and repair processes.

- **Demonstrated capacity to plan, support, and oversee turbine service projects,** which includes development of work instruction, coordination of tooling, and communication of requirements to field engineers and technicians.

PROFESSIONAL EXPERIENCE & ACHIEVEMENTS

GAS TURBINE FIELD ENGINEER/TECHNICAL ADVISOR   06/2007 to Present
International Turbines, Inc., Chicago, IL and various international locations

Charged with maintaining, repairing, and overhauling gas turbine generators, compressors, and mechanical drive packages at client sites across the world. Commissioned and decommissioned equipment; led instrumentation and control systems inspections and maintenance.
- Team Lead coordinating scheduled maintenance and repairs for multiple simultaneous assignments.
- Organized and implemented cultural awareness seminars for new personnel.

Accomplishments:
- ⇨ Led a Frame 6FA combustion inspection and end cap replacement at Italy's COFATHEC power station
- ⇨ Directed a LM2500 gas turbine upgrade and centrifugal compressor installation on a PEMEX oil platform

CHIEF ENGINEER   04/2005 to 06/2007
Mesa Medical Center, Mesa, AZ

Recruited to lead final construction phase of the Mesa Medical Center, a $198M, 400K-square-foot project. Oversaw utility, safety, fire prevention, Hazardous Materials (HAZMAT) and waste, emergency, medical equipment, and security plans. Supervised 10 engineering plant operators and facilities maintenance personnel on two 600-ton Johnson Control Chillers, 16 air handlers, 2 cooling towers, and a Siemens HVAC automated system controller.
- Coordinated diverse staff of project managers responsible for overseeing various aspects of construction.
- Accountable for $30M final phase budget and related assessments of human capital and resource management.

Accomplishments:
- ⇨ Designed and implemented the preventative maintenance program for all major and minor equipment
- ⇨ Scheduled and directed 200+ project managers each week to complete tasks on time and under budget

(CONTINUED)

ROBERT HATHAWAY

173 Pierce Avenue | Macon, GA 31204 | 478-742-2442 | info@careerprocenter.net

PROFESSIONAL EXPERIENCE & ACHIEVEMENTS (CONTINUED)

SENIOR REPAIR, PLANNING, AND ESTIMATING OFFICER (1996-2007)   09/1986 to 03/2007
United States (U.S.) Navy, International Locations

Maintained accountability for the safe and efficient operation of four General Electric LM2500 gas turbine engines and three Allison 501k 34 gas turbine engine generators and related support systems. Supervised a team of 70+ personnel to oversee daily operations of the shipboard power plant and all necessary repairs and maintenance. Managed environment pollution control, maintenance, and material management programs.

Accomplishments:
⇨ Diagnosed mechanical/electrical problems, supplied technical assistance, and proposed corrective action
⇨ Qualified each of the plant's controls, including electrical, propulsion/auxiliary, and the switchboard
⇨ Provided in-depth training to engineers regarding repair, operations, and casualty control of the plant
⇨ Completed training in every phase of GE and Allison 501k 34 gas turbine engine inspection

Early Career Experience:
Main Propulsion Division, Lead Petty Officer – U.S. Navy (1990-1993)
Boiler Technician, Second Class Petty Officer – U.S. Navy (1986-1990)

PROFESSIONAL DEVELOPMENT

General Electric Training and Certifications:
GE Gas Turbine Engines Field Engineer Direct Hired Program

United States Navy Training and Certifications:

Diesel Marine and Aviation Fuels Testing and Analysis ▪ Boiler Water/Feed Water Test and Treatment
Shipboard Gauge Calibration ▪ Engineering Department Senior-Enlisted Program Manager
Marine Gas Turbine Inspector Training and Certification ▪ Automatic Boiler Combustion Operation/Maintenance
Gas Turbine Engine Mechanical and Electrical Apprenticeship School ▪ Boiler Technician

EDUCATION

Certificate in Computer Application and Networks (2004)
TECHNICAL INSTITUTE, San Diego, CA

Associate's Degree in Computer Systems Information (1996)
CITY COLLEGE OF SAN DIEGO, San Diego, CA, GPA 3.0

COMPUTER SKILLS

Software: Microsoft (MS) Word, Excel, PowerPoint, and Outlook; Novell Network

JOSEPH K. LEE

ACTIVE TOP SECRET/SPECIAL COMPARTMENTED INFORMATION (TS/SCI)

173 Pierce Avenue | Macon, GA 31204 | 478-742-2442 | info@careerprocenter.net

TELECOMMUNICATIONS PROJECT MANAGER
Problem Solving/Analysis/Budget Management/Coordination

Adept at designing projects, setting standards, monitoring progress, reaching milestones, and ensuring on-time completion, as demonstrated in four separate major communications upgrades in Saudi Arabia worth $2M. Proven ability to lead $1.5B state-of-the-art telecommunications facility managing communications throughout entire Persian Gulf region. Demonstrated leadership skills while leading a 90-person team in maintaining more than 99% connectivity on telecommunications systems   and up to 3K incoming and 300 outgoing messages a day.

"[Joseph] is my number-one Technical Manager! He is the cornerstone
of this Command's success and the best Technical Manager I have ever served with."
~ Excerpt from a recent Performance Appraisal

CAREER HIGHLIGHTS

Project Management: Directed project, enabling Internet access for 3.2K personnel in their living quarters and greatly improving morale. Ensured continuous communications connectivity throughout naval operations in the Caribbean and Central and South American area. Managed operations of more than 300 circuits, providing Command and Control (C2) support to operational leaders throughout the Middle East.

Technical Expertise: Identified, isolated, analyzed, and corrected faults rapidly; restored 5.2K outages while maintaining 98% circuit reliability. Analyzed program operations, saving $10M in new leases and improving Defense Information Systems Agency (DISA) planning estimate discrepancies by 70%. Managed more than 300 voice and data circuits as well as message support for aircraft carriers and organizations onboard.

Research and Development: Researched, developed, and implemented new training program; improved personnel's ability to perform duties, resulting in 99% connectivity rating and promotion rates as high as 98%.

Coordination and Facilitation: Coordinated $6.2M outsourcing of the technical control and message center functions in Guam while managing 90 people. Handled more than 3K incoming and 300 outgoing messages per day while deployed to the Persian Gulf; maintained a 99.2% connectivity rating. Discontinued 10 antiquated communications circuits in London, saving $500K.

PROFESSIONAL EXPERIENCE

COMMUNICATIONS DIRECTOR 01/2011 to Present
Camp Lemonier, Djibouti City, Djibouti

Direct 21 military and civilian personnel in simultaneously completing four major projects worth $2M. Projects include implementing Fee-for-Service Internet, expanding Armed Forces Television, and upgrading Emergency Call Boxes and Land Mobile Radio. Analyze existing communications programs, including Internet Protocol (IP) network, television, radio, emergency communications, and inside/outside plant fiber communications.

COMMUNICATIONS AND INFORMATION SYSTEMS (C&IS) MANAGER 06/2009 to 12/2010
Commander Fourth Fleet, Mayport, FL

Managed and coordinated communications for all U.S. naval assets operating in the Central and South American region. Evaluated and made recommendations concerning overall plans and proposals for major telecommunications programs involving the Central and South American region. Identified, tracked, and resolved potential problems with Super High Frequency (SHF), Extremely High Frequency (EHF), and Ultra High Frequency (UHF) subsystems, networks, and data links. Directed the Electronic Key Management System (EKMS).

TECHNICAL CONTROL MANAGER 01/2007 to 01/2009
NRCC, Bahrain

Directed a $1.5B technical control facility, ensuring Quality Control (QC), fault isolation, restoration, and reporting on more than 300 circuits. Managed all Navy telecommunications operations in the entire Persian Gulf region. Directed numerous systems installations, circuit transitions, and upgrades, supporting Defense Satellite Communications Systems, SHF, EHF, UHF, optic fiber, Network Operations Centers (NOCs), and Deployable KU-band Earth Terminals (DKETs).

COMMUNICATIONS MANAGER 12/2003 to 01/2007
NAS Jacksonville, FL

Managed all external communications. Prepared multiple strategic and tactical communications plans for deployment to the Persian Gulf. Ensured 99% reliability of SHF, EHF, Very High Frequency (VHF), and High Frequency (HF) communications systems as well as a 99% reliability rating of message traffic. Conducted traffic analyses, provided for data transmission, and performed tests and evaluations.

EDUCATION/PROFESSIONAL DEVELOPMENT

Master's Degree in Information Systems Management
UNIVERSITY OF CALIFORNIA, Los Angeles, CA, Cum Laude
Bachelor's Degree in Administration Management Studies and Computer and Information Science,
COLORADO STATE UNIVERISTY, Pueblo, CO
Training: Electronic Key Management System (EKMS) Manager Course • Equal Opportunity Manager Course • Satellite Operator Course • Advanced Communications Manager Course • Naval Leadership Development Program • Fleet Senior-Enlisted Leadership Seminar • C4I Systems Engineering Course

Resume Notes

Military to Federal
Resume Samples

Bryon Santos
173 Pierce Avenue
Macon, GA 31204
United States
478-742-2442
info@careerprocenter.net

WORK EXPERIENCE:

United States Army	6/2008 to Present
Fort Sill, OK	$55,000 per year
United States	40 hours per week
Tactical Communications	Supervisor: Tom Paul
	478-555-3456

OPERATIONS MANAGEMENT: Supervise, train, and evaluate performance of 10 junior-level personnel. Key member of team charged with establishing, maintaining, troubleshooting, repairing, and managing tactical communications network consisting of Satellite Transportable Terminals (STTs) and mobile unit connected to STTs to uplink data to communications satellites via TDMA link. Monitor communications feed to ensure no disruptions to flow of intelligence and critical information to military personnel in various capacities. Personally responsible for troubleshooting and resolving routine/complex Information Technology (IT) and communications issues. Consistently maintain minimum of 97% uptime rating.

PERSONAL COMPUTERS AND NETWORK SYSTEMS: Hands-on expertise with networked personal computers, operating systems, applications and antivirus software, multiple servers (Windows XP and 2003, Exchange). Apply excellent understanding of networking topologies, internetworking concepts, access lists, direction structures, and account management in installing and managing Local Area Networks (LANs) and providing network security. Demonstrate in-depth knowledge of Transmission Control Protocol/Internet Protocol (TCP/IP) and Unix/Solaris system administration, configure Cisco routers and switches, and establish and maintain firewalls and border security.

EQUIPMENT OVERSIGHT: Spearhead mobile investigative activities, monitoring radio communications and automated information management systems. Considered technically advanced in using and maintaining sophisticated telephone and computer systems, radios, Graphical Data Fusion System (GDFS) console, sensors, and other electronics. Set up, configure, and load tactical radio communications systems with KEYMAT materials used in processing cryptographic intelligence.

TECHNICAL EXPERTISE AND SUPPORT: Perform wide range of technical functions, including setup, operation, maintenance, modification, testing, calibration, and troubleshooting of communications equipment and networked computer systems. Skilled in interpreting blueprints, drawings, instructions, and technical data to determine equipment and system malfunctions that did not respond to standard corrective measures; resolve complex problems and restore equipment systems and operations. Use common test instruments, such as digital multimeters, sign generators, semiconductor testers, and oscilloscopes, as well as computers and industrial measuring, controlling, and calibration devices.

PROGRAM MANAGEMENT: Plan and direct daily activities of Tactical Operations Center (TOC) in manner that ensures seamless static or mobile operations, including information collection, processing, and dissemination to other organizations. Oversee systems used by 300+ personnel and valued at more than $7M. Manage critical property and equipment, including remote Forward Area C4I tactical operations systems, facilitating communications among aircraft and personnel for field operations and medical evacuations.

COMMUNICATIONS: In addition to facilitating open channel of communications with users, foster open, productive relationships with senior managers, peers, and subordinates. Demonstrate equally strong and well-developed technical documentation and oral presentation/training skills. Instruct and coach junior-level tactical communications specialists in applying results of systems integration testing to modify specifications and correct problems and faults, as necessary.

United States Army
Schofield Barracks, HI
United States
Help Desk Technician, 06/2004 to 04/2006
Information Assurance Officer, 04/2006 to 06/2008

6/2004 to 6/2008
$55,000 per year
72 hours per week
Contact David Meadows, 478-555-4567
Contact Lance Donovan, 478-555-1234

OPERATIONS MANAGEMENT: In providing second-level technical support and managing complex networks for regional network operations and security center, ensured compliance with Department of Defense (DoD) and Department of Army (DA) goals, priorities, and values. Combined wealth of experience and expertise in strategic planning and organizational management with knowledge of LANs/Wide Area Networks (WANs), information management systems, and applications. Installed, conducted troubleshooting, and maintained PCs and peripherals, and served as senior member on Computer Emergency Response Teams (CERTs).

NETWORK ADMINISTRATION: Administered 1,500+ user accounts in Active Directory on more than 700 computers in DoD-Department of State's (DOS) Secret Internet Protocol Router Network (SIPRNet). Monitored outages via SPECTRUM OneClick for all of Oahu and surrounding islands and resolved operational issues on DoD's Non-secure Internet Protocol Router Network (NIPRNet), SIPRNet, and Voice over Internet Protocol (VoIP) networks throughout entire Pacific region. Planned, tested, and configured multiple operating systems on these networks, and manually updated software through Remote Desktop.

SECURITY ANALYSIS AND RISK FACTOR ASSESSMENT: Assisted in conducting in-depth evaluations of network security, including incident response, analyses of events adversely affecting system security, trend analyses, and threat intelligence. This entailed analyzing and validating more than 13K systems over network. Assessed and documented vulnerabilities from network- and application-based attacks and made recommendations for preventing, mitigating, and rectifying them. Monitored firewalls and web servers for vulnerability and stability risks, documenting flaws and determining critical steps necessary for maintaining security.

SECURITY PLAN DEVELOPMENT AND IMPLEMENTATION: Applied in-depth knowledge of automated information systems principles and methods, as well as commercial security products, technical documentation, and performance management methods. Expertly used Information Systems Development Methodology in developing customized information security systems and in creating security documentation containing preliminary strategic plan, risk analysis plans and detailed risk analyses, emergency response security measures, cost analyses, plans of action, and steps for managing this comprehensive security plan.

PROBLEM SOLVING: Evaluated and dealt effectively with Quality Control (QC) issues, which entailed maintaining daily records of all work performed and reporting issues. Determined core cause of problems and resolved them in most appropriate manner. Expertly read, interpreted, and applied drawings, instructions, and technical data to ensure LAN/WAN connectivity.

PROGRAM LEADERSHIP: Prepared reports, charts, and graphs for senior managers to use in their decision making. Demonstrated in-depth knowledge of technical engineering methods, applications, practices, and principles in working on various projects. Supervised network layout installation. Contributed onsite support in testing, Quality Assurance (QA), installation, and system integration. Astutely interpreted cabling schematics and devised cost-effective solutions.

ASSESSMENTS AND COMMUNICATIONS: Assisted peers and subordinates with varying levels of technical understanding in several areas, including troubleshooting, disaster recovery procedures and processes, and system maintenance. Provided expert-level technical advice to key decision makers and assisted in developing plans, schedules, and strategies to fit new situations and enhance customer service. Analyzed and responded to complex problems with innovative solutions and thoughtful recommendations.

OPERATIONS MANAGEMENT: In providing second-level technical support and managing complex networks for regional network operations and security center, ensured compliance with Department of Defense (DoD) and Department of Army goals, priorities, and values. Combined wealth of experience and expertise in strategic planning and organizational management with knowledge of local area networks/wide area networks, information management systems, and applications. Installed, conducted troubleshooting, and maintained PCs and peripherals, and served as senior member on Computer Emergency Response Teams (CERTS).

NETWORK ADMINISTRATION: Administered 1,000+ user accounts in Active Directory on more than 500 computers in DoD-Department of State's Secret Internet Protocol Router Network (SIPRNet). Monitored and resolved operational issues, including outages, on DoD's Non-secure Internet Protocol Router Network (NIPRNET), SIPRNet, and Voice-over Internet Protocol (VoIP) networks throughout entire Pacific region. Planned, tested, and configured multiple operating systems on these networks, and manually updated software through Remote Desktop.

SECURITY ANALYSIS AND RISK FACTOR ASSESSMENT: Assisted in conducting in-depth evaluations of network security, including incident response, analysis of events adversely affecting system security, trend analyses, and threat intelligence. Assessed and documented vulnerabilities from network- and application-based attacks, and made recommendations for preventing, mitigating, and rectifying them. Monitored firewalls and web servers for vulnerability and stability risks, documenting flaws and determining critical steps necessary for maintaining security.

SECURITY PLAN DEVELOPMENT AND IMPLEMENTATION: Applied in-depth knowledge of automated information systems principles and methods, as well as commercial security products, technical documentation, and performance management methods. Expertly used Information Systems Development Methodology in developing customized information security systems and in creating security documentation containing preliminary strategic plan, risk analysis plan and detailed risk analyses, emergency response security measures, cost analysis, plans of action, and steps for managing this comprehensive security plan.

PROBLEM SOLVING: Evaluated and dealt effectively with quality control issues, which entailed maintaining daily records of all work performed and reporting issues. Determined core cause of problems and resolved them in most appropriate manner. Expertly read, interpreted, and applied drawings, instructions, and technical data to ensure LAN/WAN connectivity.

PROGRAM LEADERSHIP: Prepared reports, charts, and graphs for senior managers to use in their decision-making. Demonstrated in-depth knowledge of technical engineering methods, applications, practices, and principles in working on various projects. Supervised network layout installation. Contributed on-site support in testing, quality assurance, installation, and system integration. Astutely interpreted cabling schematics and devised cost-effective solutions.

ASSESSMENTS AND COMMUNICATIONS: Assisted peers and subordinates with varying levels of technical understanding in several areas, including troubleshooting, disaster recovery procedures and processes, and system maintenance. Provided expert-level technical advice to key decision makers and assisted in developing plans, schedules, and strategies to fit new situations and enhance customer service. Analyzed and responded to complex problems with innovative solutions and thoughtful recommendations.

EDUCATION:

Kaplan University, Information Technology
Hagerstown, MD
United States
Associate in Applied Science
In Process

Cedar High School
Des Moines, IA
United States
Diploma
2003

JOB RELATED TRAINING:

Cisco VoIP, 09/2007; Equal Opportunity Leadership Course, 04/2007; Primary Leadership Course, 02/2007; IP Addressing and Routing, 02/2007; Managing Microsoft Active Directory in a Server 2003 Environment, 03/2006;

Installing and Maintaining Microsoft Exchange 2003, 03/2006; Information Technology Specialist School, 07/2005 to 11/2005; Computer Information Systems Analyst Course, 03/2004

RELATED INFORMATION

REFERENCES:

Willard Ford
United States (U.S.) Army
Technical Officer
910-555-1234
will.ford@mail.com
Professional Reference

Janet Lee
U.S. Army
Recruiter
910-555-3456
j.lee@mail.com
Professional Reference

Edward Smith
U.S. Army
Technical Officer
910-555-9876
ed.smith@mail.com
Professional Reference

ADDITIONAL INFORMATION:

SECURITY CLEARANCE: Secret, active

PROFESSIONAL SUMMARY: Resourceful and multifaceted Information Technology (IT)/Telecommunications professional with multiple certifications, offering extensive hands-on experience in personal computer/network operations and information management security. Highly adept at applying in-depth knowledge of Local Area Network/Wide Area Network (LAN/WAN) principles, concepts, and operations in executing wide range of technical functions, to include setting up, operating, maintaining, modifying, testing, calibrating, and troubleshooting communications equipment and networked computer systems; configuring Cisco routers and switches; and establishing and maintaining firewalls and border security. Equally comprehensive understanding of infrastructure requirements, such as bandwidth and server sizing, for maintaining and managing Windows XP/2003 and Exchange servers, as well as Transmission Control Protocol/Internet Protocol (TCP/IP) and Unix/Solaris system administration. Solid track record of assessing user needs, resolving problems, analyzing risk factors, and meeting business requirements. Prized for ability to deal with users with courtesy and tact, communicating clearly and concisely in person, by phone, and in writing. Proactive, solution-focused, and challenge-oriented, with proven ability to remain focused while working under tight deadlines and handling multiple priorities with frequent interruptions to deliver outstanding performance, even for demanding and complex assignments.

CERTIFICATIONS:
+ CompTIA Security+
+ Fiber Optic Installer
+ Information Assurance, Level II

AREAS OF EXPERTISE:
+ System Administration
+ Help Desk Management

+ Information Assurance
+ Application Analyst
+ Tactical Communications Operations
+ Data Analysis
+ Information Management
+ Global Communication and Control System
+ Communications Security
+ Compliance with Established Standards, SOPs, and Directives
+ Organization Liaison
+ Asset Monitoring
+ Active Directory
+ VBScript
+ REMEDY Incident Management Console

OPERATING SYSTEMS: Microsoft (MS) Windows NT/2000/XP/Vista, MS Windows 7, MS Exchange Server 2003, MS Server 2003/2007

NETWORK APPLICATION SOFTWARE: MS Office XP/2003/2007, MS Outlook, Ghost 9, Acronis Backup and Recovery, Remedy, MS SharePoint

NETWORKING: DHCP, WINS, DNS, TCP/IP, UDP, ICMP, LDAP, Remote Access Server/RRAS, VPN, VNC, Remote Desktop Connection, Active Directory, Wireless Router, VMware ESXi Server, Active Directory Services Administration

SECURITY: Symantec Anti-Virus/Endpoint Protection, Anti-Spyware, PKI Certificates, VBS Scripting, Information Assurance, NIPRNet Spillage, eEye Retina

AWARDS AND DECORATIONS:
+ Afghanistan Campaign Medal with Campaign Star
+ Army Commendation Medal
+ Meritorious Unit Commendation (2)
+ Army Good Conduct Medal (2)
+ National Defense Service Medal
+ Global War on Terrorism Service Medal
+ Army Service Ribbon
+ Overseas Service Ribbon

Homer White

173 Pierce Avenue
Macon, GA 31204
United States
Email: info@careerprocenter.net
Day/Mobile Phone: 555-123-4567
Evening Phone: 478-742-2442

WORK EXPERIENCE

U.S. Army, Military Intelligence Battalion	2010 to Present
Atlanta, GA, United States	$34,000 per year
Cryptologic Linguist/Information Analyst	40 hours per week
Supervisor: Staff Sergeant Tamara Hart	Phone: 478-742-2442

Duties, Accomplishments and Related Skills:

INFORMATION GATHERING AND MANAGEMENT: Use multilingual language proficiencies (Spanish, Italian), and apply laws, rules/regulations, and written guidelines to collect and translate foreign communications vital to safeguarding homeland security and international relations. Specialize in working with records and documents, in performing administrative and technical procedures using computer systems to locate and review records and reconcile discrepancies, and in accessing multiple systems to conduct threat analyses.

TECHNICAL SUPPORT: Address wide range of issues/problems that require unique solutions, which entails making determinations and using sound judgment. Expertly operate Signals Intelligence (SIGINT) and controlled cryptographic equipment to detect, locate, identify, and acquire foreign Electronic Intelligence (ELINT). Provide critical assistance in searching radio spectrum to collect and identify target communications and to perform elementary signals analysis to determine signal parameters for identification and processing.

TRAINING: Incorporate experience gained through work in customer-service positions that involved frequent contact with public and involved researching and/or adjusting customer accounts (see Other Experience). Spearhead enhancements and process improvements to daily operations by coaching and mentoring other personnel in exceeding organizational expectations. Apply excellent interpersonal abilities to cultivate and maintain positive working environment and professional atmosphere.

LEADERSHIP: Draw upon in-depth knowledge of established rules and procedures in securing, analyzing, and protecting sensitive information. Entrusted with managerial oversight of intelligence data; fine-tune procedures for securing, analyzing, and protecting sensitive information with high accuracy. Adopt customer service-type approach in providing technical assistance and making recommendations.

CHANGE MANAGEMENT: Consistently use innovation to devise plans and strategies to fit new situations. Develop win-win situations by maintaining strategic focus and viewing problematic issues as challenges rather than obstacles. Expertly apply strategic planning, organizational, and time-management skills, in the process motivating others to adhere to superior standards of excellence.

U.S. Army, 183rd Military Intelligence Battalion	2008 to 2010
Fort Gordon, GA, United States	$29,000 per year
Human Resources Specialist	40 hours per week
Supervisor: First Sergeant Norman Wittman	Phone: 478-742-2442

Duties, Accomplishments and Related Skills:

PROGRAM MANAGEMENT: Considered technical expert on wide variety of administrative matters; provided advice and guidance to management on administration problems and management. Scrutinized data to interpret composite results in preparing personnel accounting and strength management reports and annual performance evaluations. Applied Human Resources (HR) concepts, practices, laws, regulations, and policies in meeting diverse needs of 250+ Military Personnel (MILPER), in accordance with Equal Employment Opportunity (EEO) and affirmative action requirements. Through leadership by example and mentoring, supervised four personnel and ensured compliance with Department of Defense (DoD) and Army security regulations, internal controls and Standard Operating Procedures (SOPs), and work processes. Reorganized Leave and Finance Section, and revamped SOPs pertaining to personal leave, increasing rate for processing these requests from previous level of 45% to 93%.

PERSONNEL ADMINISTRATION: Oversaw processing and tracking of personnel actions, suspension of favorable actions, reclassification actions, transfers, leaves and passes, discharges, decorations and awards, and military pay. Prepared and monitored Requests for Information (RFIs) cards and tags, and meal cards. Arranged and coordinated awards ceremonies. Managed MILPER data and training support files, and posted changes to Army regulations and other publications at Battalion level.

INFORMATION MANAGEMENT: Maintained personnel files in accordance with Army Records Information Management System (ARIMS). Researched guidelines, identified discrepancies in local transaction codes, resolved errors involving personnel data by reviewing records and files, and resubmitted data. Used knowledge of Military Occupational Specialties (MOS), Special Qualification Identifiers (SQI), and Additional Skill Identifiers (ASI) to update Personnel Manning Authorization Document/The Army Authorization Documentation System (PMAD/TAADS) to assign personnel to authorized positions, published duty calendars, and training programs.

AUTOMATED SYSTEMS: Inputted and controlled data using Military Personnel Office (eMILPO); read, interpreted, and reconciled eMILPO reports; determined reportable changes, category, duty status codes, and other documentation. Applied provisions and limitations of Freedom of Information Act (FOIA) and Privacy Act. Entered/retrieved information from databases; submitted actions for correction in Enlisted Distribution and Assignment System (EDAS) and Personnel Tempo (PERSTEMPO). Inputted and managed training data into Digital Training Management System (DTMS) to plan, resource, and manage both individual and collective task training at all levels.

TRAINING: Oversaw all training programs for more than 250 MILPER. Developed and implemented training management system that was praised by Army Intelligence and Security Command (INSCOM) as "best throughout the Brigade." This training management system was credited with more accurately assessing organizational training needs, tracking training programs, and monitoring professional development status and weapons qualification levels—which, in turn, ensured 100% operational readiness.

EDUCATION

Georgia State University   General Studies
Macon, GA, United States
Associate's Degree   GPA: 3.3

JOB RELATED TRAINING:
DTMS Master Trainer Course administered by Department of Army, 2010. Training in Microsoft (MS) Excel from Georgia School of Business, 2009.

ADDITIONAL INFORMAITON

PROFESSIONAL SUMMARY: Dynamic analytical and Human Resources (HR) professional with U.S. Army and private-sector experience. Combine ability to analyze and evaluate intelligence information and highly sensitive data critical to strategic and tactical planning with solid track record in HR administration, personnel actions, policies and procedures development, customer service, data management, documentation control, and office administration.

AREAS OF EXPERTISE:
+ Securing, Analyzing, and Protecting Sensitive Information
+ Signals Intelligence
+ Data Analysis
+ Research of Computerized Records
+ Technical Support
+ Applying Established Rules and Procedures
+ Human Resources Administration
+ Training
+ Recordkeeping
+ Document Control
+ Basic Accounting
+ Dispute and Issue Resolution
+ Discrepancy Reconciliation
+ Customer Service
+ Written and Oral Communications

SECURITY CLEARANCE: Top Secret/SCI, active

MILITARY DECORATIONS AND AWARDS: Army Commendation Medal, Army Achievement Medal, Army Good Conduct Medal

FOREIGN LANGUAGE FLUENCIES: Spanish, Italian

AUTOMATED PERSONNEL SYSTEMS: Electronic Military Personnel Office (eMILPO), Enlisted Distribution and Assignment System (EDAS), Personnel Manning Authorization Document/The Army Authorization Documentation System (PMAD/TAADS), Army Records Information Management System (ARIMS), Digital Training Management System (DTMS)

TECHNICAL SKILLS: Microsoft (MS) Word, Excel, Access, PowerPoint, Outlook Express

ROM RECOMMENDATION FOR ARMY COMMENDATION MEDAL: "Specialist White provided outstanding administrative support to more than 250 soldiers, Department of Defense (DoD) civilians, and contractors assigned to the 183rd Military Intelligence Battalion. He singlehandedly prepared the Battalion awards section for the Brigade inspection, spending numerous after-duty hours requalifying the Army Records Information Management System (ARIMS) for awards and daily tasks. As a result, he was commended by the Brigade for showing 100% efficiency in the ARIMS program."

OTHER EXPERIENCE:
+ Reservations Sales Agent, Delta Airlines, Augusta, GA, 2007 to 2008. Applied established rules and procedures, as well as excellent understanding of travel-related laws and regulations. Provided technical assistance to individuals and/or businesses primarily through telephone interactions. Made determinations and used sound judgment to resolve disputes and issues. Developed, analyzed, and evaluated information involving research of computerized records by accessing multiple online/database systems. Secured, analyzed, and protected sensitive personal and financial information.
+ Cashier, Miller Co., Augusta, GA, 2006 to 2007. In addition to providing exemplary customer service, managed accounts receivable and payable, general ledger, and daily cash drawer reconciliation. Analyzed accounting data and accounts to resolve complex, non-standard transactions, complaints, or discrepancies. Participated in monthly closing process, including all financial management reporting. Used automated computer systems and programs to prepare financial statements, closing and cost accounting reports, balance sheets, and account reconciliation statements.

Edwin T. Orr

173 Pierce Avenue, Macon, GA 31204 United States
Email: info@careerprocenter.net
Day Phone: 478-742-2442
Evening Phone: 478-742-2442

EXPERIENCE:

U.S. Marine Forces Europe	06/2009 to Present
Stuttgart, Germany	$72,000 per year
Operations Manager	Average hours per week: 50
Supervisor: Francis Holland	Phone: 478-555-1234

Duties, Accomplishments and Related Skills:
Serve with Marine Forces Europe (MARFOREUR) as senior-enlisted Operations Manager and advisor, analyst, and designer of multinational training programs designed to indoctrinate and train U.S. partner nation armed forces in the art and form of American forces Non-Commissioned Officer (NCO) and junior officer leadership methods and styles. Influential in the evaluation and rewriting of policies and directives to improve performance and increase operational efficiencies within MARFOREUR and associated commands.

Design, develop, and suggest policy and planning components and improvements to major command-level initiatives working with international partners through various elements and levels of foreign policy directives and military partner development. Senior advisor and instructor on operational Command and Control (C2)

ANALYSIS AND EVALUATION: Analyze and provide insight to the overall tactical approach to execute global operational strategies affecting partnerships, theater security, lines of operation and activity, policy formulation, planning hierarchy and portfolios, categories of national interest, and strategy-to-task items. Contribute to publications of guidance, summaries of comparative worldviews, competing interests, Planning, Programming, Budgeting and Execution System, and financial management. Support the assimilation for tactical-level command to execute a given strategy through operational design conducted in a permissive, non-permissive, conventional or small war in a combatant and service command Area of Operation (AOO).

RESEARCH AND INVESTIGATION: Research existing processes and rewrite policy and directives to improve efficiencies in the daily performance of staff and the related bureaucracy. Coordinate, implement, and manage improved information flow to senior management to permit faster and more accurate decision making.

ADVICE AND GUIDANCE: Facilitate the mission readiness training of the (former Soviet) Georgian military forces and Black Sea Rotational Force in the science and art of U.S. style C2. Design and implement methodology for the further evaluation of the Georgian military by U.S. military personnel to assess combat readiness and effectiveness for Afghanistan missions. Identify emerging issues and perform evaluation process and readiness review of this vital international mission.

PROGRAM MANAGEMENT: Prepare military informational briefings for operations matters to the senior MARFOREUR leadership. Develop, supervise, and present operations training to MARFOREUR staff. Manage divisional data flow of information processed through the Command, Control, Communications, Computers, Intelligence (C4I) systems. Assimilate and contribute to national strategy processing and functioning in MARFOREUR.

COMMUNICATIONS: Restructure flow, input and output of information, and the management of data within the MARFOREUR Operations Center environment to increase throughput and ease the decision-making process.

LIAISON: Collaborate with senior MARFOREUR leaders on the discipline, appearance, training, control, conduct, and welfare of the operations staff, and throughout the USEUC theater of operations.

INTERNATIONAL AFFAIRS: Facilitate and support diplomacy as a component of forming agreements with collaborating nations, alliances, and global committees to leverage the state's desires to contribute to certain strategic efforts structured around the security of likeminded nations and that support the U.S. and democracy throughout the international community and systems.

ACCOMPLISHMENTS:
* Facilitated the support and training for the Joint Chiefs of Staff (JCS)-initiated Georgian Deployment Program (support for Marines in Afghanistan) as leader for the MARFOREUR at the Joint Multinational Readiness Center (JMRC) and the Black Sea Rotational Force (BSRF) to develop international cooperative security exercises among nations throughout the Black Sea area with further positioning for humanitarian missions.
* Assessed, designed, and implemented an enduring NCO course to develop military-enlisted, officer, and junior leaders in the science and art of leadership to elevate capabilities from a Russian military-centralized style to a Western democratic persuasive style of leadership for partner nations. Influenced military training in multiple nations, including Georgia, Bulgaria, Romania, Macedonia, Serbia, Azerbaijan, and other Eastern European, Balkan, and Caucasus nations.
* Selected to analyze military operations and training throughout the North Atlantic Treaty Organization (NATO), European Command, and Service Component AOOs. Evaluated the strategic environment under the guidance of current and future operations with partnering nations and the effects on the National Security Strategy. Provided current successes, challenges, future objectives, and recommendations for improved interoperability and achieving optimal strategic, operational, and tactical actions.

U.S. Marine Corps School of Infantry East	02/2007 to 05/2009
Camp Lejeune, NC, United States	$73,000 per year
Infantry Operations Manager	Average hours per week: 50
Supervisor: Phillip Franks	Phone: 478-555-1234

Duties, Accomplishments and Related Skills:
Managed training operations of large U.S. Marines training facility to ensure basic warfighting skills were conducted daily in accordance with the school training plan with authority over class instruction, field operations, live fire ranges, and supervision of the training staff. Facilitated continual improvement of the planning, implementation, and management all school training as directed by the school orders. Served as senior-enlisted advisor to the operations executive management.

ANALYSIS AND EVALUATION: Evaluated 64 end-of-course critiques; reviewed and conducted trend analyses and presented findings and recommendations to senior management.

ADVICE AND GUIDANCE: Revamped Standard Operating Procedures (SOPs) and conducted a complete reorganization for operations, safety, and medical practices to significantly improve the conduct, effectiveness, and efficiency of students in training and permanent personnel throughout the training continuum. Ensured annual training requirements were established and met for training division staff.

PROGRAM MANAGEMENT: Directed training programs to effectively migrate Marines from initial basic training up to and through combat-ready training with management over two development paths: those identified in the core occupational specialty of infantry, and those with other (non-infantry) designations to achieve a common skill set achieving the mantra, "every Marine is first and foremost a rifleman." Provided well-trained graduates to various missions, ensuring consistently educated and skilled personnel for the many tasks carried out domestically and overseas in support of national goals. Developed and implemented an emergency response operations center in response to severe and destructive weather circumstances.

COMMUNICATIONS: Leveraged graduate education received (resulting in a Master's Degree in International Relations) to oversight of the training and operations missions to gain greater insight into how effective training contributes to the larger scope of national security. Guest speaker at several leadership and combat training courses.

LIAISON: Served as liaison to logistics staff to ensure all training logistics needs were on target and fulfilled.

INTERNATIONAL AFFAIRS: Organized and supervised 20 VIP visits by foreign dignitaries and delegations and senior U.S. Marines general staff.

ACCOMPLISHMENTS:
* Graduated Webster University with a Master's Degree in International Relations.

U.S. Marine Corps, First Battalion, Eighth Marines	05/2004 to 02/2007
Camp Lejeune, NC, United States	$62,500 per year
Operations Manager	Average hours per week: 80
Supervisor: Joshua Martin	Phone: 478-742-2442

Duties, Accomplishments and Related Skills:
Served as Operations Manager (Operation Chief) for a large U.S. Marines organization (battalion) with multiple supervisory roles affecting a wide range of operations, staffing, and support. Provided advanced management support as advisor to senior operations staff for the control, conduct, welfare, appearance, and discipline of up to 1,200 personnel. Deployed overseas to area of combat operations; supervised 100% logistical accountability of equipment for embarkation of the organization for transportation overseas and subsequent, seamless turnover of all systems, processes, and information to replacement personnel upon return from deployment.

ANALYSIS AND EVALUATION: Provided program evaluation and implemented improvements to the operations and training sections, resulting in upgraded skills to Marine personnel necessary to conduct C2 and combat operations in Iraq; relief efforts for Hurricane Katrina; and the conduct of naval operations aboard ships in the Mediterranean Sea, the Suez Canal, the Gulf of Oman, the Persian Gulf, and Iraq.

ADVICE AND GUIDANCE: Trained operations section staff and watch officers in effectively performing tasks to support the overall training objectives of the organization.

PROGRAM MANAGEMENT: Supervised the establishment and conduct of the combat operations center (including development of combat operations center SOPs) in Fallujah, Iraq as well as the actions of assigned personnel and the processing and flow of data and information within the center. Tracked and managed multiple operational projects. Served as Operations Watch Officer for operations supporting the relief efforts in New Orleans following Hurricane Katrina.

COMMUNICATIONS: Supervised the maintenance and accuracy of the operation section publications and prepared briefings on behalf of the operations division.

ACCOMPLISHMENTS:
* Directed successful embarkation and management of combat operations center for intensive 30-day training mission to Kuwait with full accountability for data, processes, and operational integrity of the organization.

U.S. Marine Corps Headquarters and Headquarters Squadron	05/2002 to 05/2004
Jacksonville, NC, United States	$48,000 per year
Training Manager	Average hours per week: 40
Supervisor: James Scott	Phone: 919-555-6789

Duties, Accomplishments and Related Skills:
Served as Training Manager for the Marine Corps Air Station, New River installation in Jacksonville, NC. Planned, implemented, and managed professional development for 600+ military personnel in compliance with the Marine Corps Systems Approach to Training (SAT).

ANALYSIS AND EVALUATION: Analyzed tracking needs and developed a comprehensive computer database for recording and tracking of annual training and physical fitness training requirements.

RESEARCH AND INVESTIGATION: Worked with independent agency to conduct self-investigation of existing training program and processes as prelude to overhaul of training organization and systems. Comments received from Inspector General (IG) regarding the training section were "the best he had seen" of such programs.

PROGRAM MANAGEMENT: Completely restructured and modernized the Squadron operations and training branch, enabling the effective delivery of compulsory military and civilian education necessary for promotion and overcoming previous flaws in organizational management. Staff achieved measurable improvements in skills and performance levels. Subsequent formal inspections by senior staff of the training and operations processes resulted in a superior grade of "noteworthy" in recognition of the reorganization. Managed all aspects of training division operations, tracking, and compliance. Implemented and managed a martial arts program.

LIAISON: Collaborated closely with 30+ individual section offices to coordinate all annual and "pop-up" training requirements and delivery. Fostered a sense of ownership across the organization.

ACCOMPLISHMENTS:
* Nominated for and received Navy and Marine Corps Commendation Medal for efforts in restructuring and revamping the military and civilian training and personnel promotions process.
* Led organization to achieve a 97% qualification rating on the annual review, up from a previous 65%.
* Successfully completed Bachelor's Degree in History from Campbell University.

EDUCATION:

University of Pittsburgh   Major: History

International Relations: Theory and Practice, 3 Sem Hrs; Political Economy, 3 Sem Hrs; Globalization, 3 Sem Hrs; International Organization, 3 Sem Hrs; U.S. Foreign Policy, 3 Sem Hrs; Negotiations, 3 Sem Hrs;

Introduction to International Relations, 3 Sem Hrs; War and Diplomacy, 3 Sem Hrs; Research Methods, 3 Sem Hrs; Politics of Development, 3 Sem Hrs; International Political Economy, 3 Sem Hrs

Pittsburgh, PA, United States   Minor: Government
Bachelor's Degree   GPA: 3.57
Completion Date: 05/2004   120 Semester Credits Earned

Job Related Training:

RELEVANT TRAINING:
Lean Six Sigma Course, (Pending Completion 2012)
Marine Corps University Command and Staff War College, 05/2012 Graduation
Senior-Enlisted Joint Professional Military Education (JPME), 2009
Marine Corps Tactics and Operations Group-Operations and Tactics Instructor Course, 2008
Master Gunnery Sergeant Symposium, 2007
Infantry Operation Chief, 2005
Senior Non-Commissioned Officer (NCO) Advanced Course, 2000
Curriculum Developers Course, 1995

Additional Information:
Current Top Secret/Sensitive Compartmented Information Security Clearance (TS/SCI), 2011

SUPERVISOR QUOTES AND RATING TEAM COMMENTARY:
"Powerful command presence. Deftly manages simultaneous tasks for current and future operations. Upbeat in the performance of his duties; serious in the accomplishment of the mission."
MAJ SAL CONNER, Operations Officer, U.S. Marine Corps School of Infantry

PROFESSIONAL SUMMARY:
Highly experienced U.S. Marine Corps (USMC) Senior Non-Commissioned Officer (SNCO) with 30 years of experience in operations management, training, foreign policy, and international relations. Passionate leader with a history of elevating the skills and performance of those in proximity while upholding the highest standards of performance as a Marine and serving with unquestioned professionalism as a delegate to foreign military officials and dignitaries. Consistently perform at superior levels in diverse situations under frequently stressful or hazardous conditions. Widely recognized by the most senior staff as a diligent, resourceful professional, adept in handling a range of challenges from staff administration and operations management to foreign policy implementation of the most sensitive and nationally important programs.

PROFESSIONAL HIGHLIGHTS:
* Rapidly assimilated role as senior-enlisted leader within Marine Forces Europe (MARFOREUR) in comprehending and advancing the national strategies of Congress and the Joint Chiefs of Staff (JCS) by designing and implementing instructional and behavioral programs for foreign military personnel in the ways and methods of Western-style Command and Control (C2).
* Successfully pursued and achieved advanced degree (Master's) in International Relations and embraced role as representative and military liaison for U.S. interests in multiple missions to diverse countries.
* Achieved excellence in operations management and training during multiple assignments in challenging roles, both domestically and overseas. Recognized by senior leadership with multiple awards, medals, and certificates for achievements in advancing the USMC role with global impact.
* Personally mentored hundreds of staff to achieve advanced education and military promotions while overhauling several organizational operations and training programs, resulting in the implementation of advanced and sustainable skills while effectively saving lives and improving mission results.

* Served multiple overseas and domestic combat and humanitarian assignments with superb results as measured by on-the-ground achievements such as 100% compliance in logistics handling of transiting groups and recognition of performance in formal reviews.
* Completed Marine Corps University Command and Staff War College in May, 2012, greatly contributing to skills regarding joint command strategies.

AWARDS:
* Navy and Marine Corps Commendation Medal (3)
* Navy and Marine Corps Achievement Medal
* Navy Unit Commendation (5)
* Navy Meritorious Unit Commendation (6)
* Joint Meritorious Service Award
* Secretary of the Navy Letter of Commendation

Kevin MacDonald

173 Pierce Avenue, Macon, GA 31204 United States
Email: info@careerprocenter.net
Day Phone: 478-742-2442

WORK EXPERIENCE

U.S. Air Force (USAF) Defense Contract Management Agency (DCMA), Northrop Grumman	06/2011 to Present
Atlanta, GA, United States	$75,000 per year
Government Flight Representative (GFR)	Average hours per week: 45
Supervisor: Major Ernest Templeton, USAF	Phone: 478-742-2442

Duties, Accomplishments and Related Skills:

The Defense Contract Management Agency (DCMA) works directly with defense suppliers to ensure supplies and services are delivered on time, are delivered at projected cost, and meet all performance requirements. As the Government Flight Representative (GFR), develop safety program to limit danger to personnel during maintenance, repairs, and test flights.

PROGRAM MANAGEMENT AND ANALYSIS: Oversee safety program for depot-level maintenance performed on KC-10 Extender aerial tanker and E-8C Joint STARS surveillance aircraft. Analyze and evaluate the effectiveness of program operations for two contracts worth $2.1B. Develop new program policies, procedures, and regulations designed to reduce the probability of accidents during depot repairs, maintenance, and test flights. Determine compliance with contract regulations, procedures, and sound management practices. Adapt procedures to real-world contingencies.

COMMUNICATION/COORDINATION: Serve as government's representative to Northrop Grumman's Maintenance and Modification Center in Atlanta, GA. Coordinate safety requirements with contractor and prepare written reports, as needed. Complete mishap and accident reports. Issue corrective action reports, as required, to inform contractors of needed safety improvements.

SAFETY MANAGEMENT: Manage air, ground, and industrial safety program for more than 800K square feet of facilities at Kingston Airport. The spaces include hangars, repair facilities, fabrication shops, and office space. Apply knowledge of recognized safety and health principles, standards, and techniques gained during USAF career. Recognize potentially hazardous conditions and develop measures to eliminate or control these conditions. Inspect and evaluate activities of aviation organization for conformance with contract terms. Inspect the airworthiness of aircraft after they have undergone alterations or major repairs.

ACCOMPLISHMENT:
* Adapted quickly to new role, creating procedures to reduce risk to personnel and aircraft and to lead to the safe delivery of 14 KC-10 and 10E-8C aircraft per year.

USAF, Air Operations Squadron Detachment Two	06/2008 to 05/2011
Ramstein Air Base (AB), Rheinland-Pfalz, Germany	$63,500 per year
Delivery Control Manager	Average hours per week: 45
Supervisor: Charles Nelson	Phone: 478-742-2442

Duties, Accomplishments and Related Skills:

Organization provides support to military aircraft in the European Area of Operations (AOO). As the Delivery Control Manager, ensured the worldwide movement of aircraft.

OPERATIONS MANAGEMENT: Planned and coordinated the delivery of aircraft to exercises and contingency operations. Managed all aspects of delivery, including briefings, air-refueling operations, and emergency diversion plans.

Planned the mission route and handled all airspace and diplomatic clearances. Adapted plans to meet unexpected delays or problems, including aircraft at divert sites, severe weather, and maintenance issues. Led short-notice movements vital for combat aircraft maintenance.

COORDINATION: Coordinated with all branches of the U.S. military and foreign civilian and military officials while preparing aircraft movement missions. Demonstrated outstanding multinational coordination skills, repeatedly moving aircraft between Europe, the Middle East, and Africa. Interacted with officials from 12 foreign countries. Ensured tanker availability and scheduling, as needed, for aerial refueling. Improved movement procedures for aeromedical extraction team, ensuring critical medical evacuation capability.

COMMUNICATIONS: Served as liaison for Special Operations Forces in the Middle East, ensuring executive-level managers had a clear understanding of the operational status of assets in the Middle East. Provided high-level briefings and written reports for Special Forces leaders. Demonstrated outstanding oral communication skills and the ability to handle sensitive and high-visibility operations with countries such as Iraq and Afghanistan.

ACCOMPLISHMENTS:
* Directed movement of 295 combat aircraft on 39 missions, supporting operations in Iraq and Afghanistan.
* Delivered F-16 Block 50 aircraft to Iran, handling sensitive diplomatic issues.
* Coordinated the delivery of U.S. and foreign aircraft for training exercises.
* Adapted to unexpected contingencies, such as providing tanker support to five F-16 aircraft at three divert sites or ten F-18s needed for operations in Afghanistan.

USAF Air Mobility Division   05/2005 to 06/2008
Ramstein AB, Rheinland-Pfalz, Germany $60,000 per year
Refueling Operations Manager   Average hours per week: 40
Supervisor: Steven Lee   Phone: 478-742-2442

Duties, Accomplishments and Related Skills:
Organization provides global air mobility. As Refueling Operations Manager, directed the utilization of 15 aerial refueling aircraft worth more than $465M.

PLANNING AND COORDINATION: Managed aerial refueling operations in Europe, tasking high-priority missions to ensure national security objectives. Conducted planning and scheduling of tanker missions, including building the air-refueling plan in support of major North Atlantic Treaty Organization (NATO) summit. Prioritized air-refueling, airlift, and operational support missions. Maximized training and exercise participation to ensure operational readiness. Established extensive testing procedures for Standards and Evaluation program.

PROGRAM ANALYSIS: Developed air-refueling policy and procedures for European AOO. Gathered and integrated input from eight agencies to rewrite existing logistics policy. Determined the Information Technology (IT) requirements associated with the refueling program. Evaluated aerial refueling requirements and Foreign Military Sales (FMS) program requests from nine NATO countries. Coordinated initial stages of Polish refueling contract. Identified resources, including staff, funding, and equipment, required to support varied levels of program operations. Analyzed and evaluated proposed changes in mission, operating procedures, and delegations of authority; adapted to meet them.

PROCESS IMPROVEMENT: Streamlined rapid tasking process to improve alert times for aircrews. Implemented new Command and Control (C2) system to track airlift and air tanker status, improving scheduling and saving $28K per year. Demonstrated creativity and decision-making skills to adapt KC-135 for a first-ever aeromedical evacuation flight; evacuated a critically ill patient from Africa within 22 hours, saving his life.

OPERATIONS MANAGEMENT: Served as Assistant Director for organization in Djibouti, Africa. Tracked and maintained accountability for 1.5K personnel. Directed 40 counterterrorism operations and 360 flights. Ensured completion of 420 civil-military missions, including border security, school construction, well drilling, training, and civil action missions. Oversaw safe and timely execution of humanitarian missions, emergency medical evacuations, and combat support while ensuring information flow from the field to senior managers and back.

ACCOMPLISHMENTS:
* Directed 4.1K KC-135 aerial refueling flights, ensuring the ability of U.S. aircraft to meet all commitments.
* Orchestrated short-notice refueling of MC-130 aircraft, evacuating 90 U.S. citizens during Noncombatant Evacuation Operations (NEO) from Lebanon.
* Planned and scheduled refueling operations, enabling the movement of medical teams throughout a five-location Presidential tour in Africa.
* Developed air-refueling plan for continuous air coverage for the President and seven other Heads of State.

USAF 75th Air Group	05/2002 to 05/2006
Keflavik Naval Air Station (NAS), Iceland	$55,000 per year
Safety Manager	Average hours per week: 40
Supervisor: Kyle West	Phone: 478-742-2882

Duties, Accomplishments and Related Skills:
Organization ensured air sovereignty in Iceland through air defense and early warning services. As Safety Manager, identified and mitigated aviation risks.

PROGRAM MANAGEMENT: Led group's safety program, ensuring protection of more than 475 personnel, 6 organizations, and $223M in assets. Formulated, implemented, maintained, and modified safety and occupational health programs for F-15, KC-135, MC-130, and HH-60 aircraft operations. Conducted various safety inspections, ensuring compliance with Department of Defense (DoD), Occupational Safety and Health Administration (OSHA), and USAF requirements. Evaluated and approved training methods, facilities, and equipment for pilots, mechanics, and other aviation personnel. Secured the most safety training slots for any USAF Europe group, in spite of small size. Identified required resources, justifying and receiving funding for sleep deprivation prevention program. Conducted three-month study of needs in preparation for airspace negotiations. Reviewed administrative audit, finding $400K in flight pay mistakes and identifying three personnel who should have received jump qualifications.

SAFETY INSPECTION AND IMPROVEMENT: Identified safety issues and communicated the appropriate measures to resolve problems, improving mid-air collision avoidance, bird strike hazards, and aircraft technical problems, among others. Provided recommendations to resolve safety issues. Investigated ground, weapons, and flight accidents. Searched for clues, studied variables, questioned witnesses, and retraced sequences to uncover the sources of the mishap. Ensured validity of information gathered and examined data to identify possible causes. Determined critical factors and recommended alternatives to minimize future losses. Wrote summaries of mishaps and issued corrective actions.

COMMUNICATIONS: Advised and persuaded executive-level managers on the importance of adhering to safety programs. Ensured compliance with and communication of safety rules and regulations throughout base and with civil aviation authorities nationwide. Conducted safety briefings to flight and ground personnel. Took safety communications from work to the home, targeting Driving Under the Influence (DUI), suicide, and substance abuse, resulting in fewer incidents.

ACCOMPLISHMENTS:
* Led group to a zero percent ground mishap rate—the best in the Air Force (AF).
* Oversaw 2.2K HH-60 hours, 1.5K F-15 flights, and 679 KC-135 aerial refuelings with zero class A or B mishaps.
* Analyzed HH-60 mishap, identifying fleet-wide problem and initiating appropriate technical fix.
* Coordinated with civil aviation and devised air-collision avoidance procedures, improving awareness of AF flights nationwide.
* Led bird strike hazard avoidance to lowest ever with one strike in 2005.
* Transferred 8.5K pounds of munitions safely, doubling weapons storage capability.
* Rewrote Mishap Response Plan, adapting the plan to organizational, staffing, and manning changes.

USAF 95th Air Refueling Wing	05/2000 to 05/2002
Mendenhall, UK	$50,000 per year
Assistant Director of Operations Planning	Average hours per week: 40
Supervisor: Edwin Marks (Retired)	

Duties, Accomplishments and Related Skills:
Organization provides air-refueling and operational support throughout European Area of Responsibility (AOR). As Assistant Director of Operations Planning, managed 5 programs and 18 plans simultaneously.

PROGRAM MANAGEMENT: Managed five programs: Battle Staff, Exercises, Tactical Deception, Functional Area Management (FAM), Operational Security (OPSEC), and Joint Contact Team (JCTP) programs. Developed lifecycle cost analyses of projects, including determining necessary resources for exercises and committing 100 aerial refueling aircraft, crews, and resources to appropriate U.S. and NATO exercises. Managed $97K in exercise costs. Analysis and evaluation of OPSEC program led to identification of significant vulnerabilities, resulting in purchase of $75K shredder as well as new policies and briefings.

PLANNING AND COORDINATION: Led 75-person planning group in development of contingency, exercise, and base support plans. Advised on the distribution of work among positions and the appropriate staffing levels and skills mix for planning completion. Coordinated 200% training and mission-capable rate increase. Directed logistical plan to relocate operations during runway closure, utilizing three British bases for six separate flight missions. Consolidated lessons-learned input from 24 units into 1 comprehensive deployment and process improvement plan for organizations preparing for deployment to Afghanistan. Developed tanker-planning guide, ensuring proper utilization of aircraft.

COMMUNICATIONS: Demonstrated ability to communicate with a wide variety of personnel equally well one-on-one or in large group settings. Ensured 2.8K personnel received OPSEC briefings in two-week period.

ACCOMPLISHMENTS:
* Wrote NEO Plan encompassing 37 organizations and 7K personnel in response to heightened force protection requirements following 9/11.
* Led Plans and Programs Division to an "Excellent" rating on compliance inspection.
* Created Security Awareness Team, integrating five programs to improve security operations.
* Authored numerous operational plans, prioritizing needs and ensuring compliance with AF regulations.
* Awarded Frontline Manager of the Year Award; ranked #1 of 33 managers.

EDUCATION

Georgia State University	Major: Aeronautical Science
Atlanta, GA, United States	Minor: Aviation Management
Master's Degree	GPA: 3.75/4.00
Completion Date: 04/2005	39 Semester Credits Earned

RELEVANT COURSEWORK, LICENSURES AND CERTIFICATIONS:
Airport Operations and Management, 3 Sem Hrs; Aircraft and Spacecraft Development, 3 Sem Hrs; Aviation Labor Relations, 3 Sem Hrs; Air Transportation System, 3 Sem Hrs; Airport Operations Safety, 3 Sem Hrs; Human Factors in Aviation/Aerospace Industry, 3 Sem Hrs; Aviation/Aerospace System Safety, 3 Sem Hrs; Industrial Safety Management, 3 Sem Hrs; Aircraft Mishap Investigation, 3 Sem Hrs

Georgia University College	Major: Political Science
Macon, GA, United States	
Bachelor's Degree	
Completion Date: 08/1999	

JOB RELATED TRAINING:
Air Command and Staff College, 40 weeks; Squadron Officer School, 7 weeks; Defense Contract Management Agency (DCMA) Government Flight Representative Course; Production, Quality, and Manufacturing, Level 1; Chief of Safety Course; Air Force (AF) Mishap Investigation Course; Operations Risk Management Application and Integration Course; Boeing KC-135 Instructor Navigator Training; Boeing KC-135 Navigator Crew Training; Joint Undergraduate Navigator Training; Information Management Basic Officer's Course

ADDITIONAL INFORMATION

Top Secret/Sensitive Compartmented Information (SCI) Clearance

PROFESSIONAL SUMMARY:
Meticulous Program and Safety Management professional with more than 10 years' experience in positions with increasing levels of responsibility and complexity in the U.S. Air Force (USAF). Proven ability to improve processes and procedures while ensuring compliance with quality and safety requirements. Adept at planning and directing multiple programs simultaneously, demonstrating expert organizational, prioritization, and decision-making skills. Outstanding communicator able to coordinate sensitive and high-priority taskings across international and interagency groups. Skilled at inspecting aviation activities and at identifying, reporting, and resolving potential hazards. Led teams to 100% mission accomplishment throughout career.

PROFESSIONAL HIGHLIGHTS:
* Created procedures to reduce risk to personnel and aircraft, leading to the safe delivery of 14 KC-10 and 10E-8C aircraft per year in accordance with $2.1B contracts.
* Directed movement of 295 combat aircraft on 39 missions, supporting operations in Afghanistan and Iraq.
* Delivered F-16 Block 50 aircraft to Iran; handled sensitive diplomatic issues.
* Ensured execution of 4.1K KC-135 aerial refueling flights, adapting to unexpected contingencies and ensuring the ability of U.S. aircraft to meet operational commitments.
* Orchestrated short-notice refueling of MC-130 aircraft, evacuating 90 U.S. citizens during NEO in Lebanon.
* Planned and scheduled refueling operations, enabling the movement of medical teams throughout a five-location Presidential tour in Africa.
* Developed air-refueling plan for continuous air coverage for the President and seven other Heads of State.
* Improved safety operations; led group to a zero percent ground mishap rate.
* Oversaw 2.2K HH-60 hours, 1.5K F-15 flights, and 679 KC-135 refuelings with zero class A or B mishaps.
* Analyzed HH-60 mishap, identifying fleet-wide problem and initiating appropriate technical fix.
* Coordinated with civil aviation, devising air-collision avoidance procedures and improving awareness of Air Force (AF) flights nationwide.
* Rewrote Mishap Response Plan, adapting the plan to organizational, staffing, and manning changes.
* Wrote NEO Plan encompassing 37 organizations and 7K personnel in response to heightened force protection requirements following 9/11.
* Led Plans and Programs Division to an "Excellent" rating on compliance inspection.
* Created Security Awareness Team, integrating five programs to improve security operations.
* Authored numerous operational plans, prioritizing needs and ensuring compliance with AF regulations.
* Awarded Frontline Manager of the Year Award; ranked #1 of 33 managers.

SUPERVISOR QUOTES AND RATING TEAM COMMENTARY:
"[Kevin is an] exceptional officer. He anticipates and acts decisively. [There is] no better Flight Safety Officer... [Kevin has] award-winning leadership...Number 1 of 8 safety officers I have ever supervised."
John Turner, Colonel, USAF, Director, 75th Group, Keflavik, Iceland

FLIGHT INFORMATION:
Senior Navigator for Boeing KC-135: 1.8K Flight Hours, 143 as Instructor, 41 as Evaluator, and 34 in Combat Support. Comply with all Federal Aviation Administration (FAA) rules and regulations.

AWARDS:
* Meritorious Service Medal (4)
* Air Medal
* Aerial Achievement Medal (3)
* Joint Service Commendation Medal
* Air Force (AF) Commendation Medal (3)
* Joint Service Achievement Medal
* AF Achievement Medal
* AF Outstanding Unit Award (3)

* AF Organizational Excellence Award
* Combat Readiness Medal (4)
* National Defense Service Medal (2)
* Global War on Terrorism (GWOT) Service Medal
* Department of the Navy Safety Excellence Award
* USAF Flying Safety Plaque
* USAFE Safety Outstanding Unit Award
* USAFE Tactical Deception Officer of the Year
* Superior Performance Award, Squadron Officer School

PROFESSIONAL LICENSES:
* Private Pilot License, 1998

MILITARY EXPERIENCE:
USAF, 2000 to Present

SPECIFIC QUALIFICATIONS:
Program and Project Management; Personnel Management; Leading Teams; Problem Solving; Planning and Coordination; Analysis; Evaluating Programs; Process Improvement; Performing Cost-Benefit Analyses; Establishing Goals and Objectives; Achieving Objectives; Distributing Work; Assigning Tasks; Advising on Staffing Levels; Developing Policies and Procedures; Recommending Improvements in Staffing, Procedures, or Work Methods; Identifying Required Resources; Reviewing Audits or Investigations; Applying Safety and Health Principles, Standards, and Techniques; Identifying Hazardous Conditions; Communicating to Resolve Safety Problems; Implementing, Maintaining, and Modifying Safety and Health Programs; Investigating Sources of Injuries; Ensuring Validity of Data Collected; Ensuring Accurate Documentation; Writing Summaries; Examining Data; Determining Critical Factors; Recommending Alternatives to Eliminate or Minimize Losses from Injuries and Illnesses; Defining Terminology; Preparing Safety Documentation; Issuing Certificates; Evaluating Training Methods, Facilities, and Equipment; Inspecting and Evaluating Aviation Activities; Monitoring Changes in Equipment, Facilities, Key Personnel, and Scope of Operations; Ensuring Compliance with Federal Regulations and Safety Requirements; Enforcing FAA Regulations; Investigating Accidents; Determining if Legal or Administrative Action Is Required; Inspecting Airworthiness of Aircraft; Inspecting Alterations or Repairs; Quality Assurance (QA); Ensuring Conformance with Design Specifications; Ensuring Compliance with Rules, Regulations, and Procedures; Negotiating; Briefing; Oral and Written Communications; One-on-One Communications; Mentoring; Counseling; Motivating Staff; Prioritization and Organizational Skills; Managing Multiple Tasks Simultaneously; Streamlining Complex Work Processes; Building Relationships; Software Proficiency and Computer Skills

NICOLE RODGERS

173 Pierce Avenue, Macon, GA 31204 United States
Email: info@careerprocenter.net
Day Phone: 478-742-2442

EXPERIENCE:

United States Marine Corps (USMC), Staff Non-Commissioned Officer (SNCO) Academy	06/2009 to 09/2011
San Diego, CA, United States	$81,300 per year
Supply Officer	Average hours per week: 40
Supervisor: Stanley Myers	Phone: 760-555-1234

Duties, Accomplishments and Related Skills:

Facility provides Staff Non-Commissioned Officers (SNCOs) with education and leadership training to enhance professional qualifications in preparation for assuming duties of greater responsibility and making greater contribution to the U.S. Marine Corps (USMC).

SUPPLY MANAGEMENT: Directed all aspects of supply operations, including management of daily responsibilities in accordance with accepted practices and organization requirements. Maintained 100% accuracy of supply inventory and administrative requirements as per current policies and standards, administering management of $1.5M+ supply account. Enhanced accountability, accessibility, and dependability of facility equipment, improving student training in Career and Management courses.

SUPPLY PROCUREMENT AND DISTRIBUTION: Collaborated with sister SNCO Academies and relevant third-party vendors for acquisition and acceptance of diverse supply categories valued at more than $1.5M. Managed Government Purchase Card Program (GPCP) and purchasing of $8K in assets. Furnished 6K management personnel with funding, materials, and supplies.

BUDGET PLANNING AND EXECUTION: Developed annual facility supply budgets, monthly reconciliations, research, and follow-up. Oversaw Mechanized Allowance Listing (MAL), Due-in and Status File (DASF), and reconciliation of 13 Consolidated Memorandum Receipts (CMRs) for facility. Directed two quarterly CMR reconciliations. Teamed with external organizations for fiscal- and supply-associated matters, as needed. Managed ongoing reconciliation of facility assets during transition to Global Combat Support System-Marine Corps (GCSS-MC). Received fiscal inspection with zero findings and no deficiencies. Initiated and administered formation of nine transient-event CMRs and two organization property CMRs.

WAREHOUSE MANAGEMENT: Generated, administered, and oversaw warehouse guidelines and procedures and ensured well-being of personnel through conformity to generally accepted safety criterion, with zero mishaps and injuries. Offered Operational Risk Assessment worksheets to support staff.

LEADERSHIP AND TRAINING: Supervised, trained, oversaw, and evaluated five supply-section personnel. Led three leadership-training sessions with support staff personnel. Served as Uniform Victim Advocate. Taught and directed leadership training for 3K management personnel.

ACCOMPLISHMENTS:
* Augmented learning environment for 3K students annually through upgrades to 21 faculty advisor rooms and 3 classrooms, adding new monitors, DVD players, and SMART Boards through project coordination, including creating plans, researching options, writing requests for additional funding, and coordinating and preparing building and supply shipments and installation.
* Accountable for facility assets valued at $1.5M+, with zero loss or discrepancies.
* Concluded closeout for Fiscal Year (FY) 2010 with 99.99% obligation rate.
* Completed and gained approval for FY 2011 budget of $134K and FY 2012 budget of $121K, tripling FY 2010 budget and enlarging FY 2011 budget by 38%.
* Oversaw with 100% accountability 1st, 2nd, and 3rd Quarter 2010 CMR with zero discrepancy.
* Negotiated $23K in additional funds for facility's material and supply unfunded budget deficiency and a further $278K for seminars, materials, and supplies; student housing; DAPS, audiovisual equipment for classrooms; and faculty advisor rooms.
* Directed annual wall-to-wall inventory, with 100% accountability of assets.
* Organized and administered execution of use of Supported Activities Supply System (SASSY) for requisition system purchases that accumulated $10K.
* Reassigned assets valued at $55.5K from Camp Pendleton's Corporal course.

USMC, Headquarters (HQ) and Support Battalion San Diego, CA, United States	09/2008 to 06/2009
Supply Officer	Average hours per week: 40
Supervisor: Bill Ash	Phone: 760-555-1234

Duties, Accomplishments and Related Skills:

Battalion provides administrative, training, and disciplinary support for personnel assigned to Marine Corps Base Camp Pendleton, San Diego, CA, and affiliated organizations in order to increase operational and functional effectiveness, administrative simplicity, and utility.

SUPPLY MANAGEMENT: Directed all aspects of supply operations, including management of daily responsibilities in accordance with accepted practices and organization requirements. Developed and administered supply account according to accepted practices and principles. Maintained 100% accuracy of supply inventory and administrative requirements as per recognized policies and standards. Teamed with organization Operations and Technology (O/T) department for acquisition and acceptance of diverse supply categories.

BUDGET EXECUTION: Collaborated with external organizations for fiscal- and supply-associated matters, as needed. Oversaw and administered MAL and 13 CMR for O/T Assistant Director.

LEADERSHIP AND TRAINING: Supervised, trained, oversaw, and evaluated 25 supply-section personnel. Maintained organization personnel records, ensuring accuracy.

ACCOMPLISHMENTS:
* Successfully revamped and implemented proper supply management for multimillion-dollar supply account.
* Corrected backlog of delinquent CMRs in two months and ensured subsequent quarterly CMRs were published accurately and on time, with 100% accountability.
* Directed administration of Training Support Division budget and consolidated all Defense Reutilization Management Office (DRMO) runs under single management.

USMC, HQ and Service Company, Security Battalion San Diego, CA, United States	01/2004 to 08/2008
Supply Chief	Average hours per week: 40
Supervisor: Fred Johnson (Retired)	

Duties, Accomplishments and Related Skills:

SUPPLY MANAGEMENT: Assisted in management of supply operations, including oversight of daily responsibilities in accordance with accepted practices and organization requirements. Designed, organized, and managed administration of supply process, including requisitioning, property accounting, property disposal, and internal property redistribution. Maintained 100% accuracy of supply inventory and administrative requirements as per current policies and standards. Teamed with organization departments for acquisition, acceptance, and liability of diverse supply categories, valued at more than $150K.

BUDGET EXECUTION: Teamed with external organizations for fiscal- and supply-associated matters, as needed. Collaborated in oversight of organization MAL, DASF, and CMRs. Oversaw sub-custody account program for more than 23 organization departments. Traced and verified accountability of 44 organization CMRs.

WAREHOUSE MANAGEMENT: Generated, administered, and oversaw warehouse guidelines and procedures and ensured well-being of personnel through conformity to generally accepted safety criterion. Reviewed warehouse Standard Operating Procedures (SOPs) for items requiring specific National Stock Numbers (NSNs) in compliance with supply administrative records and standards.

LEADERSHIP AND TRAINING: Supervised, trained, oversaw, and evaluated 10 supply-section personnel. Managed personnel and administrative areas for department. Served as organization Equal Opportunity (EO) Representative.

ACCOMPLISHMENTS:
* Overhauled warehouse operations, resulting in improvement in accountability and serviceability
* Directed two extensive wall-to-wall inventories to prepare for senior management turnover of $4.5M account.
* Readied supply account for review by organization Inspector General (IG), including all MAL, DASF, and CMR transactions, leading to "Outstanding" rating with zero discrepancies.
* Served as administrator of Marine Corps Community Services, with oversight of community services funds and fundraising account valued at more than $23K.
* Established policies to better track personnel checkout of equipment, resulting in significant decrease in equipment loss.
* Managed organization credit card purchase authorization, evaluating more than 200 credit card purchases to ensure compliance with appropriate fiscal regulations.
* Administered wide-ranging causal investigation into 10 accounts requiring immediate modification.
* Directed reconciliation of 20 organization property accounts and 31 Table of Equipment (T/E) accounts, ensuring precise accountability.
* Supervised annual wall-to-wall inventory that led to decrease of 75K+ non-accountable items from MAL and merger of more than 25 Table of Allowance Materiel Control Numbers (TAMCN) and NSN, providing increased effectiveness to property accounting section.

EDUCATION:

Hawaii Pacific University Honolulu, HI, United States	Major: Accounting
Associate's Degree	GPA: 3.03
Completion Date: 03/2011	

OTHER:

Job Related Training:

RELEVANT TRAINING:
Uniform Victim Advocate, 07/2010
Formal School Instructor, 02/2010
Staff Non-Commissioned Officer (SNCO) Academy Advanced, 04/2009
SNCO Advanced Distance Learning Program, 01/2009
Tactical Logistics Operations, 12/2008
Equal Opportunity Advisor, 06/2006
SNCO Academy, 04/2003
Ground Supply Chiefs, 12/2000
Enlisted Supply Intermediate, 10/2000
Sergeants Course, 02/1998
Basic Recruiter, 04/1997
Administration, 09/1996
Operations, 06/1996
Leadership II, 06/1996
Personnel Administration, 06/1996
Supply Management, 05/1995
Administration Plans/Policy/Procedures, 05/1994
Leadership, 05/1994
Personal Finance, 07/1993
Supply Administration and Operations Clerk, 03/1993
Basic Supply Administration and Operations, 03/1993

Additional Information:

"… Over the last two years has taken a marginal supply section at best and built an effective and productive unit recognized during a recent Commanding Officers Inspection Program (COIP) as 'one of the best.' She is in the top 45% of all GySgts I have reviewed."
SIMON FRANK, Executive Officer, Security Battalion

PROFESSIONAL SUMMARY:
Multidimensional professional offering 20 years of combined expertise in logistics, supply, administration, and budget and bookkeeping. Astute program management skills in creating, reinforcing, and reinventing projects to meet and exceed necessary goals. Solid operational management results in flawless and smooth processing of daily systems. Dynamic leader, trainer, and manager trusted by peers and superiors; experienced in team and consensus building, consistently receiving very best work and dedication from personnel. Proactive, strategic thinker with administrative and operational skills that streamline efficient and systematic operations. Talent for evaluating existing programs, identifying issues, and developing innovative solutions through a strong analytical approach, consistently increasing both productivity and accuracy. Exceptionally organized

with solid multitasking skills while maintaining high rates of productivity. Committed to highest level of professional excellence and integrity.

PROFESSIONAL HIGHLIGHTS:
* Provided 3 updated classrooms and 21 faculty advisor training rooms at Staff Non-Commissioned Officer (SNCO) Academy, replacing outdated audiovisual equipment used to conduct leadership courses. Solicited outside vendor quotes, chose appropriate vendor, justified and was granted additional $278K in funds, and coordinated purchase and installation of rooms with upgraded material. Positively affected 3K students annually and overall readiness of facility as a professional educational academy.
* Created functional table supply account and implemented required accountability programs for Operation and Training department, which had no previous supply account procedures in place for millions of dollars in assets. Utilized ATLAS program to enter Table of Equipment (T/E) gear and created Consolidated Memorandum Receipt (CMR) area within two months of arrival at department.
* Developed and maintained critical InterService Support Agreements, allowing immediate assistance to any deployed personnel in Area of Responsibility (AOR), stepping in whenever needed to expedite order and delivery.
* Discovered and corrected problem with SNCO Academy Activity Address Code (AAC), which caused facility to receive and be credited for incorrect supplies. Conducted complete wall-to-wall inventory and removed all assets from one AAC to another, correcting accounting to correctly show no phantom overages. Stopped likelihood of facility not having supplies needed to train students and become non-functional.
* Obtained increase in SNCO Academy operating funds of more than $300K, projecting current, future, and unexpected facility expenses. Allowed Academy to gather equipment and materials essential to students.

AWARDS:
* Navy and Marine Corps Achievement Medal
* Global War on Terrorism Expeditionary Medal
* Military Outstanding Volunteer Service Medal
* Certificate of Commendation (5)
* Letter of Appreciation (15)
* Meritorious Mast (5)

Cover Letter Samples

ALLEN CARSON

478-742-2442
info@careerprocenter.net
173 Pierce Avenue ✦ Macon, GA 31204

<<Date>>

<<Name>>
<<Title>>
<<Company>>
<<Address>>
<<City, State Zip>>

Dear <<Salutation>>:

I am very interested in the Project Manager position with <<NAME OF COMPANY>>, and I believe my professional achievements and aeronautics background make me ideally suited for this opening. I am currently certified as a Six Sigma Green Belt, with upcoming Black Belt and Lean certifications. Within the next eight months, I will earn both my Master of Project Management and Business Administration degrees. In addition to a Bachelor of Science degree in Aeronautics, I offer practical aviation experience as a military helicopter pilot.

After leaving the United States Air Force (USAF) in December 2011, I achieved immediate success in the private sector as a Project Manager. All of my projects are consistently planned with aggressive deadlines, yet I have driven each one to completion at or before schedule. Both my civilian and military careers demonstrate a commitment to excellence, with frequent promotions and assignments to the most challenging tasks.

Please consider the following as a partial record of my accomplishments:

▶ Served as a Blackhawk Maintenance Test Pilot and Night Vision Flight Trainer. Before achieving flight status, I acted as Crew Chief for OH-58 helicopters, maintaining an operational readiness rate of 95%.

▶ Provided product education to customers and improved the quality of the course offerings, leading to increased customer satisfaction (90% to 97%).

▶ Designed, built, and staffed a new Administrative Department in three months (three weeks ahead of schedule) with an initial budget of $1M. The new department generated $950K in revenue during the first 12 months of operation.

I believe I can contribute greatly to the development, production, and use of the latest aircraft technology. My former commander stated that I "plan and execute complex missions with little or no guidance" and that I am a "natural leader who consistently seeks to better himself." My drive, dedication, and attention to detail have been proven time and again in both my military and civilian careers. I am confident those skills would be of substantial value to {COMPANY NAME}

I look forward to hearing from you to arrange a personal interview at your earliest convenience.

Sincerely,

Allen Carson

JAMES E. LONGO

173 Pierce Ave., Macon, GA 31204 | 123-555-6789 | info@careerprocenter.net

<<DATE>>

<<NAME, TITLE>>
<<ORGANIZATION>>
<<ADDRESS>>
<<CITY, STATE ZIP>>

Dear <<NAME>>:

I am writing to explore employment opportunities within <<ORGANIZATION>>. My background includes hands-on experience in electrical power generation equipment maintenance and repair, customer service, and training support. Enclosed please find a copy of my resume for your review and consideration.

Recognized as a dedicated and results-oriented professional, I have made numerous positive contributions throughout my career, constantly striving to foster an environment of continuous improvement. Currently, as an Electrical Technician in the United States (U.S.) Navy, I maintain and repair power generation equipment, including 43 mobile power generators and associated equipment valued in excess of $1M. I troubleshoot and repair generators ranging from 2 to 60 kilowatts to ensure power support for local training exercises and worldwide operations.

My experience includes removal, installation, and maintenance of generator engines and electrical systems, and I have provided training on the operation, maintenance, and repair of electric generators and associated equipment. I have demonstrated exceptional customer support, problem-solving, and technical skills, ensuring the highest levels of system availability and reliability. I manage time and resources to ensure efficient operations, and my superiors have consistently rated me as a top performer.

My broad-based experience in maintenance support, electrical power generation technology, and customer support has positioned me for various career avenues. I feel certain I would be a viable asset to a progressive organization such as yours, capable of making an immediate and lasting contribution.

Thank you in advance for your consideration, and I look forward to your reply.

Respectfully submitted,

James E. Longo

Enclosure

LEON REELS

478-742-2442
info@careerprocenter.net
173 Pierce Avenue ✦ Macon, GA 31204

<<Date>>

<<Title>>
<<Company>>
<<Address>>
<<City, State Zip>>

Dear <<Salutation>>:

Having positively influenced the operational and strategic performance of the United States (U.S.) Army, I am writing to offer your organization more than four years of services as Assistant Manager, leading, directing, and supervising 5 culinary specialists and up to 19 food service attendants supporting food service and hospitality activities, operations, and administration, enhancing organizational goals and objectives.

As I approach my departure from serving the U.S. Army, I would like to advance my information to your organization for review and reflect on my highlighted experience, education, and service to my country for future consideration of employment with your organization.

From 2008 to the present, I have supervised Food and Hotel Services, providing culinary training, certification, and licensure and qualifying 19 food service attendants in administration and operations for daily cleanliness and maintenance of a large-scale dining facility serving more than 1,200 personnel per day.

Below are a few of the highlights representing my career achievements:

- Deliver pivotal leadership and management in coordinating a successful VIP reception for 40+ distinguished guests and 152 top-ranking officials during an annual military conference.
- Provide training and instruction, and initiate preparation for crew/team qualification, certification, and license requirements; ensure seamless operations and food and hospitality compliance with all inspection, audit, policy, and regulatory directives.
- Achieve a 96% ranking during sanitation Supply Management Certification; trained sanitation processes to Food and Hotel Services; qualified 12 personnel and monitored performance.

I am available for interviews beginning March 1, 2012. With my successful experience and education, I am confident I would make a valuable contribution and reflect highly on your organization. Accordingly, please do not hesitate to contact me to schedule a personal interview.

Thank you in advance for your consideration. I look forward to your reply.

Sincerely,

Leon Reels

Enclosure

SUSAN PICKERTON

<<Date>>

<<Title>>
<<Company>>
<<Address>>
<<City, State Zip>>

Dear <<Salutation>>:

Having positively influenced the operational and strategic performance of the United States (U.S.) Air Force (USAF), I am writing to offer your organization seven years of professional, award-winning, and advanced caliber and experience as an Information Network Administer, Technology Manager, and Operations Supervisor.

As a results-driven, proactive leader, I excel at thoroughly analyzing network and Information Technology (IT) processes and functions; troubleshooting; devising new strategic processes and alignments to systems; efficiently mastering workflow and operations; reducing costs; mitigating risks; and providing high-level Quality Assurance (QA) relating to best practices and most effectively applied procedures.

I am a highly effective trainer, mentor, and communicator and excel at building talented teams capable of performing under high-pressure, deadline-driven, crisis-level conditions. Some of my highlights and earlier achievements include:

▶ Maintained and managed more than 40 user accounts, 30 computers, and 8 network printers while ensuring 100% Air Force Certification compliance, 2007

▶ Flawless performance as alternate Security Manager; garnered an "Excellent" annual inspection rating by Security Forces, 2008

▶ Pioneered and launched a Microsoft (MS) Excel database for decorations and performance reports, increasing on-time rates from 72% to 94%, 2008

I will separate from the USAF on 6/30/2012, and will be available for interviews beginning 9/15/2012. With my successful experience and education, I am confident I would make a valuable contribution and reflect highly on your organization. Accordingly, please do not hesitate to contact me to schedule a personal interview.

Thank you in advance for your consideration. I look forward to your reply.

Sincerely,

Susan Pickerton
Enclosure

---

173 Pierce Avenue   Macon, GA 31204   478-742-2442   info@careerprocenter.net

---

Narrative Samples

BARBARA ADAMS
173 Pierce Avenue, Macon, GA 31204
Email: info@careerprocenter.net
Phone: 478-742-2442

VACANCY ANNOUNCEMENT: 12345
Financial Manager

Skill in written and verbal communication with internal staff and external organizations.

To be a successful manager of an organization, one must have the ability to effectively and authoritatively direct and influence the actions and behaviors of others in order for organizational goals to be achieved. I am an excellent communicator and highly skilled in interpersonal relations. For seven years, I have managed a staff fluctuating in size between 5 and 500 personnel. As a leader, I respond appropriately to the situation at hand and to the needs and expectations of those involved. In order to be effective, I have developed a keen insight into my industry and my business environment. I realize the workforce is changing, and I make consistent, fundamental changes in my own attitudes and approaches in order to lead others effectively. I see myself as a facilitator, not an order giver. I am sensitive to the needs of my staff, because true sensitivity motivates employees. I take the time to identify employee needs because when an employee understands that he/she will achieve by helping the agency to achieve, he/she will reward the company with commitment, loyalty, and productivity—a win-win situation for all. I treat all employees with respect and develop relationships based upon trust, mutual commitment, and honesty. I encourage diversity in the workplace in both hiring and promotion practices and I value performance and excellence in the workforce. As a manager, I emphasize that our departmental performance is only as good as the people who comprise the team. I believe each individual is a stronger performer and better employee through working with the group as a whole, and I encourage deep respect of fellow employees throughout all levels of the organization.

In my position as Financial Manager, I am in communication daily with the Ryerson Company's policy director, weekly with the Finance Committee, monthly with the Executive Committee, and others on an "as-needed" basis. I provide funds status and budget updates to the appropriate individuals and committees regularly on Ryerson's financial operations. I also communicate with General Services Administration's (GSA) Heartland Finance Center on a regular basis to support services provided by GSA in payroll and accounting. This communication affords timely and accurate resolution to time-sensitive activities, errors, and or adjustments to financial operations. For example, one major error occurred in which incorrect data was entered into the Pegasys accounting system and caused Ryerson to be $1.2M "in the red" in appropriations. I discovered this and through my knowledge and previous contact, was able to quickly notify the finance center to correct this error. I also have regular communication with Ryerson's Office of Management and Budget (OMB) resource analyst. I have open communication with the resource analyst about Ryerson's budget priorities and on apportionment/reapportionment requirements. I also am in touch with the Congressional staff that oversees Ryerson's budget in Congress.

As Lead Accountant in Xanthan Corporation's General Ledger (GL) section, I communicated with mid-level and senior officials of the Treasury Department, Department of Defense (DoD), State Department (DOS), U.S. embassies abroad, and a sampling of public and private organizations. These communicative efforts were to resolve deposit, disbursement, and collection differences that were central to my GL functions. I briefed mid-level and senior officials of the Treasury Department, Department of Defense, State Department, U.S. embassies abroad, and a sampling of public and private organizations on resolving deposit, disbursement, and collection differences. I was designated as representative to the Treasury Department on behalf of the Government On-Line Accounting Link System. In this capacity, I promulgated Xanthan Headquarters' (HQ) needs and recommendations for enhancements and improvements. In addition, I represented the division during policy meetings and acted in the absence of the division director, providing feedback to the division director both orally and via written correspondence to update him on my actions. While at Xanthan Corp., I also served as the Primary Systems Accountant; I prepared and submitted written requirements to HQ programming support staff. As a result of said submission, defining system requirements benefited the division twofold: data integrity and reporting accuracy had been sustained; and the requirement set forth in Treasury Financial Manual I-TFM 2-3300: Reports of Agencies for which the Treasury Disburses (Transmittal Letter No. 569) had been satisfied.

BARBARA ADAMS
173 Pierce Avenue, Macon, GA 31204
Email: info@careerprocenter.net
Phone: 478-742-2442

VACANCY ANNOUNCEMENT: 12345
Project Manager

Earlier in my career, as a System Accountant with the Veterans Benefits Administration (VBA), I served as one of the focal points for the VBA's Cost Management Information System (CMIS). I interacted with 58 field station Points of Contact (POCs) on data collection, testing, and implementation of the system (CMIS). The first phase of building the structure was completed and I served as the application expert for the system and coordinator of data with the DATA Warehouse Group.

BARBARA ADAMS
173 Pierce Avenue, Macon, GA 31204
Email: info@careerprocenter.net
Phone: 478-742-2442

VACANCY ANNOUNCEMENT: 12345
Executive Assistant, GS-9/11

Experience managing administrative operations or tasks.

Throughout my 20-plus year career, I have repeatedly demonstrated my talent to manage, oversee, and supervise high-level and high profile administrative tasks. My record shows repeated success, resulting in progressively increased responsibilities and promotions. I have strong organizational skills with the ability to quickly diagnose unproductive workflows and processes and re-organize systems and workstations for maximum productivity. I appropriately delegate, so that even the most ambitious tasks and projects are achievable through hands-on oversight and short-term objectives, including steps with timeframes. I effectively analyze current processes, evaluate alternatives and options, and implement creative solutions to meet organizational objectives.

I successfully managed high-profile congressional offices for two high-ranking members as a top-level Executive Assistant, providing the leadership, training, and coaching required for creating highly effective and motivated teams of up to 15 people. I provided high-level executive assistance to congressional representatives traveling throughout the world and to foreign heads of state traveling to the U.S. I also managed a four-person administrative team at the National Energy Cooperative Association, providing mentoring, counseling, and leadership for effective team-building and top performance.

I initiated a complete new computer system installation and conversion, a reorganization and overhaul of the records management systems, and an innovative shipping and mailing software program and tracking system. I have designed and implemented correspondence tracking procedures and processes, establishing new workflow processes for improved efficiency. I progressed from secretary to executive assistant to the top politicians in Washington, firmly demonstrating competence in every task and endeavor. My skills in executive administration have led to very successful fundraising and effective constituent support.

The breadth of administrative tasks and projects I have managed and performed over the last 20 years is extensive. I wrote and typed correspondence and produced mass mailing campaigns, providing clear communication and perfect proofreading. I developed and used extensive databases to track fundraising activities, correspondence, and client lists, ensuring accurate data input, management, and up-keep. I organized travel at the highest level, making arrangements for congressional representatives on official trips with the Departments of State and Defense. I have coordinated large (greater than 2,000 people) events, providing the organizational leadership and attention to detail in all requirements for success. I have been entrusted to take meeting minutes and dictation at the highest levels, accurately learning about and recording information for effective dissemination. I designed and distributed news and press releases, communicating with the press and constituents effectively. I managed projects for large, complex events, including visits from heads of state, handling the minutia of details required for successful travel, agenda, protocol, and social events. I also provided the logistical and project planning for congressional speeches and caucuses.

BARBARA ADAMS
173 Pierce Avenue, Macon, GA 31204
Email: info@careerprocenter.net
Phone: 478-742-2442

VACANCY ANNOUNCEMENT: 12345
Supervisory Financial Specialist

Knowledge of Generally Accepted Auditing Standards and Accounting Principles (GAAS/GAAP), accounting concepts, and fiscal procedures.

Throughout my 15+ years with the federal government, I have obtained a sophisticated and contemporary grasp of not only Generally Accepted Auditing Standards (GAAS) and Generally Accepted Accounting Principles (GAAP), but also the specific federal government financial and accounting structures, including budget formulation, execution, the legislative process for authorization and appropriation, accounting, reporting of obligations and outlay, financial analysis and presentation procedures, and financial mechanisms. As a federal employee entrusted with the accurate and ethical and management of public funds, I take very seriously my responsibility to use timely, reliable, and comprehensive financial information when making decisions that have an impact on citizens' lives and livelihood. I follow an established leadership structure that provides for long-range planning, requires audited financial statements, and strengthens accountability reporting. Because of this awesome responsibility, I studied, learned, and developed a comprehensive understanding of general financial and accounting structures; financial and program management regulations, policies, objectives, and concepts; as well as the techniques of the federal government and Congress, and am familiar with all legislative fiscal restrictions affecting agency operations, including The Chief Financial Officers (CFO) Act of 1990 (Public Law 101-576). In addition, I interpret the Dawson Group's Financial Manual, Treasury Financial Manual, Comptroller General Decisions, Office of Management and Budget (OMB) circulars, as their policies apply to operations within the agency.

These skills have been obtained through a career in which I have held positions of increasing responsibility as I progressed to my current position as a GS-14 Financial Manager, a position in which I oversee and examine financial systems for the Dawson Group. I provide expert advice and guidance on the interpretation of all aspects of the Congressional legislation, regulatory directives, and procedural requirements formulation, justification, presentation, and execution of the assigned Dawson programs. I constantly review, study, and interpret Congressional legislation, including the preparation of narrative and other statistical justification in support of budget requests, preparation of testimony, and/or supporting data for Dawson officials scheduled to appear before Congressional appropriations committees, responding to Congressional budgetary questions, and realigning Dawson's programs to conform to Congressional directives. Part of my duties include serving as a principal advisor to the Chief Financial Officer (CFO) on all matters relating to accounting, programming, budgeting, and managerial financial reporting.

I oversee a comprehensive financial and budgetary performance review program and continually compile information on planned changes in overall policy and practices and the effects they will have upon established budgets, the integrity of funds, the rate and balance of obligations and expenditure, and the correlation of program schedules with related budgets. I negotiate funding requirements to meet programmed operational commitments while interpreting financial trends and take responsibility for the formulation and/or revision and dissemination of all accounting, budget review, and financial reporting policies, procedures, and guidelines.

In my current position as Financial Officer of Marigold Financial, Ltd., I have taken various external training courses to enhance my knowledge base of federal financial regulations. Several courses have enabled me to better implement federal regulations and policies within the division. These courses are: SF224 Update Seminar; Implications of Federal Appropriations Law; Advanced Appropriations Law; Understanding and Using the Standard General Ledger; Reconciling Differences; and Fundamentals of Cash Management.

As Financial Manager of Marigold, I have developed and implemented procedures governing all aspects of operations and reporting. The Marigold financial manual is the result of my efforts to bring a coordinated and disciplined approach to financial operations at Marigold. My efforts have resulted in a better understanding by staff of the roles and responsibilities each plays in the process of financial operations. This has also resulted in three years of unqualified audit opinions.

BARBARA ADAMS
173 Pierce Avenue, Macon, GA 31204
Email: info@careerprocenter.net
Phone: 478-742-2442

VACANCY ANNOUNCEMENT: 12345
Project Manager

Skill in project management in financial operations.

The Federal Management Council (FMC) is an independent federal agency making recommendations to the President and Congress to regarding fiscal projections and economic ramifications of policy and procedures. I accurately and consistently provide technical support and advice on a broad range of financial areas, including budget formulation, justification, presentation, and execution; development, implementation, and evaluation of all financial management policies and procedures; financial analysis and decision-making; management of accounting, travel, payroll, and fiscal support to the Agency; submission of proper documentation for funding and procurement; and provision of funds status reports on obligations and expenses to the Finance Committee and the Council as a whole. I have been recognized for my expertise in planning and directing financial programs, policy development, and projects and my ability to provide oversight and advice in the overall financial arena.

Included in my position as Financial Manager at FMC is the requirement that I also serve as the IT manager. I have managed two complete overhauls of FMC's IT system. Each upgrade has resulted in more services and reliable operational capabilities. The staff can now use services from home to telecommute, as the archival capacity of FMC's servers is much greater than previously, and wireless services are available within the office. I have ensured FMC has the latest traditional software and the latest available disability accommodation software for use by all staff. The progressiveness of capabilities allows the staff to be mobile and agile in the performance of the mission of the agency.

In my former position as Lead Accountant in the General Ledger section, I provided guidance and training on present and forthcoming assignments and projects. I periodically assigned tasks and oversaw the integrity and completion of work. This promoted the efficient operation of the division, ensured that I stayed abreast of accounting procedures, policies, and regulations, and afforded the junior members of the staff an opportunity to gain essential knowledge of those procedures that governed the financial operations within the accounting environment. I consistently interpreted and implemented established accounting operational procedures related to overall functionality of the department. These procedures were implemented daily in operating the General Ledger section of accounting and performing the fiduciary duties assigned in disbursement, collection and reporting of funds controlled by Headquarters. All accounting/payroll data was processed through an on-line real-time accounting system through a personal computer interface. I used various applications to control funds, generate internal and external reports, and interface with other organizations. I reconciled on a continuing basis all general ledger accounts, the Reporting System, and the On-line Payment System. Financial reports on payroll, taxes, retirements, and other accounting cycle reports are analyzed for accuracy.

I analyzed, reconciled, and reviewed financial reports and systems affecting a laboratory installation managed by The Institute of Technology. Quarterly, I evaluated the management of funding, accounting data, property, and systems interfaces. This evaluation was a subset of the aggregate contract evaluation that determined The Institute of Technology's rating for bonuses. Periodically, I conducted on-site visits to ensure accounting operations were in compliance with Financial Management Manual guidelines. I forwarded recommendations based on the review of operations to management for concurrence and overall implementation.

Numerous projects had to be managed in conjunction with day-to-day operations. I completed a project relating to un-liquidated budget authority for loaned military personnel. I researched and identified obligated funds that were no longer necessary for payment of bills in past fiscal years. The outcome was de-obligation of $95,000 in authority at Headquarters and thousands of dollars across the agency. Also, in relation to this project, I persuaded the military services to become current on billing for personnel loaned to federal agencies. This project served the entire agency, as I

BARBARA ADAMS
173 Pierce Avenue, Macon, GA 31204
Email: info@careerprocenter.net
Phone: 478-742-2442

VACANCY ANNOUNCEMENT: 12345
Project Manager

---

was the focal point for ten centers on reimbursable military personnel. I also performed lead functions in auditing the overtime system of divisions, the upgrading of payroll accounting system functions, and the transfer and consolidation of payroll functions.

In another example, I worked with the Financial Center and Treasury Financial Management Service on the implementation of the Treasury Offset Program at FMC Headquarters. I directed the staff in the accounting division to press our efforts to attain 100% compliance on tax identification numbers (TINS) and increased use of the Automated Clearing House (ACH) payment method. I promoted these initiatives to increase the division efficiency in gathering financial data, payroll streamlining, making payments and preparation of the Headquarters Center financial statements.

In my System Accountant role, I coordinated and implemented projects with the Treasury Department and Headquarters' computer support personnel and accounting division staff. All systems had internal control components, which I evaluated for accuracy of system data and daily operations. I identified deficiencies or anomalies and designed modifications to correct problems arising from system malfunctions. I redesigned the structure for handling column placement of financial data on the automated ST123 system. This change satisfied the compliance issue mandated by the Treasury Financial Manual by the April 1, 2005, deadline. I also redesigned the status of program authority report at Headquarters. This redesign afforded a shorter turnaround window in my approval or disapproval of allotment withdrawals and corrections of funding errors between the division and the budget office at Headquarters. I also participated in the effort to implement a new business management system at FMC. I contributed to requirements gathering and flowcharting operations in an effort to acquire one system for the entire agency.

Index

About the Authors

Barbara A. Adams is the President and CEO of CareerPro Global, Inc. (CPG). For the past several decades, she has remained on the cutting edge of hiring trends while building the premier resume-writing team in the industry that has served more than 54,000 veterans. Barbara is the co-author of both the Master Military Resume Writer and the Master Federal Career Coach and Train-the-Trainer certifications. She also co-authored *Roadmap to the Senior Executive Service* and *Roadmap to Becoming an Administrative Law Judge*. Additionally, Barbara and her team at CPG won the Career Innovator Award in 2011 for earning and introducing ISO 9001:2008 to the career's industry.

Lee Kelley is an Iraq war veteran, former U.S. Army Captain, and award-winning author. He is also CPG's Director of Veterans Transitions and a Master Federal Career Coach who has personally helped hundreds of veterans to develop their resumes, from all branches of the military and from enlisted all the way up to three-star Generals. Lee is the winner of the "Best Military Transition Resume" TORI award for 2011. Additionally, Lee is the co-author of the *Roadmap to the Senior Executive Service*.

CareerPro Global Professional Writing Services

CareerPro Global (CPG) is one of the oldest and largest civilian, military, and federal career management services and has been assisting veterans for more than 25 years.

As the only career management service to have earned ISO 9001:2008 international quality certification, CPG has raised the bar in resume development, quality, customer service, document security, and many other aspects of business strategy.

Our process, practices, deliverables, and expertise are in a continual state of improvement, and we welcome the opportunity to share our expertise based on our quality performance throughout the years.

We created this book to give you the insight, information, confidence, and tools to help you understand how to write job-winning military to federal and military to private-sector resumes. With all the information in this book, and the samples and templates in the Appendix and on the Vet's Toolbox CD, you should be well on your way to a fulfilling career transition.

However, if you would like to discuss the option of partnering with CPG to develop your materials, we'd love to hear from you! Contact us at www.militaryresumewriters.com.

Mailing Address:	CareerPro Global, Inc. 173 Pierce Avenue Macon, GA 31204
Toll Free:	800-471-9201
Email:	service@careerproplus.com
Web:	www.militaryresumewriters.com www.federaljobresume.com www.careerproplus.com
Vet's Transition HQ blog:	www.veteranstransitionhq.wordpress.com
Vet's Transition HQ on Facebook:	http://www.facebook.com/#!/pages/Veterans-Transition-Headquarters/172400856104702
Vet's Transition HQ on Twitter:	http://twitter.com/#!/VetsHQ
CareerPro Global blog:	http://careerproglobal.wordpress.com/2011/09/30/the-resume-and-resume-process-couldn't-have-been-better/
CareerPro Global on Facebook:	http://www.facebook.com/#!/pages/Veterans-Transition-Headquarters/172400856104702
CareerPro Global on Twitter:	https://twitter.com/#!/CareerProGlobal

Testimonials

"I now realize, there is no way I could draft a masterpiece of a resume like they did. I didn't know the government's means to weed out resumes, nor did I know the key statements that are sought out. With resume in hand, I see a lot of things I was failing to do myself. CareerPro even has an underwriting department to triple-check their own work. This is a HIGHLY professional organization that knows what they are doing. The amount and quality of work is well worth it. Don't be a fool (like me); try it out before applying on your own."

J. Skinner

. . .

"I've reviewed the resume several times, and the best feedback I can come up with is, 'wow'. I know that's so useful and eloquent. Awe is not something I am usually struck with, but that is where I find myself.

So, to close the business end of this: I think this resume is perfect. I accept it. Thank you!

If you'll allow me to shift gears for a minute, I'd like to tell you what this means to me.

I'm told by some that transition is supposed to be a joyful time; they're wrong. It's terrifying, confusing, and painful. I'm a firm believer in defining the moments in my life, but I cannot deny that Master Sergeant Harvey, United States Air Force defines me. Just contemplating laying aside the uniform taps a well of emotion that is indescribable. For so long that it seems like forever, the mantle 'Airman' has informed my thoughts, my actions, my speech, and my being. Therein lies the rub.

When I look at all my EPRs and whatnot, I just can't think, 'let's translate these experiences into KSAs'. When I look at those documents, I think about laughter and tears, friends found and friends lost, good times and the suck. I know there's some skills in there, there has to be, but right now, all it is to me is visions of dear friends, family really, and a life. That's not particularly helpful in writing a resume.

So, thank you for doing such a great job of translating all of the gibberish into something useful for an organization. I couldn't have done this. I think this will open many doors for me."

Paul

. . .

"I was very appreciative of the time Deb Young, my writer, took to introduce herself and the process. She turned out an amazing resume for me. I am very pleased with the end results of her efforts."

D. Ray

"My resume writer, Kelly Poltrack, was outstanding. She took the time to fully understand my priorities, and then used her experience and expertise to pull relevant information from my military records and CV. Her insight and professionalism were critical to creating my resume. I will recommend CPG to my friends."

R. Hill

. . .

"I felt that Joseph went well above and beyond what he was contracted for and I felt he took a personal interest in all details. His service was more than just writing a resume, because he walked me through the steps in submitting the resume and all of the required attachments without my feeling that I was imposing. This additional service on his part was very much appreciated and without it, my efforts to apply for the job may have been for naught. He recognized the complexities of applying for a government job and added his expertise."

John F.

. . .

"I would recommend this service to anyone serious about getting a federal position. My hard work and experience were displayed in a magnificent way and this service helped me get my dream job."

Ben L.

. . .

"This is the 'go-to' company if you want the best Military Transition Resume that lands interviews. I received four requests for interviews the first week after sending out my new resume. Thanks again."

M. G.

. . .

"Great support and writing assistance. The rest is up to me. I would definitely recommend your services to others. Excellent process."

P. Nolan

. . .

"Bruce, it is my honor to recommend you; you did a super job with my resume, and you made me look much smarter that I really am!"

COL Mike S., U.S. Army

. . .

"Nancy, I wanted to let you know that I was selected for USDA SES CDP. There were over 650 applicants and in the end, USDA selected 78 participants for the SES CDP. There will be 4 cohorts of 19/20 members and I'm in the first cohort. We were notified in late July and orientation for the first cohort was August 3 and 4. Our first class at American University starts tomorrow. There will be a total of 8 weeklong courses over the next 11 months. I will be done with this coursework on June 22. Thanks for all your help and hard work, Nancy. Let me know if you have additional questions about the program or the selection process."

Vickie

• • •

"With me being deployed, the process was very simple and easy. I received my finished product way ahead of schedule because of the hard work and dedication of Mr. Joseph Tatner. Thanks for the great job! I will recommend you guys to my friends and family."

K. Andra

• • •

"Outstanding service... Kelly Poltrack provides outstanding help and support! She is truly an outstanding Professional Resume Writer... the best of the best!"

M. Klackle

• • •

"Ted, kudos to you, sir. Like I said, I started my new position at a pay grade much higher than any of my peers with more experience, and I was told it was due mainly to my Federal resume and KSAs. So thanks again Ted, I know you were just doing your job, but for me it was life-changing."

Chris Elkins

• • •

"Just wanted to say thank you very much for all you did, making my resume one of the best. I got the job I was after and I have the help from you and your staff to thank."

Dave Shiner

• • •

"The product I received was well beyond what I expected! Kelly made herself very open to being contacted, and provided an instant response when we didn't make contact. Overall, I am extremely satisfied, and recommend you in the future without hesitation! Thanks!"

Kevin Manual

• • •

"The service I received was amazing! Bruce was able to articulate my competencies in a manner consistent with government expectations, all the while staying true to my unique qualities and experiences. He helped me fill in important blanks I might have overlooked and offered wonderful guidance and recommendations in regard to style and presentation. He stayed in constant communication with me and always followed up promptly by phone and email, addressing any concerns I had about the process. Finally, he had a great sense of humor and was truly a joy to work with on such an important project."

M. Karon

• • •

"I tried writing my own resume and although the effort provided me some needed insights, it didn't produce an effective or professionally appealing product. After CareerPro Global completed its collaborative work with me and produced a professionally written resume, I've received numerous calls and inquiries. Recently, I received a 'complimentary' resume review from a competitive service with the obvious intent to offer a rewrite, but in the end, they described my resume as 'an excellent product'. I've [recommended] CareerPro Global to many of my friends and colleagues."

Maj General M. Gibson

• • •

"Satisfaction is the focal point of their business. Could not be happier with the product they delivered."

R. Rodriguez

• • •

"Chris and Lee are the epitome of professionalism. Eric helped me scope what career fields were best suited for my application based on my life experiences. Lee was superb at pulling information from me, formatting it, and developing compelling narratives that made my resume 'POP' and stand out. Definitely recommend them to all."

Robert Scott

• • •

"Upon contacting CareerPro Global, I received a call back that, to my surprise, lasted over 45 minutes. Everyone I have spoken with has taken the time to explain all the processes and tricks of government hiring to me in wonderful detail. My first conversation with the writer of my resume, Joseph Tatner, lasted over an hour and the information I received in that call alone was very valuable. After completing the required forms, receiving a first draft from Mr. Tatner, and going through the revision process, I am confident that I have a resume that sets me apart from the competition. I look forward to working with CareerPro Global again for any future resume needs I have, and I recommend them wholeheartedly to my associates who need government resumes."

Adam Drake

• • •

"Terrific experience. Lee Kelley was easy to work with and delivered a top-notch product. I have already recommended your services to several of my colleagues. Thanks again."

L. McNeeley

"This was an accelerated project; I think from initial contact to application submittal, the process took just seven (7) days. Result: a top-quality, 26-page package, and an interview now scheduled for May 24. I know I'm qualified, but the application package verified it."

M.C.

• • •

"I wanted to thank you and your organization for the experience and professional assistance I received from Bruce Hillman. His work was fantastic—really top drawer! As you could imagine, after 30 years in the Army, numerous deployments, and many headaches and heartaches, turning that experience over to a person that I have not met was not easy. His prose was magnificent. He took all of the gibberish that I provided and turned it into a world-class product. I have used other resume companies and have not received the same results, or trust. My many thanks as I begin this new chapter in my life. I feel greatly prepared with this product."

W. Wood

• • •

"Fran: Anyone who asks for my resume advice will be given your name and number, along with the highest possible endorsement. Cheers!"

W. M. Colonel, USAF

• • •

"Bruce, this resume looks unbelievable!!!! I am extremely happy and it has surpassed my expectations! I will take a closer/harder look at both documents tomorrow and send you any final edits I have (I doubt there will be many)."

Julia

• • •

"Joseph: I completed the online application process. It went smoothly. I really, really appreciate your great effort and outstanding services. I completed the survey below and could not find a score higher than 10 on the ratings scale. I also completed the testimonial section. If I get feedback on the application, I'll let you know. Again, I greatly appreciate your outstanding effort on this project."

Tony Jones

• • •

"Mark Holmes has been just super to work with. He is brilliant; he has put up with my reviews, comments, cynicism, and downright fears of rejection throughout this process. Everyone I have shown his work to has said, 'outstanding; beautifully written!' There can be no greater compliment than to receive this type of feedback. It is too bad that talent like Mark's goes so often unrecognized by those who will actually read his work..."

Name Withheld

"Mark, you have got to be near genius when it comes to this type of writing. I can do technical publications and technical papers, but resumes are a totally different breed of critters. Translation: If I can't dazzle you with my technical brilliance, let be baffle you with my bull... I can sling words with the best of them in the techno-arena, but sales is beyond me. Especially in today's job market when the competition is so fierce. To sell a resume is a skill far removed from mere technical writing for mortals. I want you to know my thoughts firsthand, since I doubt he will be so bold as to share my comment with you! I have no objections admitting a 'professional' perfected my resume!"

H. G.

• • •

"I am now with Booz Allen Hamilton earning 10K more than I was making with SAIC and, as a result of the relocation, I was able to move in with and marry my fiancée. It's all a direct result of the great job you did on my resume. I cannot begin to thank you enough. I'm very happy. I am considering a deployment to Afghanistan, and even internally, the other Booz offices want my most current resume. I also want to look at the rest of the market for deployments to see what I can possibly earn. So it's time to update it. :) Thanks once more for everything."

Jason Alridge

• • •

"Response from an agency within the Department of Navy: September 16 – mailed 'old resume' – October 1 – updated profile with new resume – October 5 – got email request for DD-214s for an internship program. Thanks so much for this opportunity."

Phil Ristcao

• • •

"Dorice: Thanks! Love the new job! I wanted to send you a note but the job has kept me hopping...which is a good thing. Thanks for all your help and support. I will definitely reach out to CPG when my next job promotion opportunity comes along."

Dan Herche

• • •

"Service was excellent and I recommended your services to individuals who needed their resumes to be completed. I will always come back to your company for anything I would need help with or questions to better myself with a good career. I am so pleased with the way that your folks handled everything, from payments to communicating with the writer to ensuring projects were completed in a timely manner. Good and professional staff at CareerPro Global; keep up the good and hard work!"

Joey Blass

• • •

"I am truly pleased with the service, attention, commitment, dedication, honesty, guidance, and product received from both Anna Anderson and Susan Harris. I've told so many people about my experience, and would recommend anyone desiring to advance or pursue a position within the federal government to utilize these services. You've exceed my expectations. You've gone above and beyond. I look forward to working with you again!"

Dana Legette

• • •

"Despite an extremely short suspense coupled with my family emergency, Joseph went above and beyond to assist me in preparing for this next phase of my life. Thank you and God bless. Thank you, Eric and Chris, for being so customer-oriented. This was a wonderful experience."

Gloria Norwood

• • •

"The care and treatment of my project was not only a great learning experience but the direction offered was exceptional!"

Peter Edge

• • •

"This was an investment in my career at a pivotal stage of my life. My team obviously had the expertise I needed to give me an edge in applying for federal government positions. They were highly professional, but personable, and very patiently and willingly answered all my questions."

Cheryl Hogarth

• • •

"Anna, I'm very pleased with all the work you did in preparing my Federal resume. In respect to the Revenue Officer position with the IRS I applied for, I received an email inviting me to take the Revenue Officer Self-Assessment. I'm going to be taking that tomorrow."

Kevin Beathan

• • •

"This service was extremely helpful with the federal job postings; I was extremely pleased. Peggi and Chris knew just what was needed for me to apply for these jobs. It is working! Thanks for everything."

Robin Duncan

• • •

"The product I received was so well written and put together that it gave me a renewed sense of confidence in my job search. Thanks, CareerPro!"

MM

"My tech writer, Joseph Tatner, was excellent. I could tell from his responses that I had nothing to worry about. I will definitely be asking for him again."

Marsha Camp

. . .

"Mr. Steffan was a tremendous help in crafting both my MTR and my USAJobs resume. I would highly recommend his services to my soldiers and anyone else in the transition process. He communicated to me on a routine basis and kept me abreast of any changes. I'm extremely pleased with the result."

Barry Brinker

. . .

"Susan did a phenomenal job! Despite my hairy travel schedule, she was available with instant responses due to our time difference."

Jennifer Bilodeau

. . .

"I am pleased with the service that was provided by CareerPro staff with completing projects in a timely manner. Prices were very affordable and the writing services were excellent. Also, I am now working on a career job that I really love. Thanks to CareerPro Global for making my dreams come true."

J. B.

. . .

"CareerPro Global provided me with an exceptionally professional resume and cover letter that I am very proud to send out. Customer service was top-notch and their commitment to excellence is unmatched! I highly recommend CareerPro Global to assist anyone with building a resume that stands out from all the others. Thanks to Mark for his hard work!"

C. P.

. . .

"The final product was astounding. Information relevant to the vacancy announcements were well interpreted into my resume. I will definitely recommend this service to all my friends who will separate or retire in the near future."

Mark Shores

. . .

"Been so excited, I forgot to email you. Lockheed Martin offered me the job on Thursday, and I officially accepted it today. Susan, it was your resume that did it. I had a three-hour interview and was told so many times by so many people how impressive my resume was. I can't thank you enough. I am so grateful to you, I can't tell you. They want me to start in Jan., so I will have only Dec. to get moved. I will be getting two paychecks until April 1, so that makes the move worth it. Their compensation package is out of this world. Thanks again so much and I promise to keep in touch."

Amanda

• • •

"My writer, Deborah Young, was very helpful and supportive. She was able to craft a great Federal resume with the information provided. She remained in contact with me during the whole process and was able to answer any questions I may have had. Overall, I am really pleased with the service and would definitely use it again."

Matt Leatherwood, JR